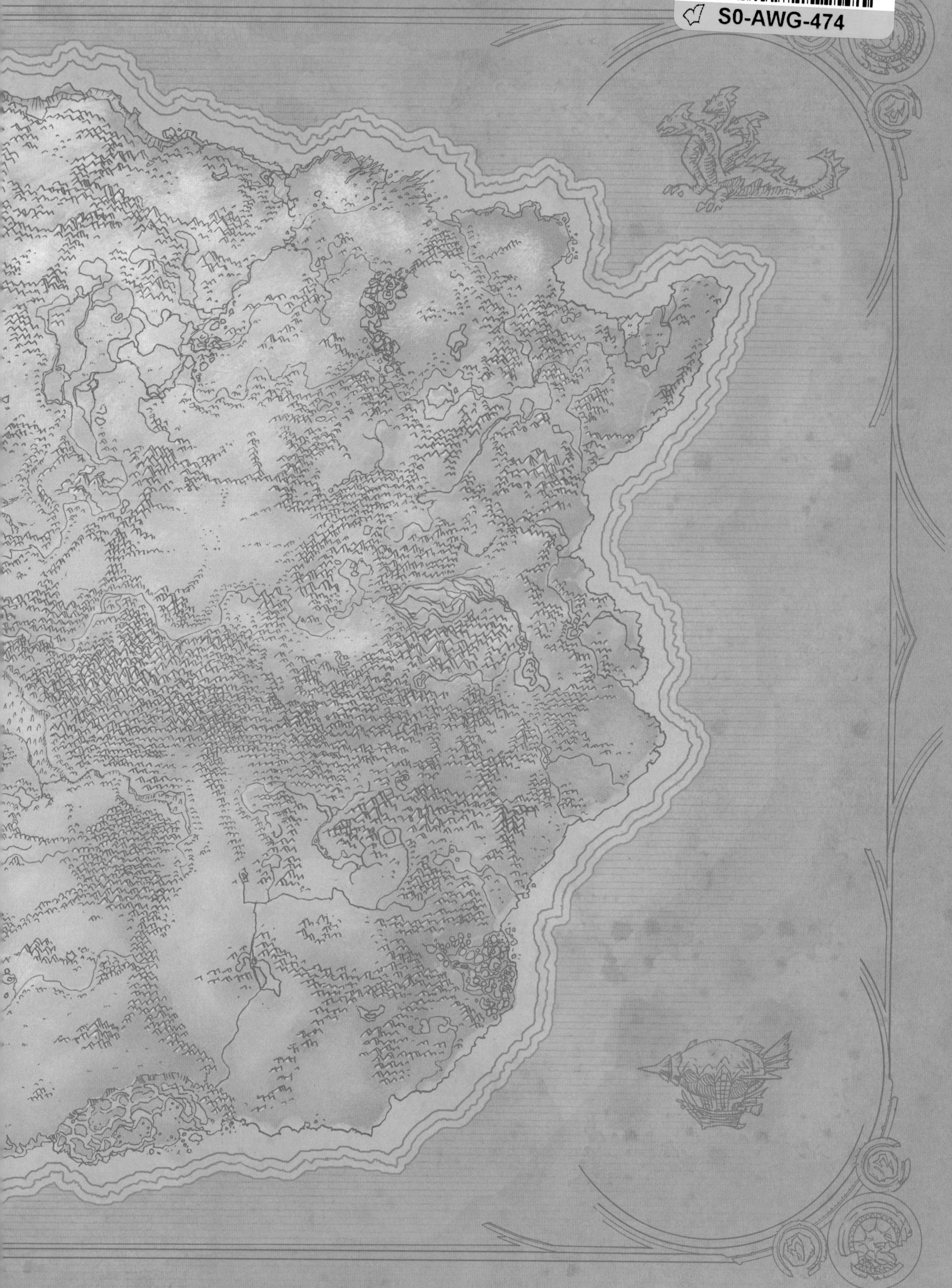

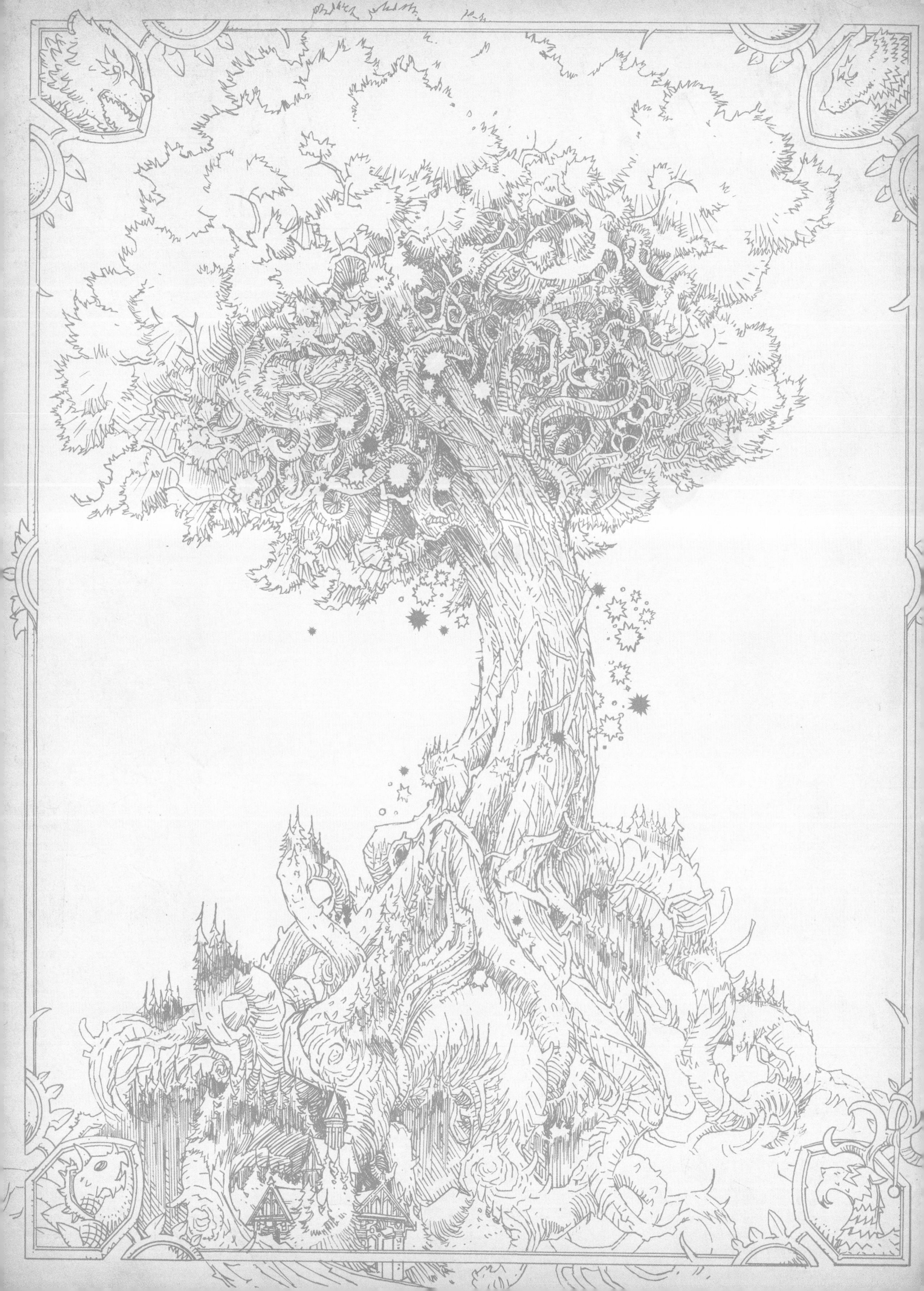

CHRONICLE: VOLUME I

Written by
CHRIS METZEN, MATT BURNS,
and ROBERT BROOKS

Full-color illustrations by
PETER C. LEE

Additional art by
JOSEPH LACROIX

BLIZZARD ENTERTAINMENT

Written by CHRIS METZEN, MATT BURNS, and ROBERT BROOKS
Additional Story ALEX AFRASIABI, CHRISTIE GOLDEN, RICHARD A. KNAAK,
DAVE KOSAK, MICKY NEILSON, BILL ROPER, JAMES WAUGH
Creative Direction and Design DOUG ALEXANDER, LOGAN LUBERA
Editors CATE GARY, ROBERT SIMPSON • *Lore* SEAN COPELAND,
EVELYN FREDERICKSEN, JUSTIN PARKER • *Production* MICHAEL BYBEE,
RACHEL DE JONG, PHILLIP HILLENBRAND, IAN SATERDALEN
Licensing MATT BEECHER, JASON BISCHOFF, BYRON PARNELL

Special thanks to: the *World of Warcraft* game team, Xiaohu Alcocer, Dana Bishop, Tina Fu, Brissia
Jimenez, Emily Mei, Frank Mummert, Tommy Newcomer, Max Ximenez

Maps, cosmology chart, borders, and spot art by JOSEPH LACROIX
Paintings by PETER C. LEE

DARK HORSE BOOKS

Publisher MIKE RICHARDSON • *Editor* DAVE MARSHALL • *Assistant Editor* EVERETT
PATTERSON • *Designer* DAVID NESTELLE • *Digital Art Technician* CHRIS HORN

Published by
Dark Horse Books
A division of Dark Horse Comics LLC
10956 SE Main Street
Milwaukie, OR 97222

DarkHorse.com
To find a comics shop in your area, visit comicshoplocator.com
First edition: March 2016
ISBN 978-1-61655-845-1

9 10 8
Printed in the United States of America

BLIZZARD.COM

CONTENTS

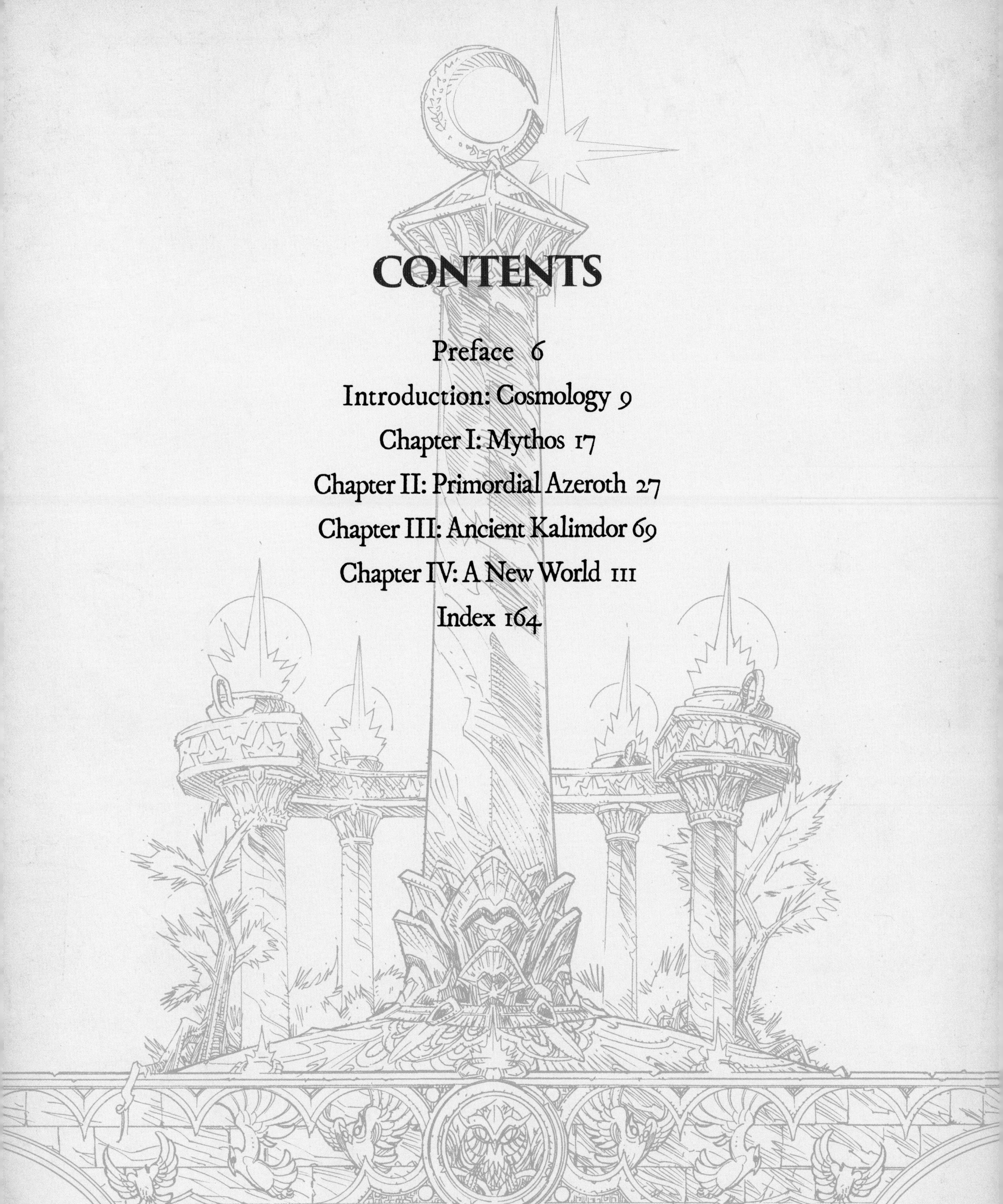

PREFACE

It's been amazing to watch the Warcraft universe grow and take shape over the past twenty years or so. What started out as a relatively simple game setting has become a lasting, vibrant world in its own right, one that is visited daily by millions of players from all around the globe.

The world of Azeroth has been shaped by hundreds of craftsmen, designers, artists, and writers since its earliest inception. It is the product of many talented hands and many passionate voices, all bent toward creating a world so rich in detail, theme, and characterization that . . . *well* . . . you'd want to pull on your +6 Boots of Butt-Kicking and give your all to defend it.

At the core of it all lies a real sense of . . . *history*. The overarching story of Warcraft is a vast, intertwining patchwork of myths, legends, and world-shaking events that ultimately contextualize the players' heroic efforts in the ever-expanding world they share.

Twenty years of storytelling. Tens of thousands of moments, characters, races, and monsters, all forming dense strata of concepts and ideas over time. This book—this *chronicle*—is meant to bring it all together and reinforce the overarching narrative that lies at Warcraft's heart. Writing this was an opportunity to unite the frayed story ends and smooth out the rough edges of this fictional history.

Ultimately, this grand (and super nerdy) editorial undertaking gives us an amazing perspective on Warcraft's recurring themes and conflicts:

How societies often clash before seeing a common humanity in each other . . .

How earnest, well-intentioned heroes can often succumb to temptations of power . . .

How failing to take responsibility for mistakes of the past can lead to calamity in the present . . .

These are just a few of the motifs that form the common thread of Azeroth's great history, expressed across disparate cultures, factions, and individuals over mythic spans of time. *Cycles within cycles . . .*

It's from this top-down view that we can more clearly see the dangerous yet glorious horizons ahead. And even in the face of all this . . . *history* . . . I'm fairly certain that the adventure is only just beginning!

Chris Metzen
SVP, Story and Franchise Development
Blizzard Entertainment
August 2015

INTRODUCTIONS

I first encountered the world of Azeroth in the year 2000. Blizzard Entertainment was looking for an author to turn the story line of its *Warcraft Adventures: Lord of the Clans* into a novel. I had six weeks to write a book set in a world with which I was completely unfamiliar. Thanks to the unfailing support and enthusiasm of Chris Metzen (who was always reachable to answer such burning questions as "What color is orc blood?"), those six weeks laid the groundwork for a business relationship that remains one of constant joy, adventure, sheer fun, and magic.

So in love with Azeroth was I after writing *Lord of the Clans* that I learned to play my first video game—*World of Warcraft*—mainly so I could spend more time there. And soon, we're all going to get to visit Azeroth in another medium entirely—the realm of movies.

In the meantime, I, like every other reader of this book, intend to sit down and curl up with this exhaustive and beautiful history of a vividly imagined world that still manages to draw me in, even though I've played *WoW* almost since its launch and written eight novels set within Azeroth's borders. (Okay, mostly . . . I went to Draenor for one of them.) There's always something to learn, a new character to meet, and a new story to tell. It's like catching up with an old friend.

May you feel the same.

"For Azeroth!"

—Christie Golden

When I was first asked to pen tales for Warcraft, the game was already something of a phenomenon, but I don't think even those at the top of the Blizzard hierarchy expected the worldwide sensation they would create just a couple of years later.

I'd been fortunate enough to be there early on in the rise of Dragonlance—*The Legend of Huma* was the first novel not written by Margaret Weis and Tracy Hickman—and I'd marveled at the legions of loyal fans at Gen Con and signings. I also had my own series, *The Dragonrealm*, with its share of dedicated followers. Yet nothing compared to what I experienced when my novel *Warcraft: Day of the Dragon* came out in 2001. The reaction was as immediate as it was huge. The appreciation of the readers came from every corner of the globe, a sign of just how dedicated the fan base for Warcraft had already become.

Over the past decade plus, I've only seen that dedication continue to swell. Azeroth is a world so rich and real that it's no surprise that millions not only have enjoyed it but also have kept coming back. It's been a pleasure to be part of this phenomenon and see my stories—and characters—added to Azeroth's already very full history, a history that continues to grow.

A history that's gonna need a volume 2 before long . . .

—Richard Knaak

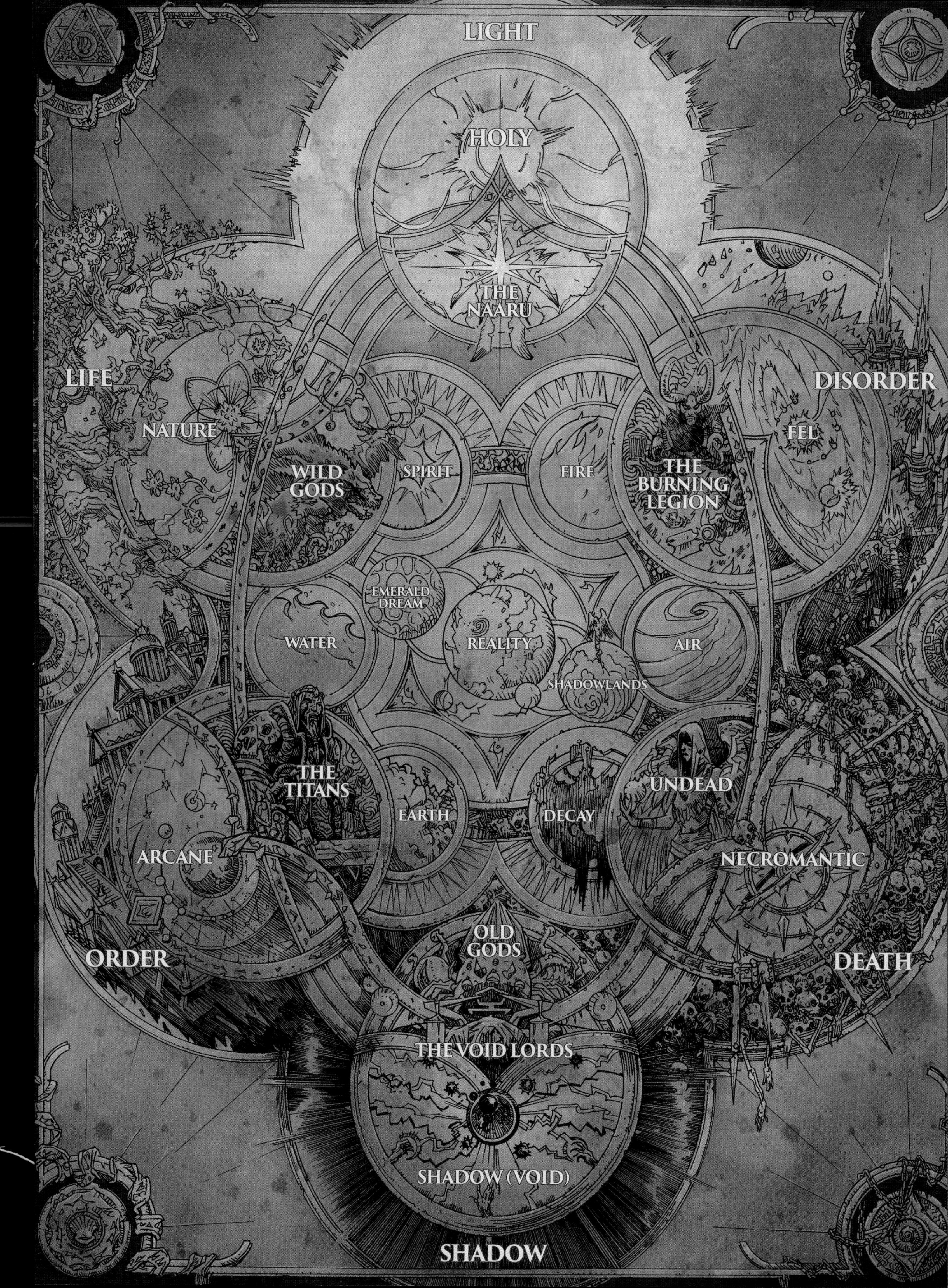
LIGHT
HOLY
THE NAARU
LIFE
DISORDER
NATURE
FEL
WILD GODS
SPIRIT
FIRE
THE BURNING LEGION
EMERALD DREAM
WATER
REALITY
AIR
SHADOWLANDS
THE TITANS
UNDEAD
EARTH
DECAY
ARCANE
NECROMANTIC
OLD GODS
ORDER
DEATH
THE VOID LORDS
SHADOW (VOID)
SHADOW

INTRODUCTION: COSMOLOGY

Azeroth is but one small world in a vast universe, a realm filled with potent magics and mighty beings. Since the dawn of time, these forces have influenced Azeroth and the surrounding cosmos, setting the stars in motion and shaping the destiny of countless worlds and mortal civilizations . . .

The Cosmic Forces

Light and Shadow

Light and Shadow are the most fundamental forces in existence. Although contradictory by their very nature, they are bound together on a cosmic scale. One cannot exist without the other.

Pure Light and Shadow dwell in a realm outside the borders of reality, but shades of their presence are found in the physical universe. Light manifests as holy magic, while Shadow (also referred to as "the Void") appears as shadow magic.

Life and Death

The forces of Life and Death hold sway over every living thing in the physical universe. The energies of Life, known commonly as nature magic, promote growth and renewal in all things. Death, in the form of necromantic magic, acts as a counterbalance to Life. It is an unavoidable force that breeds despair in mortal hearts and pushes everything toward a state of entropic decay and eventual oblivion.

Order and Disorder

The forces of Order and Disorder govern the cosmic systems of the physical universe. Order is most commonly perceived in reality as arcane magic. This type of energy is innately volatile, and wielding it requires intense precision and concentration. Conversely, Disorder is manifested as highly destructive fel magic. This brutal and extremely addictive energy is fueled by drawing life from living beings.

The Elements

The elements of fire, air, earth, and water serve as the basic building blocks of all matter in the physical universe. Shamanic cultures have long sought to live in harmony with, or assert dominion over, the elements. To do so, they call upon the primordial forces of Spirit and Decay. Those who seek to bring balance to the elements rely on Spirit (sometimes referred to as the "fifth element" by shaman, or "chi" by monks). This life-giving force interconnects and binds all things in existence as one. Decay is the tool of shaman seeking to subjugate and weaponize the elements themselves.

Elemental Duality

Many shamanic cultures have discovered that the elements can influence a variety of emotional states. For this reason, mortals often associate the elements with different feelings, both positive and negative.

FIRE
Positive Trait: Passion
Negative Trait: Fury

EARTH
Positive Trait: Stability
Negative Trait: Stubbornness

SPIRIT
Positive Trait: Bravery
Negative Trait: Naiveté

AIR
Positive Trait: Cunning
Negative Trait: Madness

WATER
Positive Trait: Tranquility
Negative Trait: Indecisiveness

DECAY
Positive Trait: Efficiency
Negative Trait: Ruthlessness

REALMS OF EXISTENCE

THE GREAT DARK BEYOND

The Great Dark Beyond represents the physical universe. It is an infinite living realm composed of innumerable stars, worlds, and mortal civilizations.

Azeroth—the world of Warcraft—is merely one of the countless worlds drifting through the vast reaches of the Great Dark Beyond.

THE TWISTING NETHER

The Twisting Nether is an astral dimension that lies in parallel with the Great Dark Beyond. The forces of Light and Void bleed together at the boundaries of the Twisting Nether, engulfing this realm in perpetual strife. At times, the volatile magics that pervade the Twisting Nether intrude upon the physical universe, warping reality beyond measure.

THE EMERALD DREAM

The Emerald Dream is an ethereal realm of spirits and untamed nature that exists alongside the world of Azeroth. Incredible beings known as the keepers forged the Emerald Dream to act as a map for the evolutionary path of Azeroth's flora and fauna. The two realms are bound as one: as life ebbs and flows across the physical world, the spiritual energies that saturate the Emerald Dream keep pace with it.

Although tied to the physical world, the Emerald Dream is a place that most mortal minds would find alien and surreal. But some of those minds, by channeling druidic magic, can enter a state of dreaming and consciously navigate the Emerald Dream. Their thoughts can also shape and influence portions of this verdant spirit realm, but the imprint that these dreamers leave behind is never permanent.

In the dreamways, time and distance are mutable. Spirits flow like living winds through lush tracts of constantly shifting primordial woodlands. What appears tangible one moment becomes intangible the next; seemingly impermeable landmarks transform in the blink of an eye.

THE SHADOWLANDS

Like the Emerald Dream, the Shadowlands are tangentially linked to the world of Azeroth. Yet whereas the Emerald Dream represents life, the Shadowlands represent death. They are nightmarish realms of decay, labyrinthine spiritual planes teeming with the souls of the dead who have passed from the world of the living.

The origins of the Shadowlands remain uncertain, but they have existed ever since mortal life first arose in the physical universe. Many believe that mortal souls are drawn into this dark place at the point of death, where they remain forever after. Still others hope that their souls will go on to a brighter place, rather than languish for eternity within the cold confines of the Shadowlands.

Denizens of the Cosmos

Void Lords

The void lords are monstrous entities composed of pure shadow energy. These beings are cruel and merciless beyond mortal comprehension. Driven by an insatiable hunger, the void lords seek to devour all matter and energy in the physical universe.

In their natural state, the void lords exist outside reality. Only the most powerful of these entities can manifest in the physical universe, and only for limited amounts of time. To maintain their presence in reality, the void lords must consume untold amounts of matter and energy.

Naaru

The naaru are benevolent creatures of living holy energy. They are perhaps the purest expression of the Light that exists in the Great Dark Beyond. The naaru have vowed to bring peace and hope to all mortal civilizations and waylay the dark forces of the Void that seek to engulf creation.

Titans

The titans are colossal godlike beings composed of the primordial matter from which the universe was born. They roam the cosmos like walking worlds, imbued with the raw power of creation itself. The titans use this incredible force to find and awaken others of their kind—others who still slumber within the far corners of the Great Dark.

The Burning Legion

The Burning Legion is the single most destructive force within the Great Dark Beyond. The fallen titan Sargeras created this vast demonic army to scour all creation. The Burning Legion moves from world to world, decimating everything in its path with devastating fel magic. No one knows exactly how many worlds and mortal civilizations the demons have annihilated in their unholy Burning Crusade.

The demons that fill the ranks of the Burning Legion are highly resilient. Their spirits are tethered to the Twisting Nether, making them extraordinarily difficult to destroy permanently. Even if a demon dies in the physical universe, its spirit will return to the Twisting Nether and manifest in corporeal form once again. To truly destroy a demon's spirit, the creature must be killed in the Twisting Nether itself, in places where that volatile maelstrom bleeds into mortal worlds, or in areas inundated with the Burning Legion's energies.

Old Gods

The Old Gods are physical manifestations of the Void. They are nightmares incarnate: mountains of blighted flesh and writhing tentacles that grow like cancers within the worlds of the Great Dark. These malignant entities serve the void lords, and they live only to transform the worlds they infest into places of despair and death.

Wild Gods

The Wild Gods are primal manifestations of life and nature. They are creatures of two realms. The Wild Gods inhabit the physical world of Azeroth, but their spirits are bound to the ethereal Emerald Dream. Many Wild Gods appear in the form of gargantuan animals, such as wolves, bears, tigers, or birds.

Elemental Spirits

The elemental spirits are primitive and chaotic beings of fire, earth, air, or water. They were some of the first sentient creatures to inhabit the nascent worlds of the waking universe. The elemental spirits appear in an almost infinite variety of shapes and sizes. Each of these creatures has a distinct personality and temperament, traits that are heavily influenced by a spirit's elemental nature.

The presence of the fifth element—Spirit—also affects the disposition of these elemental beings. A world with an overabundance of Spirit may give rise to native elementals who are passive and lack physicality. Conversely, a world with too little Spirit may birth elementals who are highly aggressive and incredibly destructive.

Undead

The undead are former mortals who have died and become trapped between life and death. These tragic beings derive power from the necromantic energies that pervade the universe. Most undead are driven by vengeance and hatred to destroy the one thing that they can never have again: life.

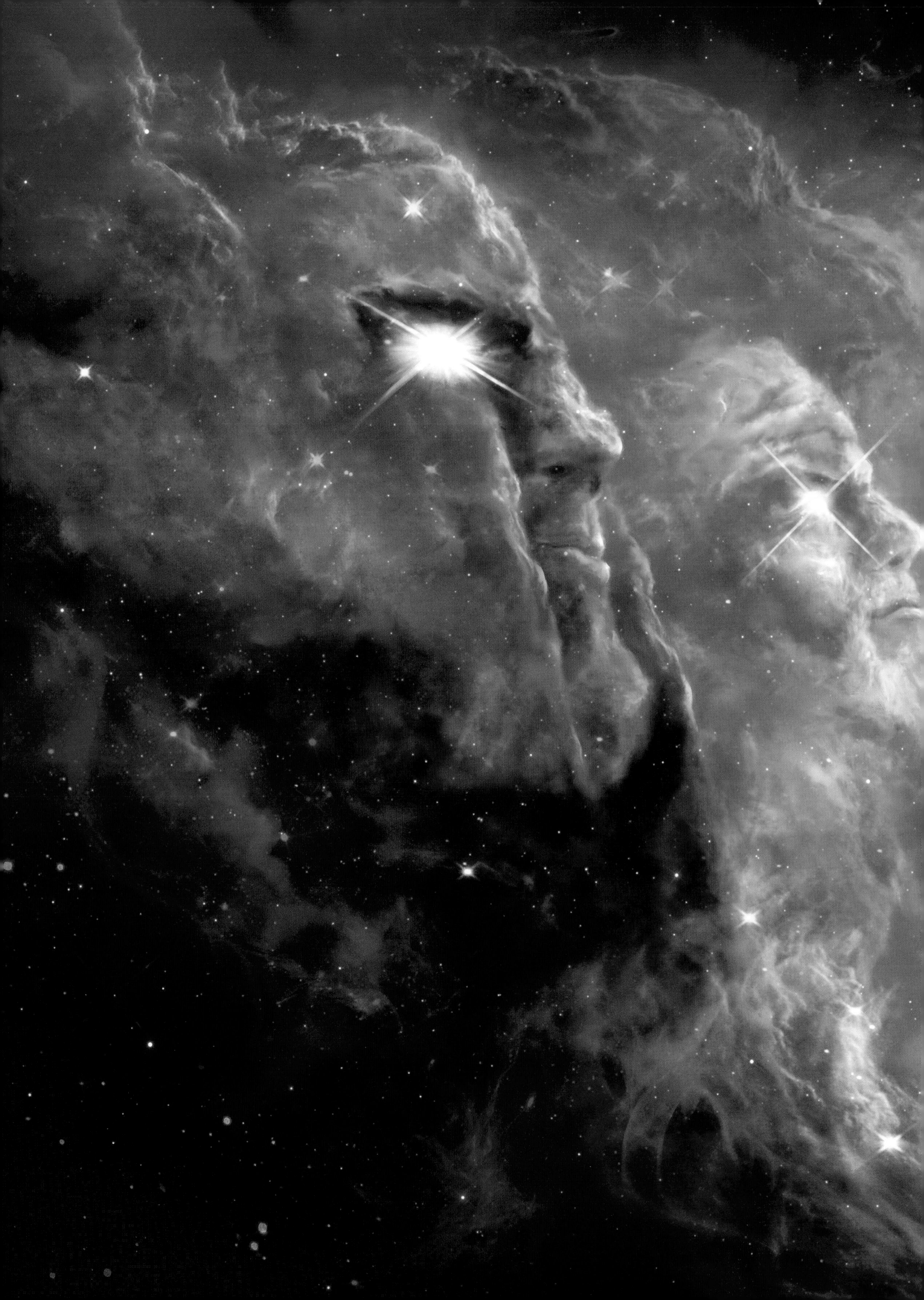

CHAPTER I

MYTHOS

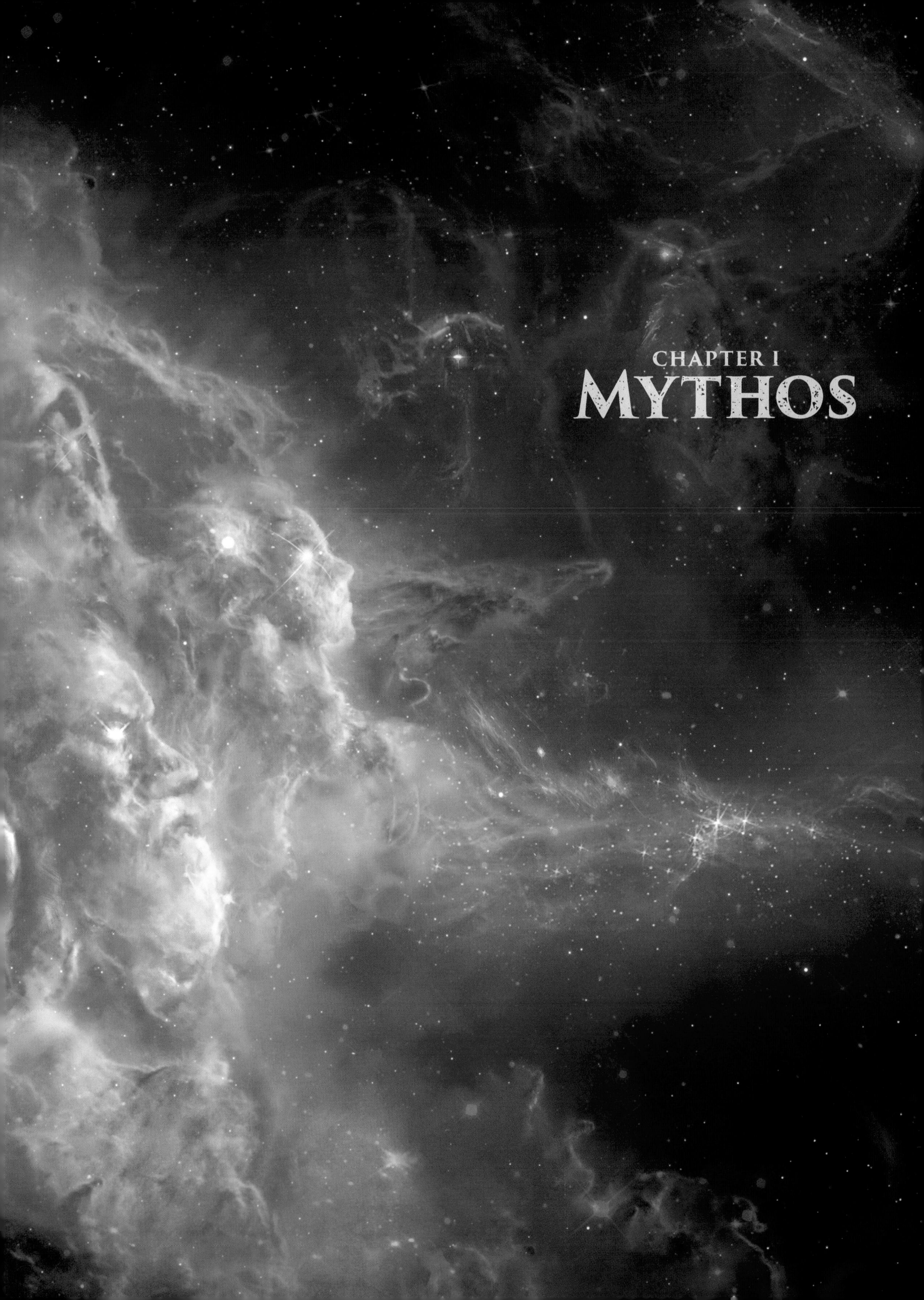

CHAPTER I
MYTHOS

ORIGINS

Before life began, before even the cosmos took shape, there was Light . . . and there was Void. Unfettered by the confines of time and space, the Light swelled across all existence in the form of a boundless prismatic sea. Great torrents of living energy flitted through its mirrored depths, their movements conjuring a symphony of joy and hope.

The ocean of Light was dynamic and ever shifting. Yet as it expanded, some of its energies faded and dimmed, leaving behind pockets of cold nothingness. From the absence of Light in these spaces, a new power coalesced and came to be.

This power was the Void, a dark and vampiric force driven to devour all energy, to twist creation inward to feed upon itself. The Void quickly grew and spread its influence, moving against the flowing waves of Light. The mounting tension between these two opposing yet inseparable energies eventually ignited a series of catastrophic explosions, rupturing the fabric of creation and birthing a new realm into existence.

In that moment, the physical universe was born.

The energies released by the clash of Light and Void raged across the nascent cosmos, raw matter merging and spinning into primordial worlds without number. For long epochs, this ever-expanding universe—the Great Dark Beyond—broiled in a maelstrom of fire and magic.

The most unstable energies coalesced into an astral dimension known as the Twisting Nether. Light and Void collided and bled together at the edges of this realm, throwing it into turmoil. Although tangentially linked to the Great Dark Beyond, the Twisting Nether existed outside the borders of the physical universe. Even so, the Twisting Nether's volatile energies would occasionally tear through the veil of the Great Dark, flooding into reality and warping creation.

The cataclysmic birth of the cosmos also flung shards of Light throughout reality. These shards suffused the matter of myriad worlds with the spark of life, giving rise to creatures of wondrous and terrible diversity.

The most common forms of life to appear were the elemental spirits—primordial beings of fire, water, earth, and air. These creatures were native to nearly every physical world. Many of them reveled in the turmoil that held sway over the early ages of creation.

Occasionally, clouds of fractured Light gathered and gave shape to beings of far greater power, of far greater potential. Among these were the naaru, benevolent creatures composed of scintillating holy energies. When they gazed out across the immeasurable universe, they saw a realm of limitless possibilities. The naaru vowed to use their mastery over holy magic to spread hope and nurture life wherever they could find it.

Even more extraordinary than the naaru were the colossal titans. Their spirits—known as world-souls—formed deep within the fiery core of a small number of worlds. For ages, these nascent titans slumbered, their energies suffusing the celestial bodies they inhabited.

When the titans finally awoke, they did so as living worlds. Cosmic winds howled across their gigantic forms, bodies shrouded in a cloak of stardust, skin crisscrossed with silvery mountain peaks and oceans shimmering with latent magic.

With eyes that shone like brilliant stars, they observed the fledgling cosmos and became enraptured by its mysteries. Whereas the naaru set out to safeguard life, the titans embarked on a different journey. They wandered the distant corners of the Great Dark, searching for others of their kind.

This grand, far-reaching voyage would one day alter the course of creation and shape the destiny of all living things.

THE TITANS AND THE ORDERING OF THE UNIVERSE

No one knows when or why the first titan awoke, but legends hold that his name was Aman'Thul.

Though Aman'Thul was alone, he knew in his heart that others of his kind must exist. Thus, he explored the worlds of the Great Dark Beyond, intent on finding more titans. His quest was arduous and lonely, but it was ultimately fulfilling. In time, he discovered other nascent world-souls. Aman'Thul lovingly nurtured these newfound kin and roused them from slumber. Those who awakened devoted themselves to his noble search.

Aman'Thul and his siblings later became known as the Pantheon. They were benevolent by nature, creatures aligned with order and stability. The Pantheon possessed a natural affinity to the latent magic in the universe. Fully aware of their incredible power, they bound themselves to a code of temperance toward the civilizations they encountered, even those of the unruly elemental spirits.

The titans of the Pantheon came to realize that order was crucial to finding others of their kind. On each world they encountered, they employed techniques to ascertain whether a world-soul was present. The Pantheon would first pacify the world's raging elemental populations. Then, they would reshape the world, forming great mountains, fathomless seas, and roiling skies. Lastly, the titans would seed myriad life-forms across the newly ordered world. In doing so, the Pantheon hoped to call forth the world-soul and help bring it to maturity. Most of the time, however, the worlds visited by the titans proved inert.

The Pantheon vowed to maintain and protect all of these worlds, even those that did not contain a slumbering spirit. To do so, they empowered primitive life-forms to uphold the integrity of their ordered worlds. The Pantheon also embedded colossal machines in the surface of the worlds that they had shaped. Through these devices, the titans could monitor their worlds—and purge them of life should their evolutionary paths succumb to disorder.

To aid the Pantheon, Aman'Thul called upon a mysterious race known as the constellar. These celestial beings observed the many worlds ordered by the titans, staying vigilant for any sign of instability. When it was necessary, the constellar could initiate a fail-safe procedure to scour life from a world in the hopes of resetting its evolutionary process.

Over the ages, the Pantheon discovered fewer and fewer world-souls. Yet they remained undaunted. They knew that the universe was vast beyond measure, and even after epochs of exploring the stars, they had only plumbed but a small corner of creation.

Unbeknownst to the titans, malign forces were also hard at work in the distant reaches of the Great Dark.

THE PANTHEON

Aman'Thul—Highfather of the Pantheon
Sargeras—Defender of the Pantheon
Aggramar—Lieutenant of the Great Sargeras
Eonar—The Life-Binder
Khaz'goroth—Shaper and Forger of Worlds
Norgannon—Keeper of Celestial Magics and Lore
Golganneth—Lord of the Skies and Roaring Oceans

THE VOID LORDS AND THE BIRTH OF THE OLD GODS

From the moment the cosmos came to be, dark spirits within the Void sought to twist reality into a realm of eternal torment. These entities were known as the void lords, and they had long watched the Pantheon and their journey from world to world. Envious of their power, the void lords sought to corrupt one of the world-shaping titans into an instrument of their will.

To achieve this goal, the void lords struggled to manifest in the physical universe. As they did so, their energies seeped into reality, warping some of the unsuspecting denizens of creation. Yet the noble and virtuous titans proved impervious to this insidious corruption. Eventually, the void lords moved to exert their influence over a titan in its most vulnerable state: before it had awakened.

The void lords did not know which worlds contained slumbering titan spirits. Thus they pooled their power and hurled dark creatures throughout the physical universe, hoping some would smash into a world-soul. An unknown number of the void lords' creations hurtled through the Great Dark. They contaminated mortal worlds and everything else they touched in their blind search for a nascent titan. In time, these wicked beings would come to be known as the Old Gods.

Although the titans were aware that Void energies existed in the universe, they had no knowledge of the void lords or the Old Gods. The Pantheon's attention was consumed by another, more immediate threat: demons. These ferocious creatures had been born from the Twisting Nether. Held in the thrall of unbridled hate and malice, they hungered for nothing less than the destruction of all life in the universe.

THE RISE OF DEMONS

Just as in the Great Dark Beyond, life had also arisen in the Twisting Nether. The creatures that emerged from this turbulent realm were known as demons. They had been formed as a result of the Light and Void energies that had bled together at the borders of the Twisting Nether. The demons embraced their furious passions and reveled in pushing the boundaries of their power, heedless of the consequences. Many of these aberrations indulged in the highly volatile energy that pervaded the Nether. Some learned to wield the all-consuming powers of fel magic. Before long, these bloodthirsty demons clawed their way into the physical universe, terrorizing mortal civilizations and bringing ruin to world after world.

Demons came in many forms. Some, like the two-headed void hounds, roamed the trackless wastes of the Nether like ravenous beasts. Others, such as the monstrous abyssals and infernals, were mindless amalgamations of matter and fel energy, created by more powerful and intelligent demons.

Among these greater demons were the nathrezim, otherwise known as dreadlords. Cunning and manipulative, they dedicated their existence to mastering the arts of shadow magic. The nathrezim relished infiltrating mortal civilizations, sowing unrest, and turning nation against nation. As these societies devolved and crumbled from within, the nathrezim would corrupt their populations, twisting innocents into new and horrific breeds of demon.

The mighty annihilan, or pit lords, took a more direct approach to conquering worlds. These monstrous butchers existed only to brutalize and torture the mortals who crossed their path. The pit lords often enslaved the lesser demons that stalked the Nether, using them as fodder to besiege the mortal civilizations of the Great Dark Beyond.

The Pantheon soon learned of the demonic incursions that flared at the far corners of creation. Fearing that these demons would disturb the Pantheon's quest to find and awaken other world-souls, the titans dispatched their mightiest warrior, the noble Sargeras. Without hesitation, the great-hearted titan set out and pledged he would not rest until he had cleansed the universe of all demonic influence.

SARGERAS AND AGGRAMAR

Even among the extraordinary members of the Pantheon, Sargeras displayed unmatched courage and strength. These traits would suit him well for the harrowing task of hunting demons. Girded by his unshakable conviction, he launched himself into the Great Dark.

Sargeras was soon drawn to worlds inundated with erratic and volatile energies. In these places, the influence of the Twisting Nether had spilled into the physical universe, allowing vast numbers of demons to manifest.

For ages, Sargeras traveled to these beleaguered worlds, fighting to spare their mortal inhabitants from invading demons. He saw his foes reduce entire civilizations to smoldering husks, warping their denizens into hateful and depraved aberrations. Witnessing this staggering loss and ruin filled Sargeras with an overwhelming sense of helplessness. Before embarking on his mission, he had never imagined such evil could exist in the universe.

Nevertheless, the unruly demons were disorganized and incompetent. Sargeras easily defeated his foes, winning victory after victory. As his battles dragged on, he became aware that some demons had learned to wield Void energies. Through investigating these dark powers and where they originated from, Sargeras discovered that malign intelligences were spreading corruption throughout the cosmos.

These intelligences were the void lords, and they were far more powerful than demons. The presence of the void lords left Sargeras deeply troubled. He pondered what the powers of the Void were planning, and what their existence could mean for the universe.

Despite his unsettling discovery, Sargeras continued waging his war on demons. The work of the Pantheon progressed without hindrance. They searched for nascent titans, ordering new worlds in the process. Sargeras often looked upon these budding worlds. Seeing life bloom, free from demon influence, gave him a sense of satisfaction. His love for life galvanized his will to confront the void lords and undo their sinister plans for creation—whatever those plans might be.

In time, the demons redoubled their efforts, engulfing ever more worlds in death and devastation. To Sargeras's dismay, he realized that he had fought many of these demons before. After he had defeated them in the physical universe, their spirits had simply returned to the Twisting Nether. Eventually they had been reborn in new bodies.

The only way to kill demons permanently was to slay them in the Nether, or in areas of the Great Dark saturated with that volatile realm's energies. Sargeras, however, was yet unaware of this fact. He knew only that his current tactics were ineffective. It was not enough to destroy his foes. He needed a means to contain them.

Concerned about this development and the continued influx of demonic activity, the Pantheon sent another titan to aid their champion. His name was Aggramar, and though he was inexperienced in battle, he proved a quick study. He earned Sargeras's admiration and became the titan warrior's trusted lieutenant. For many millennia they fought shoulder to shoulder, an impenetrable bulwark against the ravaging demonic onslaught.

With Aggramar able to hold his own in battle, Sargeras had time to closely study the properties of the Twisting Nether and find a way to contain demons. Though he hadn't yet grasped the volatile realm's full scale, he had learned how to manipulate and shape some of its energies. Sargeras used this knowledge to forge a prison within the Nether. Known as Mardum, the Plane of Banishment, it would act as an impregnable pocket dimension from which nothing could escape. No longer would demons be reborn after defeat. Now, they would be contained within this prison, where they would languish for all eternity.

As Aggramar and Sargeras continued their campaign, the prison overflowed with captive demons and their destructive fel energies. Soon, these energies became so great that they began tearing at the veil between the Nether and the physical universe. The prison appeared in distant reaches of the Great Dark as a burning, verdant star.

Sargeras's and Aggramar's valiant efforts soon brought peace to the cosmos. Demonic incursions would remain a constant threat to the Great Dark, but they became increasingly rare. The titans' worlds prospered, and life, in all of its complexity, flourished.

THE WILL OF THE VOID

As the Pantheon searched for slumbering world-souls, Sargeras and Aggramar continued their hunt for errant demons. The two champions agreed that they could protect more worlds if they worked apart, only calling on each other for aid in times of dire need. Thus, they went their separate ways.

It was during this epoch that Sargeras discovered the full horror of the void lords' plans.

He was drawn to a remote corner of the Great Dark, where cold Void energies radiated out from a black and desiccated world. There, Sargeras found enormous beings he had never seen, festering across the world's surface. These were the Old Gods, and they had embedded themselves in the world and shrouded it in a veil of Void energies.

With growing horror, Sargeras realized that this was not just any world. He heard the world-soul dreaming within its core. But these were not the joyous dreams Sargeras recognized from other world-souls—they were dark and horrific nightmares. The Old Gods' tendrils had burrowed deep, enveloping the slumbering titan's spirit in shadow.

A conclave of nathrezim had also discovered this black world. They came to dwell among the Old Gods, basking in their dark power. Sensing their evil, Sargeras captured and ruthlessly interrogated the nathrezim. The broken demons revealed what they had learned about the Old Gods and the intentions of the void lords. If the powers of the Void succeeded in corrupting a nascent titan, it would awaken as an unspeakably dark creature. No power in creation, not even the Pantheon, could stand against it. In time, the warped titan would consume all matter and energy in the universe, bringing every mote of existence under the void lords' will.

Sargeras, the undefeated champion of the titans, knew fear for the first time. It dawned on him that just as the Pantheon had been searching for world-souls, so, too, had the void lords. Sargeras had never dreamed that Void energies could so utterly consume a slumbering titan.

Yet the proof was right before his eyes.

Rage and anguish burned through Sargeras's soul. He smote the nathrezim with a single blow—his fury so great that he utterly obliterated the demons' forms. Sargeras turned his attention to the black world itself. His heart ached with sorrow, for he knew there was only one way to stop the dark titan from rising.

With a heave of his blade, Sargeras split the world in two. The resultant explosion consumed the Old Gods and their energies, but it killed the nascent titan as well.

Sargeras immediately returned to the rest of the Pantheon and summoned Aggramar to his side. Before the gathered titans, Sargeras recounted his discoveries. The other Pantheon members were stunned by what they had learned, but even more so by Sargeras's rash action. They chastised him for so needlessly killing one of their kin. Had he called on their aid, they argued, they could have purged the world-soul of corruption.

Although Sargeras tried to convince them that what he had done was necessary, he came to realize it was futile. The other titans had not seen what he had seen. They would never understand why he had taken such drastic measures. Apart from Aggramar, the other titans had no firsthand knowledge of the Void or demons. They could not fathom the depths of such malice and corruptive power.

Heated arguments flared between Sargeras and the rest of the Pantheon concerning how best to deal with the threat posed by the void lords. Above all, Sargeras feared that if the Old Gods had corrupted one world-soul, they might have corrupted many others as well. It might be too late to stop them.

Sargeras expressed his growing fear that existence itself was already flawed—an idea that he had come to terms with following his encounter with the Old Gods. Only by burning away all of creation could the titans stand a chance of thwarting the void lords' ultimate goal. In Sargeras's mind, even a lifeless universe was better than one dominated by the Void. Life had taken root in the cosmos once before. Perhaps after the physical universe was scoured of corruption, life would take root once again.

This idea horrified the rest of the Pantheon. Eonar, the Life-Binder, reminded Sargeras that the titans had sworn to protect living things whenever possible. Nothing could be so dire as to warrant systemic extinction. Even Aggramar stood against his mentor, arguing that there must be another way to defeat the void lords. He urged Sargeras to abandon this dark plan and reason out another solution.

Overcome with despair and feelings of betrayal, Sargeras stormed away from the other titans. He knew full well that his kin would never see reason. And if they would not help him expel the void lords' corruption, then he would do it himself.

This was the last time the titans of the Pantheon would see him as one of their own.

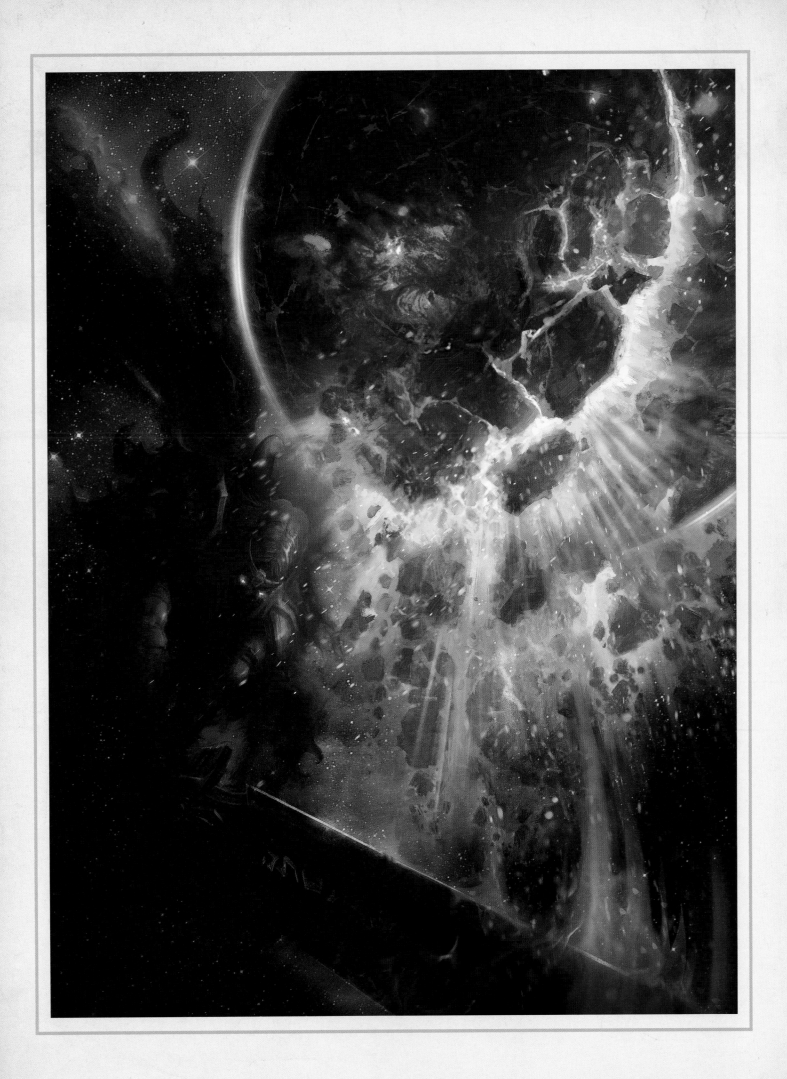

SARGERAS DESTROYS THE CORRUPTED WORLD-SOUL

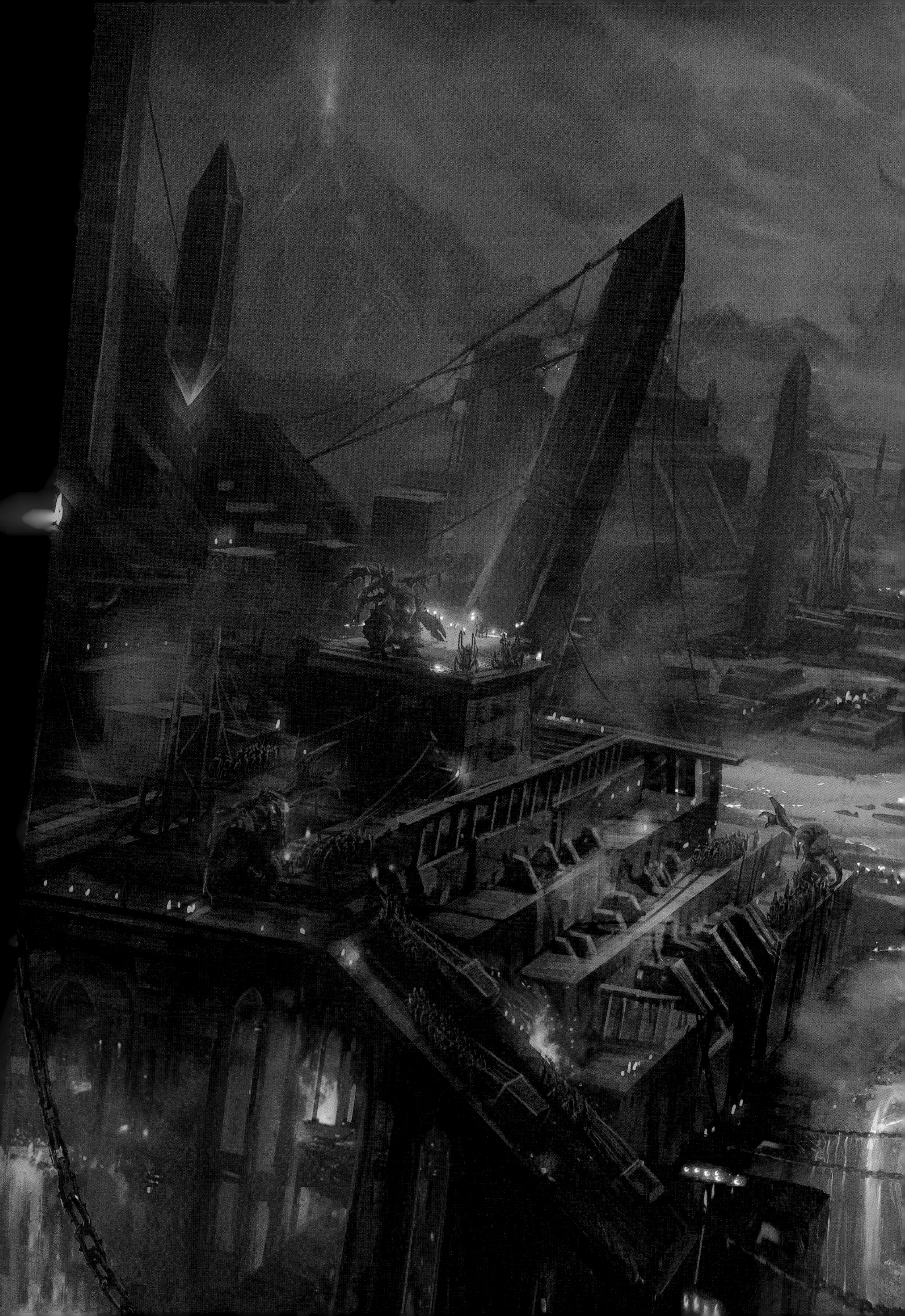

CHAPTER II
PRIMORDIAL AZEROTH

CHAPTER II
PRIMORDIAL AZEROTH

REIGN OF THE ELEMENTS

For many long ages, the Pantheon continued searching the cosmos for nascent titans, bringing order to countless worlds in the process. Yet despite their efforts, they did not find any more of their kin. At times, the titans of the Pantheon wondered if their search was in vain, but always they resolved to press on. They knew in their hearts that more world-souls existed, and this hope filled them with purpose.

Though the Pantheon did not know it, their intuition was correct. A miraculous new world was taking shape in an isolated corner of the Great Dark. Deep within this world's core, the spirit of a mighty and noble titan stirred to life.

One day, it would be known as Azeroth.

As the nascent titan developed, elemental spirits roamed across the world's surface. Over the ages, these beings became ever more erratic and destructive. The burgeoning world-soul was so vast that it had drawn in and consumed much of the fifth element, Spirit. Without this primordial force to create balance, Azeroth's elemental spirits descended into chaos.

Fire, earth, air, and water—these were the forces that lorded over the infant world. They reveled in unending strife, keeping the face of Azeroth in constant elemental flux. Four elemental lords, powerful beyond mortal comprehension, reigned supreme over innumerable lesser spirits.

Of the elemental lords, none could match the ruthless cunning of Al'Akir the Windlord. He often sent his elusive tempest minions to spy on his enemies and sow distrust among their ranks. Using feints and ruses, he would pit the other elementals against each other, only later to unleash the full fury of his servants on his weakened foes. The winds would howl and the skies would darken with storms at his approach. As lightning blasted the world's surface, Al'Akir's whirlwind elementals would come screaming from the heavens, enveloping his foes in monstrous cyclones.

Ragnaros the Firelord despised Al'Akir's cowardly ways. Compulsive and brash, the Firelord embraced brute force to annihilate his enemies. Wherever he went, volcanoes would burst through the world's crust, spewing forth rivers of fire and destruction. Ragnaros longed for nothing more than to boil the seas, reduce the mountains to slag, and choke the skies with ember and ash. The other elemental lords fostered a deep hatred of Ragnaros for his brazen and devastating assaults.

Therazane the Stonemother was the most reclusive elemental ruler. Ever protective of her children, she raised towering mountain ranges to ward off her enemies' assaults. Only after they

OVERLEAF: THE BLACK EMPIRE

had worn themselves thin against her impenetrable fortifications would the Stonemother emerge, wrenching open giant chasms in the earth and swallowing entire elemental armies whole. Those who survived would meet oblivion at the fists of Therazane's most powerful servants: walking mountains of unforgiving crystal and stone.

The wise Neptulon the Tidehunter was careful not to fall for Al'Akir's schemes or to commit his minions to fruitless attacks against Therazane's citadels. As the armies of fire, air, and earth clashed across the face of Azeroth, the Tidehunter and his elementals would divide and conquer their rivals in brilliant routs. When his foes fled, Neptulon would crush them beneath tidal waves that dwarfed even Therazane's highest mountain holdings.

The apocalyptic battles between the elemental lords raged for untold millennia. Dominion over Azeroth constantly shifted between the factions, each one striving to remake the world in its own image. Yet for the elementals, victory was secondary to the conflict itself. To them, the world's calamitous state was sublime, and their only desire was to continue their endless cycle of chaos.

COMING OF THE OLD GODS

The elemental lords reveled amid the primordial bedlam until a group of Old Gods plummeted down from the Great Dark. They slammed into Azeroth's surface, embedding themselves in different locations across the world. These Old Gods towered over the land, mountains of flesh, pockmarked with hundreds of gnashing maws and black, unfeeling eyes. A miasma of despair soon enveloped everything that lay in their writhing shadows.

Like gargantuan, cancerous pustules, the Old Gods spread their corruptive influence across the landscape. The lands around them seethed and withered, turning black and lifeless for leagues upon leagues. All the while, the tendrils of the Old Gods wormed into the world's crust, slithering deeper and deeper toward the defenseless heart of Azeroth.

Organic matter seeped from the Old Gods' blighted forms, giving rise to two distinct races. The first were the cunning and intelligent n'raqi, also known as the "faceless ones." The second were the aqir, insectoids of incredible resilience and strength. As the physical manifestations of the Old Gods' will, both of these races would serve their masters with fanatical loyalty.

Through their new servants, the Old Gods expanded the borders of their remote dominions. The n'raqi acted as ruthless taskmasters, employing the aqir as laborers to erect towering citadels and temple cities around their masters' colossal bulks. The greatest of these bastions was built around Y'Shaarj, the most powerful and wicked of the Old Gods. This burgeoning civilization was located near the center of Azeroth's largest continent. Y'Shaarj's holdings, along with the other Old God domains, would soon spread across the world and become known as the Black Empire.

The rise of the Black Empire did not go unnoticed by the elementals. Seeing the Old Gods as a challenge to their dominion, the elemental lords moved to excise the entities from their world. For the first time in Azeroth's history, the world's native spirits worked in unison against a common enemy.

Al'Akir's tempests joined with Ragnaros's fiery servants, creating monstrous cyclones of flame. These blistering firestorms raged over the world, reducing the Black Empire's citadels to ash. Elsewhere, Therazane raised jagged rock walls to corral her enemies and shatter their temple cities.

Neptulon and his tidal minions then swept in, crushing the n'raqi and the aqir between unyielding stone and the fury of the seas.

Yet for all their fervor, the elementals could not topple the Black Empire. No matter how many n'raqi and aqir died, more and more would spawn from the Old Gods' putrid forms like larvae from a hive. The n'raqi and the aqir engulfed the land like an unstoppable pestilence, shattering the elementals' forms.

In the end, the Old Gods enslaved the elementals and their lords. Without the native spirits to counter the n'raqi and the aqir, the borders of the Black Empire crept over much of the desiccated world. Perpetual twilight descended upon Azeroth, and the world spiraled into an abyss of suffering and death.

THE DISCOVERY OF AZEROTH

Meanwhile, in the depths of the Great Dark Beyond, Aggramar continued his quest to eradicate all signs of demonic influence. His battles led him from one world to another, from one demon-beset civilization to the next. Though Aggramar bore the full weight of this task alone, his resolve never wavered. He believed with all his heart that Sargeras would one day return and see that the Pantheon's cause was right.

It was during his long and lonely journeys that Aggramar sensed something extraordinary: the tranquil dreams of a slumbering world-soul, billowing across the cosmos. The song of life led him to a world that the Pantheon had not yet discovered, a world they would later name "Azeroth."

Nestled within the world's core was one of Aggramar's kin—one far more powerful than any yet encountered. The spirit was so mighty that Aggramar sensed its dreams even through the din of activity that rattled across the world's surface.

Yet as Aggramar drew closer to Azeroth and beheld the world, horror seized him. Void energies shrouded the world's surface like a layer of diseased flesh. From the ruined landscape rose the Old Gods and their Black Empire. Miraculously, the nascent titan's spirit remained uncorrupted, but Aggramar knew it was only a matter of time before it succumbed to the Void.

Aggramar sought counsel with the rest of the Pantheon, informing them of his discovery. Clearly, this was proof that Sargeras had been right about the void lords and their plans. Aggramar urged the other titans to take action with all due haste before Azeroth was lost forever.

Eonar was quick to champion Aggramar's cause. She compelled the other Pantheon members to think of the world's potential. If brought to maturity, this new titan could exceed even Sargeras's considerable might, she argued. Indeed, it could become their greatest warrior, one capable of neutralizing the void lords once and for all. But more than that, Azeroth was one of them—a lost and vulnerable member of their family. The Pantheon could not abandon their own sibling to the clutches of the void lords.

Eonar's words stirred the hearts of the rest of the Pantheon. They unanimously agreed to save Azeroth, no matter the cost.

Aggramar formulated a bold plan of attack: all members of the Pantheon would travel to Azeroth and purge the Black Empire that had claimed it. They would not, however, take action directly. Due to their colossal forms, Aggramar feared the Pantheon would irreparably damage, or even kill, the world-soul. Instead, he proposed creating mighty constructs to act as the Pantheon's hands and prosecute their will against the Black Empire.

Under the guidance of the great forger Khaz'goroth, the Pantheon crafted an army of enormous servants from the crust of Azeroth itself: the aesir and the vanir. The aesir were fashioned from metal, and they would command the powers of storms. The vanir were formed from stone, and they would hold sway over the earth. Collectively, these mighty creatures would be known as the titan-forged.

The members of the Pantheon imbued a number of their servants with their specific likenesses and powers to lead the rest of the titan-forged. These empowered beings were called the keepers. Though they would develop their own personalities in time, they would forever after bear the mark and abilities of their makers.

Aman'Thul gifted some of his vast abilities to Highkeeper Ra and Keeper Odyn. Khaz'goroth bestowed his mastery over the earth and forging to Keeper Archaedas. Golganneth granted Keepers Thorim and Hodir dominion over the storms and skies. Eonar gave Keeper Freya command over Azeroth's flora and fauna. Norgannon lent a portion of his intellect and mastery of magic to Keepers Loken and Mimiron. Lastly, Aggramar imparted his strength and courage to Keeper Tyr, who would become the greatest warrior of the titan-forged.

With this new army molded from the world's crust, the Pantheon went to war. The time to shatter the Black Empire and free Azeroth from its malign influence had come . . .

Wrath of the Titan-Forged

Led by the keepers, the titan-forged slammed into the Black Empire's northernmost holdings. The resilience and strength of the Pantheon's armies made them an unstoppable force. They unleashed the wrath of gods upon their enemies, scouring legions of n'raqi and aqir and sundering their temples.

The arrival of the titan-forged caught the Old Gods completely off guard. They reeled in response to these stone- and metal-skinned invaders, but they were determined not to lose control over Azeroth. To reassert their dominance, the Old Gods called upon their greatest lieutenants: the elemental lords.

The enraged elemental lords and their minions beset the titan-forged on all sides. Ever wary of fighting a unified elemental army, the keepers resolved to divide and conquer their enemies. Thus they split their own forces and dispatched each group of titan-forged to make war on a specific elemental lord.

Tyr and Odyn volunteered to confront the most destructive elemental lieutenant: Ragnaros the Firelord. Their battle raged for weeks, engulfing the land in fire and magma. Yet the keepers' resilient metal forms kept them safe from Ragnaros's fiery onslaughts. Through sheer strength and force of will, Tyr and Odyn pushed Ragnaros back into his volcanic lair in the east. In a land of boiling acid seas and skies choked with ash, the two keepers defeated the Firelord.

Meanwhile, Archaedas and Freya unleashed their powers upon Therazane the Stonemother. To protect herself and her minions, the elemental ruler retreated into the towering stone spire that she called home. Archaedas used his dominion over the earth to weaken the citadel's foundations and shatter the craggy giants who guarded it. Freya then made colossal roots sprout from the ground to entangle the fortress. They wormed through stone and crystal, buckled the citadel's walls, and brought them down on Therazane's head.

Ra, Thorim, and Hodir waged war with Al'Akir the Windlord. Using their mastery over the skies and storms, they forced the elemental lord back to his lair among the highest peaks of Azeroth. Lightning set the heavens aflame as Al'Akir struggled to hold off his foes. In the end, the three keepers turned the elemental lord's own power against him, defeating Al'Akir atop his lofty domain.

Neptulon the Tidehunter and his minions rushed to aid the other embattled elemental lords, but they were waylaid by Loken and Mimiron. The two keepers used their wits to harry and outmaneuver Neptulon's forces at every turn. Ultimately, Loken unleashed his arcane powers to freeze and shatter the water elementals' forms, while Mimiron crafted enchanted bonds to imprison Neptulon himself.

Although the elemental lords had been defeated, the keepers knew that they could not utterly destroy the beings. The spirits of the elementals were bound to Azeroth itself. If they were killed, their corporeal forms would simply manifest again in time.

Ra soon found a solution. He set out to imprison the elementals, much as the great Sargeras had done to demons. Ra first called on the aid of the gifted titan-forged sorceress Helya. They worked in concert to craft four interlinked domains within a pocket dimension known as the Elemental Plane. Ra and Helya then banished the elemental lords and nearly all of their servants to this enchanted prison realm.

Ragnaros and the fire elementals were exiled to a smoldering corner of the Elemental Plane known as the Firelands. Therazane and the earth elementals were locked within the crystalline caverns of Deepholm. Al'Akir and the air elementals were imprisoned among the cloudy spires of the Skywall. Lastly, Neptulon and the water elementals were sucked into the fathomless depths of the Abyssal Maw. Only a few elementals would remain on the surface of Azeroth. With their leaders gone, these beings scattered and abandoned the war.

Having contained the elementals, the keepers turned their attention to the Black Empire's aqiri legions. Many of the insectoids dwelled in vast catacombs that snaked beneath the surface of the devastated world. Archaedas bent the stones and soil to his will, collapsing the aqiri burrows and driving the creatures aboveground. Upon emerging from their lairs, the insectoids found themselves surrounded by the titan-forged.

The battles between the titan-forged and the aqir proved unexpectedly vicious. In time, the keepers destroyed most of the aqiri race. Small pockets of the insectoids, those that had tunneled deep underground, escaped the keepers' wrath. Yet they were too weakened to mount a counterattack.

THE TITAN-FORGED BATTLE THE ELEMENTAL LORDS

THE BLACK EMPIRE

YOGG-SARON

NEPTULON

Y'SHAARJ

C'THUN

AL'AKIR

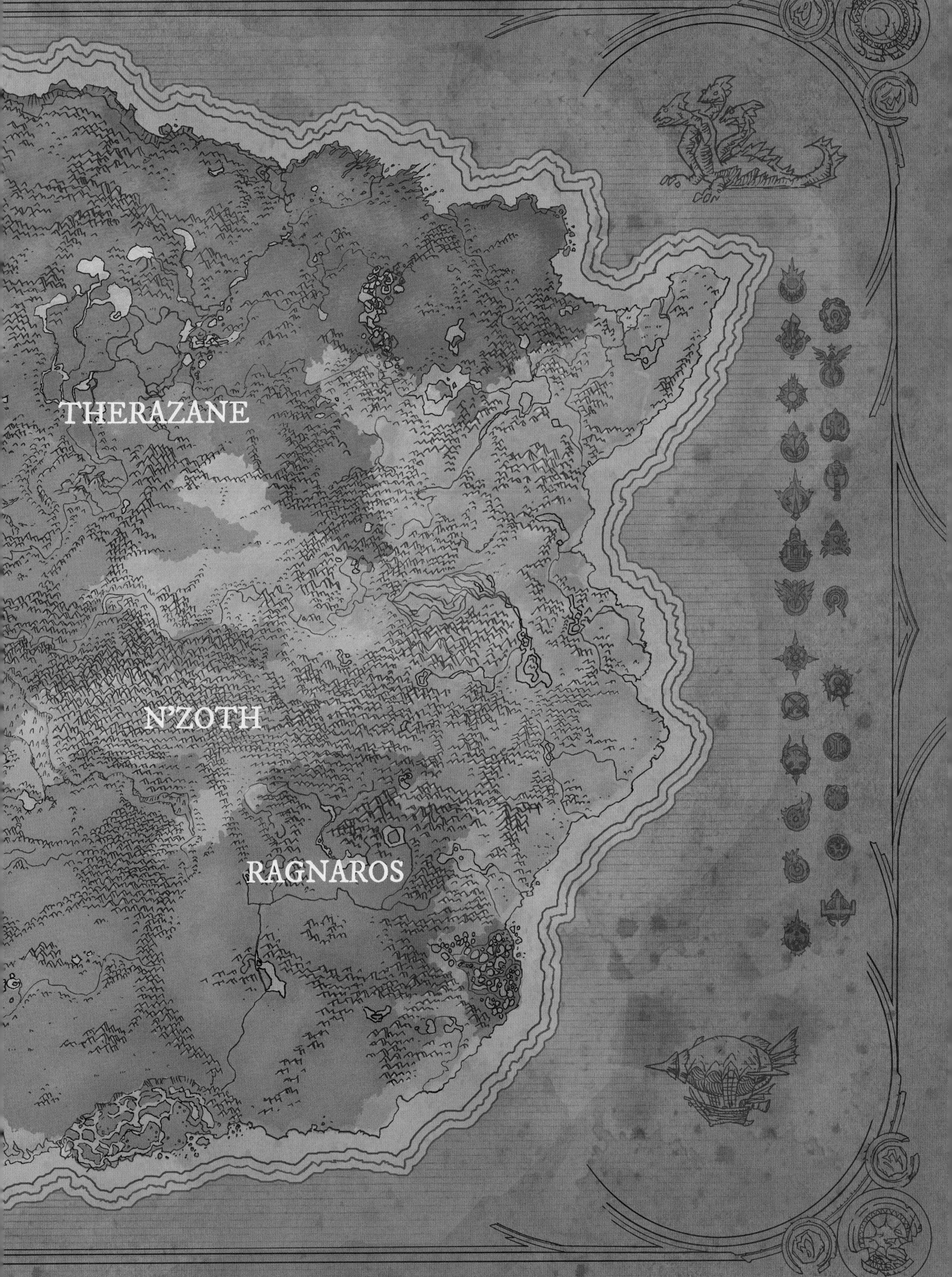
THERAZANE
N'ZOTH
RAGNAROS

Fall of the Black Empire

The victories over the aqir and the elementals heartened the keepers, but they knew that their greatest battles were still to come. As one, they turned their righteous gaze on the heart of the Black Empire: the sprawling temple city built around the Old God Y'Shaarj. By toppling the most powerful n'raqi bastion on Azeroth, the keepers believed they could crush their enemies in one swift stroke.

The keepers and their allies waded through one swarm of n'raqi after another as they battled their way toward the mountainous form of Y'Shaarj. The broken and mangled bodies of titan-forged and n'raqi alike riddled the landscape by the time the invaders breached the city and assaulted the Old God itself.

Y'Shaarj was more powerful than the keepers had expected. It poisoned the minds of the titan-forged, drawing out their fears and darkening their thoughts.

The Pantheon grew concerned that the Old God would overwhelm their servants. Despite the risk of harming the world, they decided to take direct action. Aman'Thul himself reached down through Azeroth's stormy skies and took hold of Y'Shaarj's writhing body. With a heave of his mighty arm, he tore the Old God from the crust of the world. In that moment, Y'Shaarj's gargantuan bulk was ripped apart. The immensity of the Old God's death rattle shattered mountaintops and obliterated hundreds of titan-forged where they stood.

Y'Shaarj was dead, but its tendrils had bored more deeply through Azeroth than Aman'Thul had ever imagined. In excising the Old God from the world, he had inadvertently ripped an eternal wound in Azeroth's surface. Volatile arcane energies—the lifeblood of the nascent titan—erupted from the scar and roiled out across the world.

Horrified by this turn of events, the Pantheon realized they could not risk killing the other Old Gods in such a manner. The malignant creatures had embedded themselves so deep into the world that tearing them out would destroy Azeroth itself.

The Pantheon knew that the only course of action was to imprison the Old Gods where they lay and contain their evil forever. It would be a difficult task, but it would be possible with the aid of the keepers. At the Pantheon's behest, the titan-forged devised a plan to shatter the last vestiges of the Black Empire forever. They would battle each of the Old Gods directly. Once they had weakened the creatures, Archaedas would create subterranean chambers to contain them. Mimiron would then fashion colossal machineries to lock the Old Gods in place. When this work was done, Loken would imbue each prison with a great enchantment that would neutralize the Old Gods' evil.

With their plans formed, the titan-forged began their campaign. Great battles tore across the land as the titan-forged fought their way southeast to the bastion of N'Zoth. After overwhelming the Old God, the keepers used their powers to encase the creature in an underground prison.

Next, the titan-forged marched southwest to the sprawling temple city that had grown around the third Old God, C'Thun. The keepers and their allies purged swarms of n'raqi before assaulting the Old God itself and subduing it. Much as they had done with N'Zoth, the keepers entombed the entity beneath the earth and constructed a prison of their own devising over its form.

Only one Old God remained, the vicious and cunning Yogg-Saron. It would not fall so easily. As the titan-forged closed in on Yogg-Saron's crumbling northern stronghold, the Old God unleashed the greatest of its generals: the C'Thraxxi.

OVERLEAF: MAP OF AZEROTH UNDER THE BLACK EMPIRE'S CONTROL

The C'Thraxxi were monstrous war bringers, larger and more resilient than other n'raqi. They possessed great strength and brutal intellect, and their dark powers and maledictions could drive even the titan-forged to madness.

The giant, tentacle-faced C'Thraxxi whipped the remnants of the Black Empire into a frenzy. They swarmed the titan-forged on all sides, thinning their ranks. By the time the keepers and their allies reached Yogg-Saron, their forces were greatly diminished. They found that they lacked the strength of numbers to defeat the Old God. Yogg-Saron would have destroyed the titan-forged completely if not for the heroic efforts of Odyn.

Although scarred and battered by war, Odyn summoned his waning strength and inspired the titan-forged to launch a counterattack. He commanded Loken to weave a grand illusion spell that forced the C'Thraxxi to see themselves—and even Yogg-Saron—as the enemy. As the Black Empire's forces turned on one another, Odyn swooped in to cut down his confused foes. The other titan-forged followed his lead, and together they succeeded in pacifying Yogg-Saron. As they had done with C'Thun and N'Zoth, the keepers buried the entity beneath the earth, locking it away in a monolithic enchanted prison.

THE WELL OF ETERNITY AND THE WORLD FORGES

For the first time in Azeroth's history, a tentative peace settled over the world. The titan-forged had banished the chaotic elemental lords to another plane of existence. They had also purged the Black Empire and muted the terrible power of the Old Gods. Against all odds, Azeroth had been saved.

But there was much work to be done. The keepers' most pressing concern was the horrific scar left behind when Aman'Thul had torn Y'Shaarj from the world's crust. A constant stream of volatile arcane energy bled from the colossal rift, lashing out across the world. The keepers knew that, if left unattended, these energies would consume Azeroth over time.

The keepers labored day and night, crafting magic wards around the gaping wound to stanch the escaping lifeblood. Eventually, the tumultuous energies calmed and settled into balance. All that remained of the scar was an immense lake of scintillating energy that the keepers would call the "Well of Eternity." Thereafter, the power of this wondrous fount would be infused in the ailing world, helping life to take root and bloom across the globe.

With the wound healed, the keepers sought to strengthen Azeroth's nascent world-soul and stabilize its life force. To do so, Archaedas and Mimiron combined their powers to craft the Forge of Wills and the Forge of Origination. These two extraordinary machines would work in tandem, infusing Azeroth's slumbering spirit with cosmic energies. The Forge of Wills would be embedded in the northern reaches of the world, and it would shape the world-soul's budding sentience. The Forge of Origination would be installed in the southern reaches of Azeroth, and it would regulate the rhythms of the deep earth and fortify the world-soul's form.

After these two machines were constructed, the keepers went to work. Odyn oversaw efforts to install the Forge of Wills within a vast northern mountain range that would become known as the Storm Peaks. The Pantheon appointed Odyn the Prime Designate for his valorous deeds in the war with the Old Gods. The task of watching over Yogg-Saron's prison and maintaining the Forge of Wills would fall to him. Odyn and the other keepers immediately began building the great fortress of Ulduar to serve as the main bastion of the titan-forged on Azeroth. The fortress would house not only Yogg-Saron's prison, but also the Forge of Wills and other machineries of the keepers' devising.

The Forge of Wills also served another purpose: it could draw on the life essence of Azeroth itself, giving shape and sentience to creatures of living stone and metal—not only giants, but other types of titan-forged as well. This new generation of titan-forged would help the keepers bring order to the world.

As the Forge of Wills churned out these new titan-forged, Highkeeper Ra led an expedition to install the Forge of Origination in the south. He was accompanied by a number of stone-skinned creatures recently wrought from the Forge of Wills: the anubisath giants, the leonine tol'vir, and the indomitable mogu.

En route, Ra discovered that remnants of Y'Shaarj's corporeal form lay strewn across the southern reaches of the world. When Aman'Thul had ripped the Old God from Azeroth, pieces of the entity had fallen back to the surface, infusing the land with evil. The largest intact piece of Y'Shaarj was the Old God's icy heart, a mass of diseased flesh seething with Void energies.

Rather than destroy the heart, Ra built a subterranean vault to contain it and neutralize its evil. He, along with the other keepers, knew that studying the heart could help them understand the nature of the Old Gods and other Void creatures. Ra charged his mogu followers with watching over the Vault of Y'Shaarj. They would guard and care for the surrounding land as well.

Ra then continued his expedition and traveled west. There, he and his followers embedded the Forge of Origination in the land. The earth rumbled beneath Ra's feet as the gargantuan machine churned to life. The highkeeper soon sensed that the twin forges were working in synergy, sending healing energies through the heart of the world. Ra and his followers erected a sprawling fortress around the Forge of Origination. This site was called Uldum, and it would become the southernmost base of operations for the keepers.

Much like the Forge of Wills, the Forge of Origination would serve a dual purpose. In the event that Azeroth's flora and fauna succumbed to corruption, the incredible energies stored inside the great machine could be unleashed to eradicate all life on the world, allowing it to start anew.

Highkeeper Ra commanded some of the tol'vir and anubisaths to safeguard Uldum forever. He and the rest of his servants marched northwest into a land later known as Silithus. This arid and inhospitable region was home to the subterranean prison that housed the Old God C'Thun. Ra and his allies labored to expand on the prison, ultimately constructing the mighty fortress of Ahn'Qiraj. After the task was done, the highkeeper ordered his remaining titan-forged to safeguard the stronghold.

Ra himself, seeing his work completed, would spend the following ages roaming the southern regions of Azeroth, distantly observing his titan-forged and ensuring that they upheld their sacred charges.

THE ORDERING OF AZEROTH

With the twin forges embedded in Azeroth, the keepers moved to reshape the surface of the world. To this end, they called on the new generation of servants wrought from the Forge of Wills.

Each of these loyal and mighty titan-forged would play a different role in ordering and protecting the world. The craggy, kindhearted earthen would specialize in crafting mountains and carving out the deep places of the world. The clockwork mechagnomes, designed by Keeper Mimiron, would help build and maintain the keepers' extraordinary machineries. The stone-skinned mogu would dig out the myriad rivers and waterways of Azeroth. The task of safeguarding many of the keepers' holdings would fall to two different groups of constructs: the iron-skinned vrykul and the chiseled tol'vir. To shape the environment, the keepers also conscripted the powerful stone and sea giants. They would roam the breadth of Azeroth, lifting towering mountain ranges and dredging out the fathomless seas.

As the titan-forged began shaping Azeroth, Keeper Freya set out to populate the world with organic life. To do so, she crafted the Emerald Dream, a vast and ever-shifting dimension of spirits and nature magic. This ethereal plane acted as a mirror image of Azeroth, helping regulate the evolutionary path of the world's flora and fauna. A confluence of spirits and strange, otherworldly beings populated the Dream, frolicking in the surreal paradise that was their home. The mystical Dream defied mortal perceptions of reality. Concepts like time and distance held no sway within this realm of intangibles. A day on the physical world could feel like decades in the Dream.

Freya then wandered the world, searching for areas where the Well of Eternity's energies had coalesced. These regions created optimal conditions for the development of new flora and fauna. Freya shaped immense enclaves of nature at these places of power. She molded life of astounding diversity, seeding it around the world. The sites where Freya had done her work were located at the polar extremes of the world. They included regions that would later become known as Un'Goro Crater, Sholazar Basin, and the Vale of Eternal Blossoms.

The greatest creatures to emerge from these enclaves were colossal animals known as the Wild Gods. Freya adored and cared for these majestic beings as if they were her very own children. She often wandered the physical world with the Wild Gods at her side, vibrant forests and grasslands blooming in their footsteps. Yet there was one place she and the Wild Gods frequented more than any other: a massive forested peak called Mount Hyjal.

THE DREAMING WORLD

Some believe that Freya wove the Emerald Dream into being from nothing. Others claim that this strange place had always existed in some form, a dream born from Azeroth's slumbering world-soul. It is said that Freya tapped into this realm and molded what would become known as the Emerald Dream as a way to commune with the nascent titan.

THE WILD GODS

Among the greatest Wild Gods were:
Malorne—the honorable White Stag
Aessina—the Mother Wisp
Agamaggan—the Razorboar
Aviana—the Mistress of Birds
Ursoc and Ursol—the colossal Bear Lords
Tortolla—the Wise
Goldrinn—the Great Wolf
Chi-Ji—the Red Crane
Niuzao—the Black Ox
Xuen—the White Tiger
Yu'lon—the Jade Serpent

It was on the slopes of Hyjal that Freya bound the spirits of her beloved Wild Gods to the Emerald Dream. Inexorably tied to the ethereal realm, they would come to symbolize the health and vitality of Azeroth itself. Forever after, Hyjal would remain a refuge and sacred place to the Wild Gods.

As Freya's creations explored the world, they came across a number of other strange life-forms. These creatures had emerged from Azeroth's elemental past of their own free will. When the keepers had sealed off the Elemental Plane, some stragglers had escaped banishment. The fury of these spirits had ebbed over time, and they had become creatures of flesh and blood. It was from these former elementals that some forms of wildlife, such as proto-dragons, came to be.

In time, the keepers and their servants stabilized Azeroth's main landmass, a continent that teemed with plants and creatures of every kind. Twilight fell as the titan-forged surveyed the world they had shaped, and they named the primary continent *Kalimdor*: "Land of Eternal Starlight."

THE PILLARS OF CREATION

The Pantheon bestowed wondrous artifacts on the keepers to aid them with ordering the world. These relics were known as the Pillars of Creation. Ages after the keepers had completed their grand work, the artifacts would become lost and scattered across the lands of Azeroth.

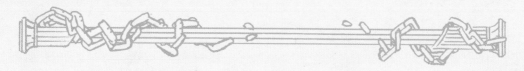

GIANTS SHAPING THE LANDS AND SEAS OF AZEROTH

THE PANTHEON'S DEPARTURE

Pleased with the keepers' efforts and assured that the slumbering world-soul was in good hands, the Pantheon prepared to venture back into the Great Dark. The discovery of Azeroth was proof that other nascent titans could exist in the universe, and the titans were eager to renew their search.

The keepers mourned the imminent departure of their makers, but they also brimmed with pride at being given the honor of safeguarding Azeroth. To commemorate the Pantheon's departure, Loken and Mimiron crafted a set of enchanted artifacts called the Discs of Norgannon, which would transcribe history as it unfolded on Azeroth. If ever the Pantheon returned, they would possess a record of what had come to pass in their absence.

In his final act before departing, Aman'Thul commissioned the constellar Algalon the Observer to serve as the world's celestial guardian. The possibility that the world-soul could become corrupted was one the titans could not ignore. Should that come to pass, Algalon had the power to initiate a procedure that would activate the Forge of Origination, purging the world of life and any corruption that was present.

With that, the Pantheon bade the titan-forged farewell and disappeared into the stars. The titans had done everything possible to heal Azeroth and assure the world-soul's maturation. All that remained now was to wait—and hope that the world-soul would one day awaken.

GALAKROND

In the ages after the Pantheon left Azeroth, myriad life-forms flourished across the surface of the world. The most savage and cunning were the proto-dragons, who dwelled in the frozen north of Kalimdor. The various proto-dragon species had a wide array of strengths and abilities. Some were gigantic winged beings of incredible fortitude, their spirits tied to the world itself. Others had unknowingly tapped into the latent elemental energies that permeated the newly ordered world.

But there was one proto-dragon whose brutality and devastating power overshadowed the rest of his kind. His name was Galakrond, and he was the largest proto-dragon who had ever soared across Azeroth's skies. So mighty was the enormous creature that the beating of his wings could flatten entire forests. Strength, however, was not his only weapon. He possessed a preternatural cunning that made him an exceptional hunter.

In time, Galakrond came to dominate the most sought-after hunting grounds in northern Kalimdor. Compelled by an insatiable hunger, he devoured everything in sight. His body swelled to an even greater size. Yet nothing could ever sate his cravings.

So terrible was his hunger that Galakrond began feasting on other proto-dragons, even the corpses of the dead. Devouring fallen proto-dragons eventually warped Galakrond's mind and body with a necrotic affliction. Misshapen limbs and dozens of eyes sprouted across his gargantuan form. Death energies wafted off of Galakrond's jagged hide, reanimating dead matter. These necrotic powers were infused in Galakrond's victims, and they rose from the dead as mindless abominations.

The ranks of Galakrond's wretched minions expanded. Soon, he and his ruined followers terrorized the skies over Kalimdor. The other proto-dragons, fractured by long-standing rivalries, failed to unite against this new threat.

Tyr, the mightiest of the keepers, was the first of his kind to notice the danger posed by Galakrond. He warned his fellow keepers of what he had seen, but he could not motivate them to act. Though the keepers had once sworn to protect the world, the war with the Old Gods and the Ordering of Azeroth had sapped their collective strength and willpower. They had become indifferent to the world at large, focused solely on maintaining their vaults and arcane machineries.

But Tyr was not deterred by his siblings' apathy. His drive to seek justice and order in the world pushed him forward. Tyr knew that if Galakrond remained unchecked, he would devour all nature, spreading his affliction to the far corners of Azeroth. Thus the keeper sought a means to destroy the giant proto-dragon and his minions.

Tyr found his answer with five of the greatest and most intelligent proto-dragons in existence: Alexstrasza, Neltharion, Malygos, Ysera, and Nozdormu. Nearly all of these creatures hailed from different strains, and each of them displayed unique powers. Even the two sisters Alexstrasza and Ysera commanded distinct abilities. The tenacious and kindhearted Alexstrasza could summon gouts of fire from her maw. The mighty Neltharion possessed incredible strength, and his piercing roar could shatter bone and rock alike. The cunning Malygos could breathe frost, encasing his foes in solid ice. The wise Nozdormu could assail his enemies with blinding storms of coarse sand. The elusive Ysera's breath could debilitate her enemies, sapping their willpower and throwing them into a deep trance.

Tyr beseeched the five proto-dragons for aid in thwarting Galakrond. The creatures were initially suspicious of the strange being who had approached them, but they soon vowed to fight by his side. Despite their differences, the five proto-dragons showed a surprising willingness to work as one.

Under Tyr's guidance, Alexstrasza and her companions warred with Galakrond and his fetid minions. Their battles raged over the snowy peaks and rocky spires of northern Kalimdor. Initially, Galakrond's jagged hide warded off the attacks of the five proto-dragons. Though disheartened by their enemy's resilience, Alexstrasza and her allies soon found his weaknesses. They assaulted Galakrond's many eyes and his soft, vulnerable gullet. By using their powers in harmony and trusting in one another, the five proto-dragons vanquished their gargantuan foe. Galakrond's lifeless husk plummeted to the ground, smashing into the frozen tundra of what would become known as the Dragonblight.

The five proto-dragons had won despite all odds, but they had only done so by working together. It was a lesson they would not soon forget. Alexstrasza and the others would carry on this ideal of unity and cooperation for ages to come.

TYR AND THE SILVER HAND

Tyr fought alongside the proto-dragons, but Galakrond proved too powerful even for the keeper of justice. In one particular battle, the monstrous creature bit off Tyr's iron hand, suffusing him with necrotic energy. Although Tyr survived, his wound would never truly heal. Many years later, Tyr would replace his lost hand with one forged of pure silver. This silver hand would come to symbolize his belief that only through personal sacrifice could one achieve lasting justice.

43

ORDERED AZEROTH

Ulduar
(Yogg-Saron)

Sholazar Basin

Wyrmrest
Temple

Mount Hyjal

Well of Eternity

Un'Goro Crater

Ahn'Qiraj (C'Thun)

Uldum

Vale of Eternal Blossoms
(Vault of Y'Shaarj)

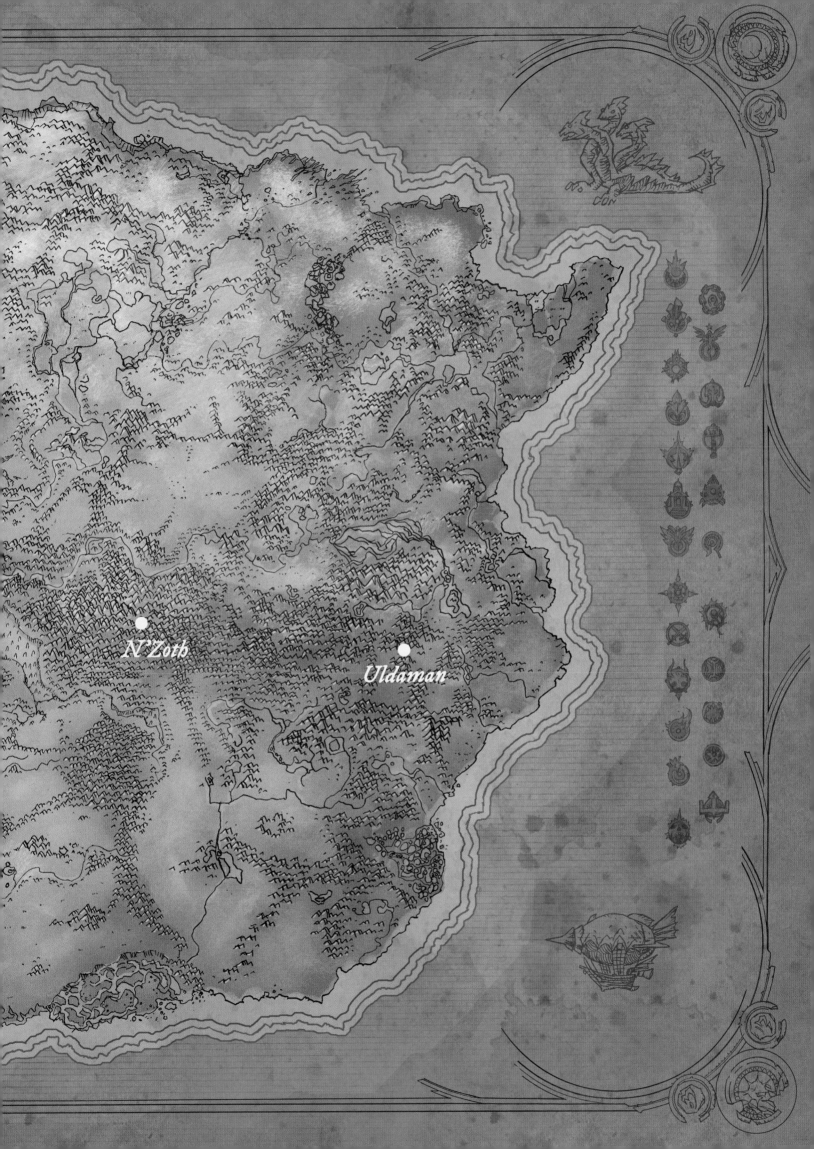

N'Zoth

Uldaman

CHARGE OF THE DRAGONFLIGHTS

While Tyr and the proto-dragons were battling Galakrond, the other keepers finally emerged from their stupor. Too late, they realized the threat that the corrupted monstrosity posed. They were heartened by the resolve of Tyr's winged allies and ashamed of their own apathy. Tyr, however, never chastised the other keepers. Instead he convinced them to imbue the five proto-dragons with powers so that they could safeguard the lands of Azeroth.

Only Keeper Odyn challenged this idea. Though he acknowledged the proto-dragons' heroism, he did not agree that Azeroth's fate should be placed on their shoulders. Odyn saw Alexstrasza and her ilk as primitive life-forms. Only the mighty titan-forged could be trusted to protect the world. Odyn argued that as Prime Designate, he had the final decision on how to proceed.

Yet Tyr and the other keepers disagreed. Through bravery and self-sacrifice, the proto-dragons had earned the right to act as Azeroth's guardians. Despite Odyn's continued protests, the other keepers moved forward with their plans.

After the proto-dragons defeated Galakrond, the keepers journeyed to the frozen tundra where the final battle had taken place. Even Ra traveled from the distant south to take part in the great ceremony that was to come. Acting as conduits of their creators' powers, the gathered keepers bestowed the blessings of the Pantheon upon each proto-dragon.

Highkeeper Ra channeled the powers of his creator, Aman'Thul, into the proto-dragon Nozdormu. Of all of Aman'Thul's myriad powers, Nozdormu was blessed with a mastery of time itself. Henceforth, Nozdormu became known as the Timeless One, and he held dominion over the interweaving pathways of fate and destiny.

The nurturing and ever-merciful Freya called upon her creator, Eonar, to empower the proto-dragon Alexstrasza. Known thereafter as the Life-Binder, Alexstrasza would devote everything she was to the stewardship of the living world. Having proved her courage and compassion in the battles against Galakrond, she was crowned the Dragonqueen and given command over her kind.

Freya also beseeched Eonar to bless Alexstrasza's younger sister, the proto-dragon Ysera, with nature's influence. Ysera was charged with keeping watch over the flowering wilds of Azeroth from within the Emerald Dream. Bound to this ethereal realm, she descended into an endless trance and became known thereafter as the Dreamer.

Keeper Loken called on his creator, Norgannon, to endow the proto-dragon Malygos with incredible arcane powers. Henceforth, Malygos would be known as the Spell-Weaver. The limitless realms of magic and hidden arcana would be his to share, explore, and protect.

Lastly, Keeper Archaedas asked his creator, Khaz'goroth, to bestow some of his vast power upon the indomitable proto-dragon Neltharion. Known afterward as the Earth-Warder, Neltharion was given charge over the mountains and deep caverns of the earth. He embodied the strength of the world and served, for many long ages, as Alexstrasza's greatest friend and confidant.

Bristling with the Pantheon's energies, the five proto-dragons transformed into immense and graceful creatures. Nozdormu's hide took on a bronze hue like a sea of shimmering golden sand. Alexstrasza's scales turned a deep and vivid shade of red. Ysera's lithe form became a vibrant green to reflect her new connection with nature. Malygos turned an icy blue color, and his very scales radiated potent arcane energies. Neltharion's rough hide became an earthy black.

From that day forward, these five extraordinary beings would become known as the Dragon Aspects.

The keepers also sought to create a new species to help the Dragon Aspects protect the world. These beings would serve the Aspects as consorts and allies. To this end, the keepers magically altered hundreds of proto-dragon eggs. From them would emerge creatures born in the image of the Aspects. This new race, known as dragons, would form five distinct flights: bronze, red, green, blue, and black.

Though each of these flights would serve a different Dragon Aspect, they would all be bound by their duty to protect Azeroth. To strengthen this bond, the keepers forged a grand tower in northern Kalimdor called Wyrmrest Temple. It would serve as the heart of the dragons' culture, a sanctuary where they could gather and discuss their activities. But above all, Wyrmrest would stand as a symbol of their unity.

The keepers, satisfied with their work, disappeared back inside their lairs, leaving the Aspects to watch over the living creatures of Azeroth.

ODYN AND THE RAISING OF THE HALLS OF VALOR

As the other keepers were conducting their ceremony to empower the Dragon Aspects, Odyn brooded within the halls of Ulduar. He was furious that his allies had acted against his wishes—the wishes of the *Prime Designate*. More than that, Odyn believed with all his heart that the Dragon Aspects would fail in their charge to safeguard the world.

For the good of Azeroth, Odyn decided to take matters into his own hands. He would create an elite army of his design, one that he could call on to protect the world should the need ever arise. To fill the ranks of this fighting force, Odyn would look to the mighty vrykul. He had always admired their innate courage and strength. He saw the vrykul, above all other titan-forged, as the perfect expression of the warrior spirit.

Upon returning to Ulduar, Tyr and the other keepers demanded that Odyn abandon his foolish plans. Yet their words had no effect on the Prime Designate. Odyn was single-minded in his focus and unbending in his ideas of what was right. He invited the other keepers to help him create his army. When none stepped forward to join his cause, Odyn announced he would pursue his quest without them.

Odyn secured one of Ulduar's wings to act as the base for his new army. To permanently separate it from the rest of the fortress and from the other keepers, he called on the titan-forged sorceress Helya. Over the ages, Odyn had come to see her as his adopted daughter. Helya wove a great spell to encase the keeper's stronghold. Then, focusing all of her power, she ripped the colossal chunk of Ulduar from the earth and lifted it into the cloudy skies. In time, this floating citadel would become known as the Halls of Valor.

From atop his fortress, Odyn bellowed out a proclamation to all vrykul. Those who proved their bravery by dying glorious deaths in battle would live again in the Halls of Valor. Their spirits would be transported to the fortress and given mighty new storm-forged bodies. These champions—these Valarjar—would serve as Azeroth's foremost guardians. Their deeds would live on in the hearts of all titan-forged forever after.

All that remained was to find a means of ferrying the spirits of the dead to the Halls of Valor. For this, Odyn studied the energies that permeated the Shadowlands. The knowledge he gained would allow him to transform some vrykul into spectral beings known as the Val'kyr. These wraithlike servants would travel between the Shadowlands and the physical world, guiding the souls of worthy vrykul to the Halls of Valor. Yet those who became Val'kyr would be cursed to live as phantom beings for all eternity.

No vrykul volunteered for the grim task of becoming a Val'kyr, and thus Odyn decided he would create his servants by force. Helya admonished the keeper for his willingness to turn the titan-forged into slaves against their will. The argument between her and Odyn grew so heated that the two nearly came to blows. In the end, Helya warned that she would return the Halls of Valor to Ulduar if Odyn did not change his mind.

Odyn saw Helya's disobedience as a threat not only to his plans, but to the future safety of Azeroth itself. Blinded by his dreams of what the Halls of Valor could become, he struck out at the sorceress. Odyn shattered her physical form and twisted her spirit into the first of the Val'kyr. Helya's howls of pain and anger rumbled across the surface of Azeroth and pierced into the very heart of the Shadowlands.

This violent transformation would forever darken Helya, but her torment was not finished. Though she loathed Odyn for what he had done to her, she found herself compelled to obey his will. Under Odyn's command, she set out to transform unwilling vrykul into the cursed Val'kyr.

For ages, Helya and her fellow Val'kyr brought the souls of heroic vrykul to the Halls of Valor. The citadel became filled with storm-infused Valarjar. Odyn trained and empowered each of these warriors. He had no remorse for breaking from the keepers, or for transforming Helya into the first Val'kyr. In Odyn's mind, everything he had done was for the safety of Azeroth and in honor of the great Pantheon.

SARGERAS AND THE BETRAYAL

The keepers went about their duties on Azeroth, unaware of a new threat that was taking shape in the distant reaches of the Great Dark.

Sargeras, having broken all ties with the Pantheon, meditated on the fate of the universe in isolation. His fear that the void lords had already corrupted other world-souls consumed him. As doubt and despair continued twisting the titan's every thought, he became more certain than ever that creation itself was fatally flawed. Finally, he concluded that the only way to spare the universe was to purge it in fire. Thus his grand Burning Crusade would begin.

To accomplish this Burning Crusade, Sargeras required a vast force of unquenchable rage. He knew of only one place that held such power and potential: Mardum, the Plane of Banishment.

Over the ages, the prison had become bloated with fel magic and vengeful demons. Their presence had warped Mardum, transforming it into a realm of nightmare. Torrents of fel energy ceaselessly bombarded the prison's walls, bathing the captive demons in a roiling sea of volatile magic.

Sargeras quelled his remaining apprehension and tore the prison asunder, spilling its wrathful denizens into the Great Dark Beyond. The subsequent explosion of fel magic was powerful beyond even what the fallen titan had imagined. Violent energies enveloped Sargeras, surging through his veins and searing his very soul. His eyes burst in gouts of emerald fire. Fel volcanoes ignited across his once-noble form, splitting his skin apart and revealing an endless furnace of blistering hate.

Yet despite these horrific physical changes, Sargeras's mind remained locked on his one all-consuming purpose. To prevent the void lords from possessing creation, life itself had to be extinguished.

In shattering the prison, Sargeras had ruptured the boundary between the Great Dark and the Twisting Nether. A monstrous celestial maw, limned in a storm of emerald fire, had ripped through the fabric of reality. It would remain a scar on creation—smoldering proof of Sargeras's madness—for all eternity.

Demons of every shape and size poured into the physical universe from this rift, howling in triumph at their release. Sargeras imbued the ravenous masses with his power, uniting them as one in an inferno of fel magic. Though many demons had previously tapped into the volatile energies of the Nether, none had ever experienced the pure might and rage found in Sargeras's fel. Some of the creatures grew in size and stature. Still others felt new cunning and intelligence unfold in their minds.

By this point, Sargeras had learned more about the nature of demons—including how to permanently destroy their spirits. He offered a simple pact in exchange for the demons' newfound power: fight at his command, or be extinguished. It was not a difficult choice.

To thwart the void lords, Sargeras unleashed his new army—his Burning Legion—upon the innumerable worlds of the Great Dark. Never before had the forces of evil been united in such numbers. Sargeras wielded enough power to make disobedience all but unthinkable. None would dream of challenging him, but more importantly, his minions grew to delight in their role as agents of extinction.

The Burning Legion fell upon its first world. Though it did not contain a slumbering titan, it was a world that had been ordered by the Pantheon in ages past. Sargeras's forces incinerated the mortal civilizations that dwelled there, wiping out dozens of sentient species. When the constellar whom the Pantheon had charged to oversee the world arrived, Sargeras himself annihilated the celestial being.

Aggramar was the first to learn of the constellar's demise. As more news of the Burning Legion's atrocities reached him, he hunted down the demonic army. Aggramar arrived just in time to witness the Legion scouring yet another world, and he saw the twisted, fire-wreathed being leading it: his mentor and greatest friend, Sargeras.

Aggramar was stunned. He demanded an explanation from Sargeras. The former champion offered none, only declaring that his Burning Crusade was the sole means to purify the universe. Anyone who stood against him, Sargeras added, would burn in the fires of his Legion as well.

Knowing that he could not sway Sargeras with words, Aggramar challenged his former mentor to single combat. Before the watching eyes of the demon masses, the two greatest warriors the universe had ever known came to blows.

Aggramar soon found himself outmatched. Like all titans, he was uniquely susceptible to fel magic. Sargeras's ferocious assaults shattered Aggramar's defenses and sent him reeling in agony. In a final desperate counterattack, Aggramar summoned all the power at his command and struck at Sargeras.

Their two blades met, igniting a furious explosion of fel and arcane power. When the torrent of warring energies finally subsided, Sargeras and Aggramar saw that both of their weapons had been shattered.

Heavily wounded by the blast, Aggramar retreated from the battle and returned to the rest of the Pantheon. Disbelief gripped the other titans as they learned what had happened. The thought of their most trusted and noble warrior falling to darkness shook their faith to the core. The Pantheon could not fathom how to stop such a threat, yet they agreed they could not sit idly by. Girded for war, the combined might of the Pantheon confronted Sargeras and his unholy Legion near a world named Nihilam.

Aman'Thul called out to Sargeras, pleading with him to abandon his mad Burning Crusade. He told Sargeras of Azeroth, a fledgling world-soul with more potential than any of the Pantheon had ever seen, a being strong enough to defeat the void lords in due time. Sargeras listened carefully but was unmoved.

Despite his earlier battle with Sargeras, Aggramar believed that something noble still lingered deep in the former champion's heart. As a last resort, he laid down his arms and approached the fallen titan. Aggramar recounted tales of their glorious battles against demons, reminding Sargeras of the sacred oaths they had sworn to protect creation. But Sargeras was set in his ways. Nothing the Pantheon could say—nothing even his cherished protégé could say—would ever change his mind.

With a howl of rage and sorrow, Sargeras struck Aggramar down, his ruined fel blade nearly cleaving the titan in two.

Infuriated by this unthinkable murder, the Pantheon launched an all-out assault on Sargeras and his Burning Legion. Stars withered and died as the battle raged across the cosmos, scarring vast stretches of reality. Nihilam, known thereafter as the Doom World, became warped and twisted by the apocalyptic conflict. The titans of the Pantheon wielded powers incomprehensible to mortal minds, yet even they could not overcome Sargeras's fel-fueled might.

The fallen titan decimated the Pantheon members with fel fire until he had broken their will to fight. To seal their demise, Sargeras summoned a massive fel storm that would consume their bodies and souls alike. Yet just as the furious onslaught of energy washed over the defeated titans, Norgannon made one last attempt to stave off oblivion.

Norgannon bent the raw energies of the universe to his will, weaving a protective shroud around each of the Pantheon titans' spirits and launching them into the Great Dark. While the titans' disembodied souls hurtled through the cosmos, Sargeras's fel storm obliterated what remained of their physical forms.

Unaware that the titans' spirits had survived, Sargeras declared the Burning Legion victorious. The Pantheon was no more, and he now had tantalizing clues about a powerful world-soul called Azeroth. Yet though Sargeras had learned the name of this nascent titan, its whereabouts remained a mystery. Nonetheless, without the Pantheon to oppose him, he knew he would find the world-soul in time.

And he knew he would have to do so before the void lords did.

THE BURNING CRUSADE

The Burning Legion had triumphed over the Pantheon, and Sargeras moved to rally even more demons to his cause. Yet the fight with the Pantheon had exposed a flaw in his seemingly unstoppable army—one that he was determined to remedy.

For all of Sargeras's vast power and intellect, he could not direct his entire army at once. Demons were vicious and bloodthirsty, but most lacked strategic thinking. Much of the Legion had fallen needlessly to the Pantheon. Sargeras wanted cunning and tactically minded commanders to join his side, and he had seen a place from which to harvest such servants: a world called Argus.

Argus was home to the highly advanced eredar, a race far more intelligent than any other Sargeras had encountered. The eredar hungered for knowledge above all else. By attaining it, they believed they could shape the universe into a better and more benevolent place.

A triumvirate of leaders ruled over the eredar, not by might or fear, but by contemplating the great questions of the cosmos and sharing the answers with their people. The mighty Archimonde had a gift for finding the strengths in those around him. His bold demeanor inspired his followers, filling them with the confidence and the courage to face any challenge. Kil'jaeden, the most brilliant of the rulers, was considered a prodigy even among the gifted eredar. Witty and cunning, he reveled in puzzling out the most confounding mysteries of the cosmos. Last there was Velen, the spiritual heart of the triumvirate. He stood as a relentless champion of peace, whose wisdom could defuse any conflict.

Individually, each member of the triumvirate would have made an excellent leader. But it was together, with each of their strengths working in synergy, that they elevated their people to heights undreamt of.

The eredar's great cohesion was the ideal solution to the Legion's weaknesses. Yet to conscript them to his cause, Sargeras would have to corrupt them entirely. In the guise of a radiant and elegant being, he communed with the eredar triumvirate. Sargeras played to their desires, promising them knowledge and unimaginable power. He showed them worlds beyond count over which they might hold dominion, primitive places that the eredar could transform into sanctuaries of peace and intellectual thought.

Sargeras vowed to share with the eredar not only the most obscure secrets of existence, but also the final answer to what he believed was the fundamental flaw in creation. In return, the denizens of Argus would devote themselves to Sargeras's grand work . . . and help him remedy that flaw.

The offer awed both Archimonde and Kil'jaeden, who were honored to be part of this grand undertaking. Velen, however, was not convinced. He sensed something strange about the seemingly beautiful and all-knowing creature who had appeared to them.

Velen meditated using an ancient artifact gifted to his race by the holy naaru long before his time—the ata'mal crystal. Through the enchanted relic, he received a horrific vision of the eredar's future if they sided with Sargeras. They would become horribly disfigured, transformed into demonic beings of depthless evil.

Velen warned his brothers of what he had seen, but they dismissed his insights and made it clear they intended to accept Sargeras's offer. Fearing that Archimonde and Kil'jaeden would kill him if he continued to dissent, Velen feigned acceptance. Though he and Kil'jaeden were particularly close friends, Velen didn't believe he could trust their bond to prevail over Sargeras's enticing promises.

Velen despaired at the fate of his people. In this moment of desperation, the same beings who had granted him his vision of the eredar's downfall reached out to him. One of the naaru, K'ure, contacted the eredar leader and offered to shepherd him and his closest allies to safety. Filled with renewed hope, Velen sought out other eredar whom he believed he could trust.

As Sargeras arrived on Argus to corrupt the unsuspecting eredar, Velen and his followers made their daring escape. They gathered aboard a massive naaru dimensional fortress known as the *Genedar* and fled their homeworld forever. From that day forward, Velen and his followers would be known as the *draenei*, or "exiled ones."

On Argus, Sargeras bent the other eredar to his unholy will. Fanatical fel whisperings surged through the minds of the world's inhabitants, drowning out their ability to reason. Sargeras also infused the eredar with fel energies, twisting their forms to resemble hideous demons.

Sargeras found quick use for his new fel-corrupted converts. The eredar settled in as commanders within the Burning Legion. Kil'jaeden and Archimonde would stand as the most gifted and powerful among them.

Sargeras molded Kil'jaeden's innate cunning and intellect to suit the Legion's designs. Known thereafter as "the Deceiver," Kil'jaeden was charged with using his wits to beguile the mortal civilizations of the physical universe and transform them into agents of the Burning Legion.

Sargeras also saw Archimonde's talent in motivating his people as an invaluable tool to strengthen the Burning Crusade. Archimonde, henceforth known as "the Defiler," would use his powerful will to drive the demonic masses to acts of extreme violence and barbarism. He would draw out and temper the furious strength in all those who served under him, remaking them into weapons of annihilation.

Under the eredar's leadership, the ranks of the Burning Legion swelled with new demonic races, gathered from the Twisting Nether and the worlds of the Great Dark. Archimonde empowered the monstrous pit lords and conscripted them to serve as living siege engines. They would inspire dread in all those they faced. The mo'arg, a highly resourceful and industrious race of demons, became the Legion's armorers. They would forge fel-infused weaponry and constructs to besiege the worlds of the cosmos. Kil'jaeden also brought in the devious succubi to infiltrate prospective worlds for conquest and gather intelligence about their civilizations. The brutal doomguard, demon warriors of unsurpassed strength and cruelty, fought as the Legion's shock troops. The

FLIGHT OF THE DRAENEI

Velen's rejection of Sargeras's grand vision and his subsequent escape enraged Kil'jaeden. Even though the draenei had vanished without a trace, the Deceiver vowed never to stop hunting them, bent on vengeance for what he saw as Velen's betrayal.

SARGERAS AND THE BURNING LEGION

zealous shivarra became the Legion's foremost mystics and advisors. They fostered a fanatical loyalty to Sargeras.

These wicked creatures, among many others, bolstered the might of the Burning Legion. Pleased with his burgeoning forces, Sargeras launched the demons into the Great Dark, renewing his Burning Crusade against creation.

In the ages to come, the Legion would scour countless other worlds and civilizations from existence.

Loken's Betrayal

Meanwhile, unbeknownst to Sargeras, the last embers of the Pantheon's power clung to life. Although Sargeras had destroyed the titans' physical forms, Norgannon's grand spellwork had preserved their souls. The disembodied titan spirits hurtled through the Great Dark toward the world of Azeroth and its keepers. There, the Pantheon hoped they could locate physical forms to inhabit. If they could not find such vessels, the titans feared their weakened spirits would soon fade into oblivion.

Upon reaching Azeroth, the depleted spirits slammed into the keepers, who had been crafted by the Pantheon's own hands. The keepers were immediately overwhelmed as the titans' powers flared in their minds. They witnessed fragmented memories of distant worlds, of lifetimes never lived and wonders never seen. But just as quickly as the influx of power had come, it dimmed.

The keepers, still retaining their original personalities, puzzled over the strange phenomenon. They knew they had been gifted with a portion of the Pantheon's power, but they were unaware that the last remnants of their beloved makers had been infused in their very bodies. The bewildered servants called out to the Pantheon for answers, but they received no reply. The deep silence troubled the keepers, and they sank into a long period of confusion and unease.

The Old God Yogg-Saron, imprisoned beneath Ulduar, sensed these fluctuating emotions. In the eons since the Ordering of Azeroth, a sharp awareness had begun to stir within the entity. Yogg-Saron had devised a plan to weaken its jailors and escape imprisonment. It would corrupt the Forge of Wills, tainting its creation matrix with a strange malady known as the curse of flesh. Any titan-forged created by the machine thereafter would fall victim to this affliction. Some would even spread it to previous generations of titan-forged. The curse of flesh would gradually transform many of these infected servants into mortal beings of flesh and blood—beings who the cunning Old God knew could be easily killed.

To implement this plan, Yogg-Saron turned to Keeper Loken. Out of Ulduar's guardians, Loken had been the most troubled by the Pantheon's silence. Yogg-Saron assailed the keeper through fevered dreams, stoking the cold fires of his despair. Yet even in his disturbed state, Loken resisted the whisperings in his mind. Ultimately, his downfall would come from a much subtler place.

As Loken drifted deeper and deeper into despair, he sought comfort from a vrykul named Sif, the mate of his brother, Keeper Thorim. Loken often met with Sif in private, telling her of his darkest fears. In time, a forbidden love blossomed between the two titan-forged.

Yogg-Saron latched onto Loken's love for Sif and twisted it into a dangerous obsession. The relationship quickly soured due to Loken's increasingly compulsive behavior. More and more, he

KEEPER THORIM DISCOVERS THE BODY OF HIS WIFE, SIF

talked of openly professing their love for each other, an act that Sif vehemently opposed. She knew that if Thorim discovered the affair, it would shatter the keepers' unity.

Ultimately, she broke all ties with Loken, demanding that he leave her in peace. The thought of losing Sif drove Loken to madness. In a fit of anger and jealousy, he lashed out at his love and killed her.

Though racked by guilt, he could not bring himself to tell Thorim of what he had done. Loken scrambled for a way to cover up Sif's death. It was in this time of need that her spirit appeared before his eyes.

Much to Loken's surprise, this visage of Sif forgave him. She also warned him of the need to act with haste, lest Thorim learn the truth. If he did, the titan-forged would descend into civil war, and every pledge Loken had made to the Pantheon would be broken.

Sif's suggestion struck Loken as devious, a characteristic he had never known her to possess. He sensed something strange in her spirit: an unseen darkness, subtle yet discernible. But Loken's fear clouded his judgment, and he pushed away his doubts.

On Sif's guidance, Loken dragged her corpse into the frigid wastes of the Storm Peaks. He informed Thorim of his wife's demise and convinced the keeper that Arngrim, king of the ice giants, was to blame. The grief-stricken Thorim unleashed his unbridled fury, slaying Arngrim and many of his followers. This event ignited a catastrophic war between Thorim's storm giants and Arngrim's ice giants. Sif's spirit continued aiding Loken as the conflict raged. Her guidance became ever more extreme and worrisome, but Loken forged ahead nonetheless. She convinced him to build an army of his own using the Forge of Wills, one large enough to protect Ulduar from the depredations of the warring giants.

Loken was even persuaded to punish his brother for starting the war. He berated Thorim for letting anger rule his emotions and for creating such a terrible rift between the titan-forged. Loken further admonished his brother, claiming that Sif herself would look upon him in shame if she could only see the things he had done in her name. This bitter condemnation threw Thorim into a deep depression. Overcome with regret, he abandoned Ulduar and languished in solitude.

With Thorim in isolation, Loken used his newly forged army to overwhelm the giants and end their conflict. All those who resisted his will were locked away in stasis chambers.

But as these battles progressed, Loken noticed something unsettling among his warriors. A dark affliction suffused their spirits. Loken called out to Sif again for advice, but this time, she remained silent. Dread overtook the keeper as he realized that her spirit had not existed at all. She was an illusion created by Yogg-Saron.

Though Loken did not know it, the false spirit of Sif had also tainted the Forge of Wills while the keeper was creating his army. Yogg-Saron's curse of flesh had taken root in the heart of the machine's creation matrix. Loken had, in his selfishness, allowed Yogg-Saron to play him as an unwitting pawn.

This discovery shattered the last vestiges of Loken's noble heart. He became obsessed with keeping his transgressions a secret, even if it meant embracing the power of Yogg-Saron. With such might at his command, he knew he could defeat the remaining keepers and destroy all evidence of his wrongdoing.

THE SEALING OF THE HALLS OF VALOR

In order to defeat the other keepers, Loken realized that he would first have to neutralize Odyn and his mighty Valarjar army. But a direct attack against their floating citadel, the Halls of Valor, would be impossible. Instead, Loken took a more insidious approach. He reached out to Odyn's adopted daughter, the Val'kyr Helya.

For millennia, Helya had dutifully followed Odyn's commands, transporting the spirits of slain vrykul to the Halls of Valor. Yet even while she did so, Helya nursed the cold anger that stirred in her phantom heart. She never forgave Odyn for turning her into a Val'kyr against her will. Helya dreamed of a day when she might avenge what had been done to her and the others who had been transformed into Val'kyr.

Loken called out to Helya and played on her simmering anger and feelings of betrayal. He promised he would break the chains of servitude that bound her to follow Odyn's will. In exchange, she would seal off the Halls of Valor from the world forever. Thereafter, Helya could usurp Odyn's role as the caretaker of all vrykul spirits. Enticed by this chance to sate her appetite for revenge, she agreed to Loken's plans.

After Loken had restored her free will, Helya called on the same powers she had used to secure the Elemental Plane in ages past. She bent the latent arcane energies swirling around Azeroth to her command, sealing off the Halls of Valor and the inhabitants within. Odyn and his mighty Valarjar struggled desperately to escape their floating citadel, but they could not break the impregnable barrier Helya had created. There the Valarjar and the keeper would remain, trapped within the golden corridors of the Halls of Valor for ages to come.

Helya, now liberated from her life of servitude, forged a new home for herself and the other Val'kyr. She created this enchanted refuge far below the Halls of Valor, binding it to Azeroth's great seas. The ocean mists soon coiled up to envelop Helya's domain and shroud it from sight. Known as Helheim, this realm would become the final destination for many vrykul spirits after death.

GUARDIANS OF SHADOW

Not all Val'kyr continued to follow Helya after Odyn's defeat. Some of these spectral beings disappeared into the Shadowlands. The few who still retained a glimmer of nobility in their souls dedicated themselves to watching over the physical world. From within the Shadowlands, these Val'kyr would at times guide the dead back to the land of the living.

Yet the darkness that had long festered in Helya's heart transformed Helheim into a place of nightmare and shadow. The souls of dead vrykul who arrived there soon found themselves turned into vengeful wraithlike beings. These cursed spirits were known as the Kvaldir. They became one with the ocean mists, bound to the ebb and flow of the tides. The eternal fire of malice and anguish that burned in their souls would drive the Kvaldir to raid and plunder the shores of Kalimdor for all eternity.

THE FALL OF THE KEEPERS

With Odyn and his Valarjar sealed away, Loken returned to Ulduar. He believed he now had ample time to orchestrate the downfall of the other keepers. Yet he soon discovered a new threat to his plans.

Mimiron had begun investigating strange anomalies in Loken's new titan-forged. The brilliant keeper suspected that some malfunction within the Forge of Wills was to blame for the impurities he had observed. Before he could pursue his theory, Loken sabotaged the keeper's workshop, killing Mimiron in what appeared to be a tragic accident. Mimiron, however, was not completely dead.

Mimiron's faithful mechagnomes discovered that their master's spirit lived on. They scrambled to build a giant mechanized body to house the keeper's fading soul. This heroic act saved Mimiron, but he was never the same again. His brush with death had broken his mind. He secluded himself in Ulduar's vast workshops, spending his days lost in the inner workings of his clockwork inventions.

Knowing Mimiron's fate would raise suspicions among the other keepers, Loken dispatched his army to neutralize his remaining brethren. First, Loken confronted Freya at her verdant domain within the Storm Peaks, the Temple of Life. Battle raged between the two keepers and their followers, sundering the temple and bleeding its precious life energies dry. Freya struggled valiantly against her foes, but she ultimately fell to Loken and the shadowy powers Yogg-Saron had granted him.

Yogg-Saron itself seized on Freya's weakened state, enthralling her spirit. The Old God compelled the broken Freya to withdraw into the halls of Ulduar. There, she would spend her forlorn days tending to a sprawling garden at the heart of the fortress.

As Loken confronted Freya, another group of his titan-forged waged war on the mighty keeper Hodir within his lair, the Temple of Winter. Two fire giants named Ignis and Volkhan led the assault. They enveloped the temple in blistering infernos, sapping Hodir's wintry strength and decimating his icy followers. Loken later arrived to subdue Hodir directly, a task he completed with ease.

Just as it had done with Freya, Yogg-Saron warped Hodir's mind. The entity forced the keeper to retreat into a frigid chamber within Ulduar, where he would remain in seclusion for millennia.

Two of the remaining keepers—Tyr and Archaedas—did not fall victim to Loken's schemes. Tyr had long suspected that a darkness was growing within the fallen keeper, a suspicion that was confirmed when he witnessed Loken's attack on Hodir.

Yet Tyr was in no position to confront Loken directly. Throngs of the fallen keeper's loyal titan-forged stalked the Storm Peaks and the halls of Ulduar. Knowing he stood little chance against this army, Tyr took Archaedas and their close friend, a titan-forged giantess named Ironaya, to the outskirts of the Storm Peaks. Among the icy cliffs, they waited and watched Loken's schemes unfold, planning their next move.

Loken dispatched his forces to hunt down Tyr and his companions. These titan-forged scoured the mountains and caves of the Storm Peaks, but they never found their prey. Believing that Tyr and his allies had fled the region, Loken asserted sole dominion over Ulduar. He altered the machineries within the fortress and used them to anoint himself the new Prime Designate of Azeroth. He also disabled the tainted Forge of Wills and banished many of his servants to the Storm Peaks. Thereafter, he sealed off the sprawling fortress of Ulduar.

Loken languished in regret within Ulduar's silent halls. Despite everything he had accomplished, he was ever fearful that the Pantheon or their appointed watcher, Algalon, would one day return to Azeroth. If that happened, they would discover Loken's horrific crimes and punish him.

But in truth, the greatest threat was right beneath Loken's feet. No longer under the watchful eyes of Ulduar's jailors, Yogg-Saron began to stir, working to free itself from its impregnable prison.

THE VANISHING OF RA

As he dealt with the other keepers, Loken always expected that Ra would emerge from the southern reaches of Kalimdor to investigate the goings-on in Ulduar. But much to Loken's surprise, the highkeeper remained silent throughout these world-altering events.

Overcome with curiosity, Loken dispatched a contingent of his army to the distant bastion of Uldum to investigate Ra's activities. These titan-forged agents never found the missing highkeeper, but they did learn from the local mogu, tol'vir, and anubisaths that Ra had mysteriously vanished.

These meetings would have a lasting impact. In journeying south, Loken's forces had unwittingly spread the curse of flesh throughout many of Ra's faithful servants.

Unbeknownst to Loken and the titan-forged, Ra had experienced a revelation . . . one so terrible that it had driven him into seclusion. When the Pantheon's power and memories had been infused in the keepers, Ra had reeled in confusion much like his siblings. Over time, however, he had concluded that this event was more than just an anomaly. The influx of power was the *last remnant* of the Pantheon's spirits.

Ra struggled to accept the fact that the Pantheon had fallen. He extracted the lingering power of Aman'Thul from himself and carefully stored it in a mountain vault near what would become known as the Vale of Eternal Blossoms. There, the highkeeper hoped to preserve what little was left of his beloved titan creator.

Ra then retreated into the catacombs beneath the land to meditate on what he had learned. With the highkeeper gone, his loyal titan-forged developed new cultures, wholly distinct from those of their northern kin. Most of the tol'vir congregated around Uldum, making the fortress their home. To the west, the anubisaths continued their sacred charge of watching over the prison of C'Thun. Similarly, the mogu remained in the east, guarding the titan-forged vaults and machineries buried beneath the earth.

THE WINTERSKORN WAR

For many ages after Loken's betrayal, the titan-forged who were exiled from Ulduar spread across northern Kalimdor. The lumbering giants gradually trickled into the mountains and seas around the region, disappearing from sight. The earthen tunneled into the deep places of the world, where they fought for dominance against a race of brutish and misshapen creatures known as troggs. Many of the vrykul remained aboveground, congregating into small clans. Some of these factions wandered the harsh northern landscape as nomads. Others established dwellings across the forested tundra of the region.

A tenuous peace existed between these groups of titan-forged, but it could not last. In time, malign forces moved to assert dominion over the lands once protected by the keepers. Among these forces were two of Loken's own creations, the brutish fire giants Volkhan and Ignis.

Volkhan and Ignis saw the Storm Peaks surrounding Ulduar as a land ripe for conquest. Yet to seize the region, they required an army. To this end, the giants turned to the fierce Winterskorn clan of vrykul.

Though many vrykul were warlike in nature, most avoided direct confrontation with each other. The Winterskorn proved to be an exception. These vrykul had developed a culture of violence and aggression, due in large part to their belief that they would one day ascend to the Halls of Valor. They thrived on conflict, whether it was between members of their own clan or with nearby groups of titan-forged.

Volkhan and Ignis took control of the Winterskorn by force and stoked the fires of their battle lust. The giants fortified the metal hides of the vrykul with enchanted armor. Volkhan and Ignis also forged powerful weapons designed to shatter the iron and stone skin of the other titan-forged.

TROGGS AND THE ORIGINS OF ULDAMAN

Following the war with the Old Gods, the keepers used the Forge of Wills to create new titan-forged to help them reshape the world. Yet their first designs proved too complex and overambitious. Rather than making the perfect servants, they had created stone-skinned savages known as troggs. The keepers quickly refined and perfected their designs. The next generation of titan-forged to emerge from the Forge of Wills would be known as the earthen.

The keepers were troubled by the troggs, but they could not bear to destroy them. Instead, Ironaya built a small subterranean vault, known as Uldaman, that would act as a stasis chamber for the troggs. Some of them escaped imprisonment and wandered the newly ordered world. Others even found their way into the domain of earth in the Elemental Plane, Deepholm.

But just as this new army embarked on its great conquest, anomalies began to appear in the Winterskorn. The vrykul's metallic skin became brittle and weak. They had begun showing the first symptoms of the curse of flesh.

Despite this setback, Volkhan and Ignis had no intentions of abandoning their campaign. They also knew that they could no longer rely on the Winterskorn alone to achieve victory. To strengthen the army, Volkhan and Ignis molded powerful molten golems and iron constructs of their own design.

This massive Winterskorn army marched first against the good-natured earthen, storming their underground lairs. The earthen were utterly unprepared to face such an overwhelming and organized force. Entire caverns were massacred to the last living creature. A small group of survivors escaped the onslaught and sought the help of Tyr, Archaedas, and Ironaya, who had thus far eluded Loken's wrath.

Incensed by what they learned, Tyr and his companions immediately journeyed to the earthen's cavernous home to aid the beleaguered titan-forged. Tyr himself led the bravest of the earthen in skirmishes with the Winterskorn, while Archaedas and Ironaya constructed defenses to ward off future attacks. In time, the earthen and their allies drove back the Winterskorn.

Although their attempt to conquer the Storm Peaks had failed, Volkhan and Ignis did not concede defeat. They returned to their blistering forges and created a new army—one even greater than before. Not satisfied with golems and constructs alone, Volkhan and Ignis crafted enchanted snares with which to enslave entire flights of proto-dragons. These creatures would serve not as mounts, but as beasts of war. The giants outfitted their winged servants with fiery weapons to strike terror into the hearts of the earthen.

The Winterskorn's next brutal assault shattered the earthen's defenses and drove them from their refuge. The earthen scattered across the icy mountain passes, but they could not escape their foes. Vrykul and golems hunted the earthen on the ground, while proto-dragons assailed them from the skies. Even Tyr, Archaedas, and Ironaya were forced to flee from the Winterskorn's fury.

Knowing that he and his allies could not defeat the Winterskorn alone, Tyr called on the five Dragon Aspects for help. The noble Aspects grew enraged upon seeing so many dead titan-forged. Their fury only deepened when they learned that proto-dragons had been enslaved. Without hesitation, the Aspects took wing and unleashed their powers on the Winterskorn's iron ranks.

Much as they had done in their fight against Galakrond, the Aspects worked in unison to overwhelm the vrykul army. Alexstrasza held the Winterskorn at bay with towering walls of enchanted fire. Malygos drained the magical essence that fueled the constructs and golems, rendering them useless. He also shattered the enchanted snares that bound the proto-dragons and set the beasts free. Neltharion raised mountains from the earth to corral and contain the vrykul and their giant masters. Lastly, Ysera and Nozdormu combined their powers to create a spell that would bring a decisive end to the conflict.

Ysera and Nozdormu enveloped the Winterskorn in a cloying mist that caused the titan-forged to fall asleep. These incapacitated creatures were then locked away in tomb cities across northern Kalimdor. They would not know the peaceful sleep of the Emerald Dream. Rather, they would languish in a timeless, unconscious slumber for thousands upon thousands of years.

In the millennia to come, the curse of flesh would continue warping the sleeping Winterskorn vrykul. When they eventually awoke, almost every one of them would discover that they had degenerated into mortal creatures of flesh and blood.

THE DISCS OF NORGANNON

With the Winterskorn defeated, Keeper Tyr at long last turned his attention to Loken. So long as Ulduar remained sealed off and the titan-forged were divided, more conflicts would arise. Tyr grimly concluded that unless he took action against Loken, Azeroth would spiral into an abyss of war and chaos.

But overthrowing Loken would require years of preparation. Tyr and his allies, Archaedas and Ironaya, concluded that they would first need to gather intelligence on Loken and his activities. To this end, they formulated a plan to steal the Discs of Norgannon from the heart of Ulduar. The relics had been recording everything that transpired on Azeroth, including Loken's betrayal. If there was any hope of undoing the damage caused by his schemes, it would be through the careful study of his actions.

Having devised a ruse to claim the discs, Tyr traveled to the gates of Ulduar itself. There, he called on Loken to relinquish control of Ulduar for the good of Azeroth, threatening dire consequences if he refused. Loken emerged from the fortress to convince Tyr that less drastic measures would suffice. A fierce argument erupted between the two keepers—exactly as Tyr had hoped. While Loken was distracted, Archaedas and Ironaya infiltrated Ulduar and stole the Discs of Norgannon.

Once they had secured the artifacts, Tyr and his companions escaped back into the icy crags and ridges of the Storm Peaks. They knew that Loken would soon hunt them down. Thus they prepared to journey south, where they hoped to find a refuge from which to plan their next move.

Before setting out, Tyr and his allies gathered great numbers of titan-forged who dwelled around Ulduar. A large group of peaceful vrykul afflicted by the curse of flesh, most of the surviving earthen, and many of the mechagnomes agreed to take part in the journey. Tyr, Archaedas, and Ironaya saw these titan-forged as innocent victims of Loken's treachery, and they promised to secure them a sanctuary before liberating Ulduar. The refugees traveled for many weeks, believing they had eluded Loken.

When Loken learned that the Discs of Norgannon were missing, panic seized him. If Tyr and his allies presented the artifacts to Algalon or the Pantheon, Loken's life would be forfeit. Out of desperation, he turned to the only creatures he knew were powerful enough to stop the mighty Tyr and recover the discs: ancient C'Thraxxi monstrosities known as Zakazj and Kith'ix.

Zakazj and Kith'ix had served as the Black Empire's most ruthless and cunning C'Thraxxi generals. Long ago, the keepers had sealed them and many of the other n'raqi away in underground chambers alongside the Old Gods. With considerable effort, Loken excavated these C'Thraxxi tombs and roused Zakazj and Kith'ix to life. He ordered the colossal abominations to kill Tyr and all who followed him. Sensing the lingering touch of Yogg-Saron in Loken's mind, the two C'Thraxxi readily obeyed.

Far to the south, in a tranquil and temperate glade, Zakazj and Kith'ix overtook the fleeing keepers and their followers. Fearing for his allies' lives, Tyr ordered Archaedas and Ironaya to lead the rest of the titan-forged farther south. Meanwhile, he would hold off the C'Thraxxi for as long as possible.

Only the barest shadow of Aggramar's old power lingered within Tyr's iron form, but the titan's noble spirit had not flagged. Tyr would not retreat, not when the lives of innocents were at risk.

As he grappled with the C'Thraxxi, torrents of both arcane and shadow energy ripped through the once-peaceful glade. The violent struggle between the lone keeper and the C'Thraxxi raged for six days and nights. Through it all, Tyr never gave ground—but neither did his foes. As fatigue set in, Tyr resolved to sacrifice himself to protect his friends. He unleashed all of his remaining power on the C'Thraxxi, expending his life force in a blinding explosion of arcane energy that shook the bones of the world.

To the south, Archaedas and Ironaya watched as the eruption of magic flared across the horizon. After the volatile energies subsided, the two titan-forged ventured back to the site of the battle. There, within a giant crater crackling with arcane magic, they found the lifeless bodies of Tyr and Zakazj.

Despite facing hopeless odds, the keeper of justice had nearly killed both C'Thraxxi. The survivor, Kith'ix, had only narrowly escaped Tyr's vengeful onslaught. The severely wounded C'Thrax had blindly fled to the west. It would not be seen again for many thousands of years.

In honor of her fallen comrade, Ironaya named the glade surrounding the crater "Tyr's Fall," which in the vrykul tongue translated to "Tirisfal." She and her followers buried Tyr and his foe where they lay. They placed Tyr's massive silver hand atop his final resting place as a memorial to his valiant sacrifice.

Although all of the refugees would carry on the story of Tyr's noble sacrifice, the vrykul in particular felt compelled to do something more. They were so moved by the keeper's deeds that they decided to settle at the battle site and stand vigil over Tyr's grave until the end of their days.

Archaedas and Ironaya honored the vrykul's wishes to settle the land of Tirisfal. The keeper and the giantess continued south with the earthen and mechagnomes in tow. They eventually stopped at the easternmost titan-forged vault on Kalimdor: Uldaman. Archaedas and Ironaya expanded the site, carving out new chambers to hold the Discs of Norgannon and vowing to protect the history of Azeroth with their lives if need be.

As the years passed, some of the earthen exhibited signs of the curse of flesh. Many of these titan-forged feared that the effects would only worsen. They asked to be placed in hibernation until a cure could one day be found. Archaedas, promising to rouse them at some time in the future, agreed. He sealed his followers within Uldaman's vast subterranean vaults.

The mechagnomes, however, remained awake. Even though they knew the curse would one day overtake them as well, they heroically vowed to watch over Uldaman and maintain its wondrous machineries.

TYR'S SACRIFICE

The mortals who would one day inhabit the area of Tirisfal would feel two conflicting energies emanating from the earth: the remaining spiritual essence of Keeper Tyr, and that of his enemy Zakazj. Some would tap into Tyr's energy; others would become attuned to the C'Thrax's dark aura.

TYR'S SILVER HAND AND ITS VRYKUL CARETAKERS

In distant Ulduar, Loken became desperate upon learning that his C'Thraxxi had failed to kill his foes. He assumed that with the mighty Tyr dead, Archaedas and Ironaya would not attempt a direct assault upon Ulduar. But the Discs of Norgannon still posed a threat to him. Stealing or destroying the artifacts was no longer an option—Archaedas and Ironaya could easily seal off Uldaman from intruders.

Instead, Loken attempted to replace the Discs of Norgannon with an archive of his own design, one that he dubbed the Tribunal of Ages. He adjusted the historical events contained in this new repository to his liking and expunged his sins from the record. Though he assumed he had been successful, his archive proved to be flawed. The histories stored within were warped even beyond Loken's understanding.

Loken then took one final drastic measure to prevent retribution from Archaedas and Ironaya. He believed that his enemies would eventually summon the constellar Algalon. To stop this, Loken altered the titan communication devices in Ulduar. This assured that no living creature would be able to contact Algalon. Only Loken's own death would draw the constellar to Azeroth. The fallen keeper assumed that his demise would come at the hands of Archaedas and Ironaya. If so, he was confident that Algalon would take his revenge for him by wiping out every living creature on Azeroth's surface.

CHILDREN OF GIANTS: THE RISE OF HUMANITY

With the Winterskorn asleep in their deep vaults and many of the earthen sealed within Uldaman, the remaining vrykul clans dominated the lands of northern Kalimdor. Over the course of eons, their disparate cultures flourished in unique ways. They developed their own identities and customs as they spread across the unforgiving north.

One of the mightiest clans to arise was the Dragonflayer. Much like the Winterskorn, these vrykul found that their iron hides were gradually turning to flesh over time. Initially, the clan leaders sought to balance out their diminishing strength by enslaving the ancient proto-dragons, just as the Winterskorn had done in previous centuries.

But unlike the Winterskorn, the Dragonflayers did not see the proto-dragons as mere beasts of war. They used the fearsome drakes as hunting companions, and they also rode them as battle mounts. Over time, these proto-dragons became an inseparable part of the clan's culture. They were also a necessary weapon against the vrykul's mortal enemy: a fierce race of bear-men called the jalgar, the progenitors of modern-day furbolgs.

Under King Ymiron, the Dragonflayer clan finally gained the upper hand against its foes. In a coordinated offensive, the vrykul attacked and drove the jalgar into Kalimdor's lush central forests. Yet on the heels of this victory, tragedy struck. The curse of flesh took another turn.

Dragonflayer women began giving birth to small, malformed children—a development that spread fear and superstition among the clan. Some of the vrykul even blamed Ymiron for the affliction, but the king had his own belief about who was responsible. In his mind, the mythical keepers were behind the curse of flesh.

65

The keepers, whom many vrykul viewed as their godlike creators, had not been seen or heard from in generations. Ymiron convinced his people to renounce the silent and aloof keepers, who had clearly abandoned them to the curse of flesh. He promised to unite *all* vrykul under his banner. As his first decree, Ymiron ordered his followers to cleanse the clan by destroying all of the malformed infants.

Many of the Dragonflayers obeyed Ymiron's brutal orders. Some, however, could not bring themselves to murder innocent children. They sought to hide their stunted offspring in a place of legend, a land far to the south where a lost clan of vrykul was said to have journeyed with Tyr, Archaedas, and Ironaya.

A number of Dragonflayers ventured south, taking their diminutive newborns in search of this fairy-tale refuge. Most were never heard from again. But others did find their way. With heavy hearts, they left their beloved sons and daughters in the care of the vrykul who inhabited Tirisfal.

In the ages that followed, the afflicted children and their offspring would continue degenerating into mortal beings called humans. Many of the other titan-forged—mechagnomes, tol'vir, mogu, and giants—would suffer a similar fate. Very few of the keepers' servants would fight off the affliction. Just as Yogg-Saron had hoped, the curse of flesh would weaken the titan-forged. But it would also give rise to mortal qualities of necessity that the Old God had never anticipated: courage, resolve, and heroism.

Unaware that these potent traits would one day shape the fate of the world, Yogg-Saron and the other Old Gods focused on escaping their prisons. Freedom, however, would take thousands of years to attain.

For now, more immediate dangers stirred in the lush heart of Kalimdor. A new power—a savage native race born in the early ages of the world—was on the rise. They called themselves trolls, and it would not be long before they learned of the malignant entities imprisoned beneath the earth.

THE DRAGONFLAYERS AND THE LONG SLUMBER

The Dragonflayers struggled to purge themselves of the curse of flesh in many ways. Despite all of their efforts, they would remain addled and weakened by the affliction. Eventually, these vrykul would place themselves in hibernation in the hopes of staving off the curse of flesh.

CHAPTER II: PRIMORDIAL AZEROTH

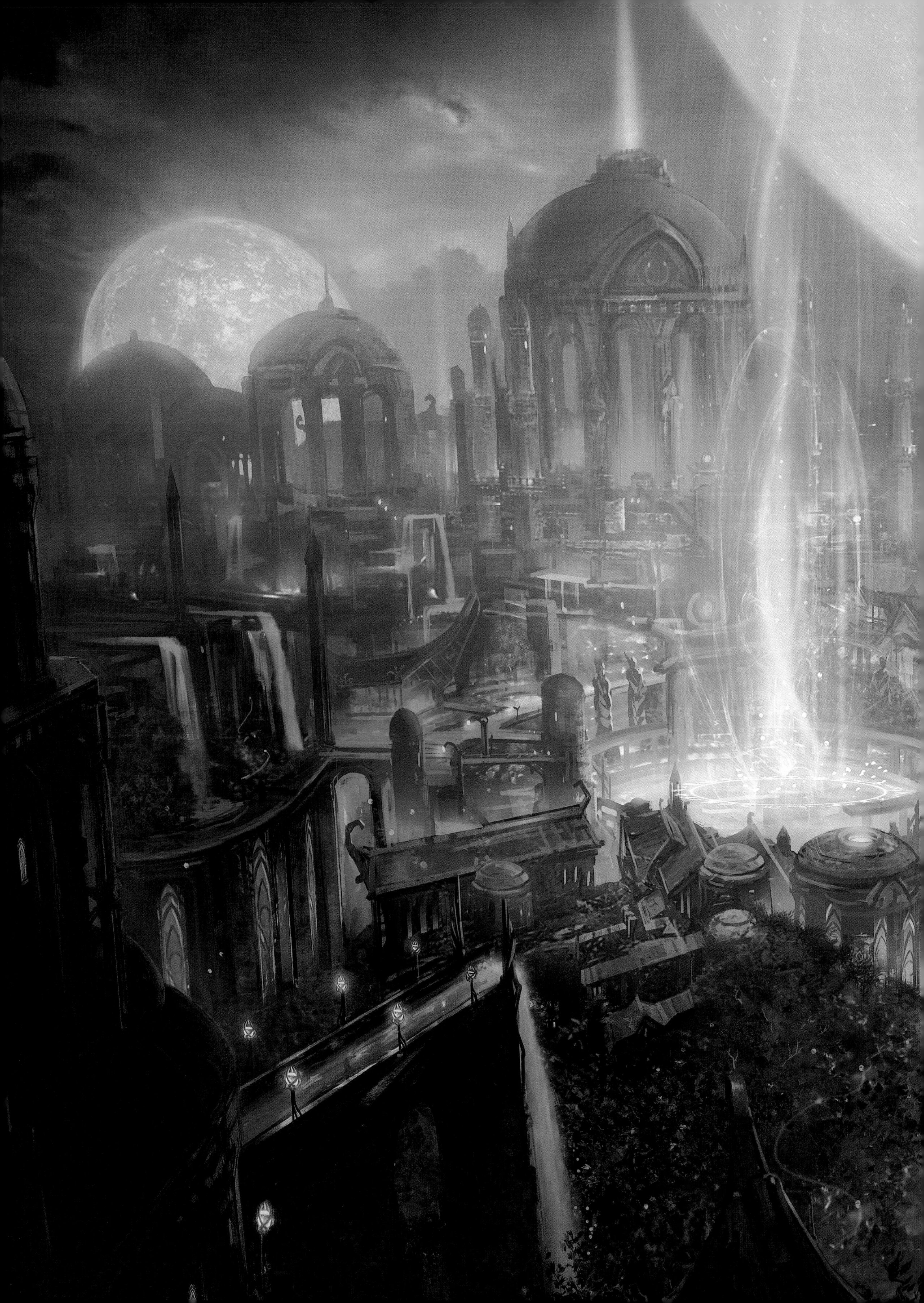

CHAPTER III

ANCIENT KALIMDOR

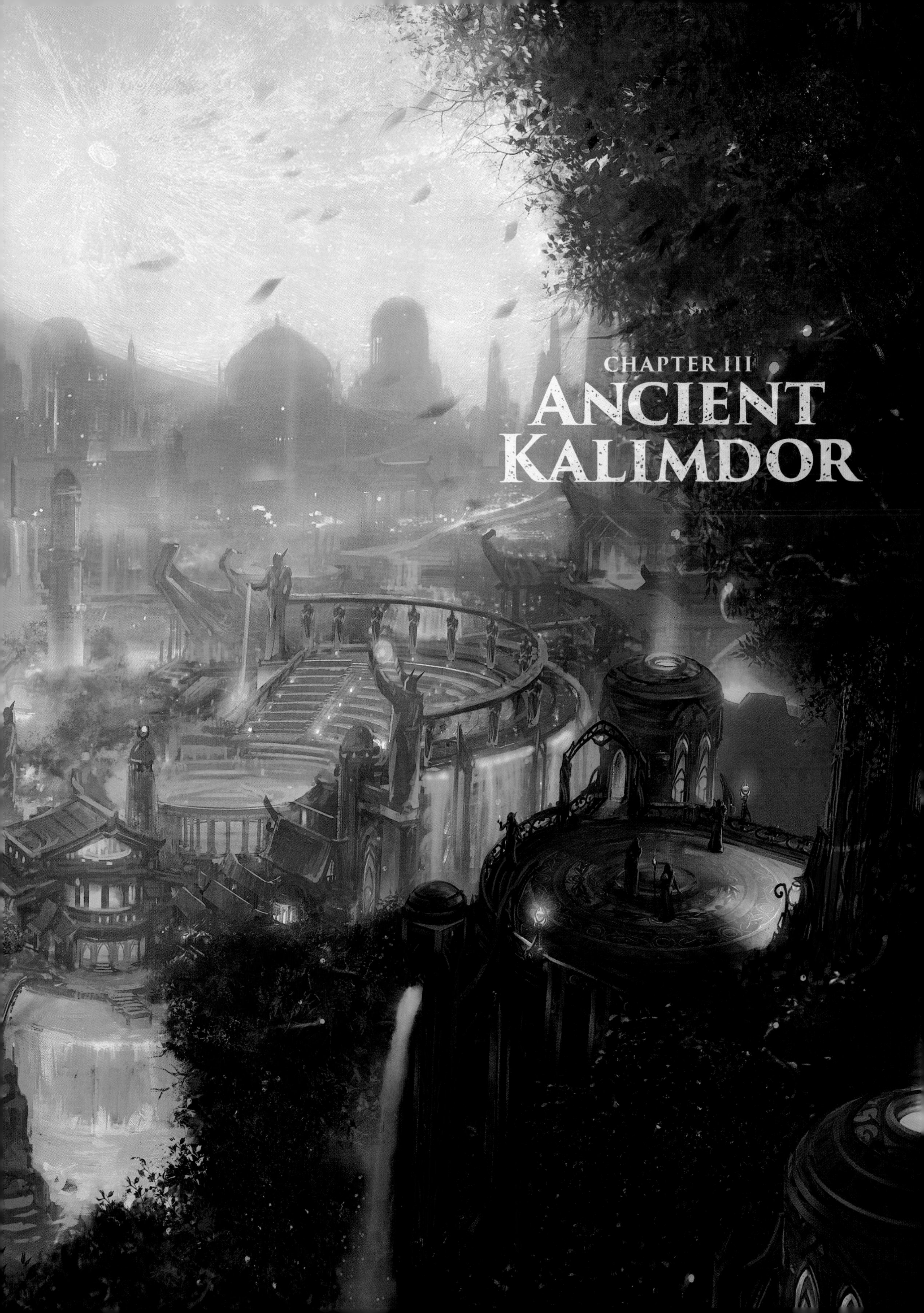

CHAPTER III
ANCIENT KALIMDOR

THE EMPIRE OF ZUL AND THE AWAKENING OF THE AQIR
16,000 YEARS BEFORE THE DARK PORTAL

For generation after generation, life bloomed across the ordered world of Azeroth. Nowhere was this more evident than in the dense woodlands around the Well of Eternity. The fount of Azeroth's arcane lifeblood accelerated the cycles of growth and rebirth. Before long, sentient beings evolved from the land's primitive life-forms.

Among the first and most prolific were the trolls, a race of savage hunter-gatherers who flourished in Azeroth's jungles and forests. Though the trolls were of only average intelligence, they possessed incredible agility and strength. Their unique physiology also allowed them to recover from physical injuries at an astonishing rate, and they could even regenerate lost limbs over time.

The early trolls developed a wide array of superstitious customs. Some practiced cannibalism and devoted themselves to warfare. A rare few sought knowledge through mystic practices and meditation. Still others honed their ties to a dark and powerful form of magic known as voodoo. Yet no matter their individual customs, what all trolls shared was a common religion that revolved around Kalimdor's elusive Wild Gods. The trolls called these powerful beings "loa," and they worshipped them as deities.

Due to their reverence for the Wild Gods, the trolls gathered near a series of peaks and plateaus in southern Kalimdor. This was home to many of their honored loa. The trolls gave the holy mountain range the name Zandalar, and soon they built small encampments upon its slopes.

The most powerful group of trolls was called the Zandalar tribe. Its members claimed nearly all of Zandalar's tallest plateaus, believing them to be sacred ground. Atop the highest peaks they constructed a small cluster of crude shrines. In time, these grew into a bustling temple city known as Zuldazar.

OVERLEAF: THE NIGHT ELF CAPITAL OF ZIN-AZSHARI

THE ZANDALARI TROLL CAPITAL, ZULDAZAR

Over the next several centuries, other tribes arose to challenge the Zandalari for territory and power. The most notable of these were the fearsome Gurubashi, Amani, and Drakkari. The Gurubashi and Amani in particular laid claim to enormous swaths of land in Kalimdor's lush jungles and woods. On occasion, tribes clashed, often over hunting grounds. Yet major conflicts were few, and rarely lengthy. Trolls were such skilled and fierce fighters that any real conflict would cost both sides dearly. Untouched land was plentiful in all directions, and the various tribes quickly learned it was wiser to resettle than risk war.

Only one place was forbidden by the tribes' witch doctors and priests: a small mound of blackened stone at the base of the Zandalar Mountains. The loa warned the tribes' mystics of severe consequences should they disturb the black stones. For many years, none of the trolls dared disobey.

But curiosity eventually won out.

A group of rebellious trolls plumbed the forbidden mound. They discovered that the black stones were not mere rocks—they were the jagged hide of a monstrous creature. None of the trolls had ever seen anything like it. They believed it to be an undiscovered loa, and a powerful one at that, considering that the other spirits were frightened of it. The trolls performed vile rituals and living sacrifices to awaken the slumbering monstrosity.

Roused by the blood offerings, a gigantic C'Thraxxi general emerged from its long slumber and ruthlessly slaughtered all those who had revived it. The trolls were unaware that this was Kith'ix, the being who had survived the encounter with Keeper Tyr. Gravely wounded, the C'Thrax had fled southwest to what would be known as the Zandalar Mountains before collapsing into a deep hibernation. Reeling from its presence, the ancient loa inhabiting the area had buried Kith'ix beneath the earth so that no other creature would disturb it.

The awoken C'Thrax looked upon troll civilization with contempt, for it was but a pale shadow of the Black Empire of eons past. Kith'ix knew it would delight the Old Gods to see this pitiful civilization rent to ashes. The C'Thrax reached out with its mind and found a race of creatures it could control—the aqir. In the ages after the fall of the Black Empire, these insectoids had remained hidden in small warrens and tunnels beneath the ground.

Kith'ix rallied the aqiri swarms, driving them to make war and establish their dominance over Azeroth once again. As the C'Thrax expanded its power and recovered, the insectoids began building a vast subterranean empire known as Azj'Aqir. Kith'ix patiently watched and waited as the aqiri ranks swelled in number. When the time was right, the C'Thrax led the insectoids from their underground empire, and they swept across the land.

The trolls' experience as hunters made them formidable foes, but the aqiri threat was unlike any they had ever faced. Numerous smaller tribes fell before the unrelenting insectoids' legions.

As the aqir encroached perilously close to the Zandalar Mountains, the Zandalari moved to act. They united the disparate troll tribes into a single mighty force, which they called the Empire of Zul. The members of this newly forged society would put aside their differences and work together to destroy the aqir.

The Zandalari took on the role of commanding the troll armies. With their temple city looming high in the mountains, they could detect enemy movements and direct attacks at weak points. Under the Zandalari's guidance, the other trolls used ambush tactics in the surrounding jungles to whittle down the enemy's numbers. Elsewhere, revered priests summoned the loa to assail their enemies. These ferocious Wild Gods joined the troll warriors in battle, ripping through the aqiri ranks and even wounding Kith'ix.

The aqir were forced to retreat before they could mount a proper siege on the sacred mountains. Kith'ix, gravely wounded by the loa, fled to the northeast with a contingent of its closest aqiri followers. There, it planned to regain its strength while the insectoids continued their war against the trolls.

Though they had driven the aqir away, the Zandalari knew that their enemy still posed a grave threat. The insectoids, if left unchecked, would attack outlying troll territories.

At the Zandalari's behest, the other tribes moved out to hunt down the aqir. The trolls quickly learned it was not enough to simply kill the insectoids. If any aqir escaped underground, they would establish a new colony and rise up again later. To permanently end the threat, no corner of the continent could be left unguarded. Thus, the Zandalari convinced the most power-hungry troll factions to establish new strongholds across Azeroth. Chief among these groups were the Amani, Gurubashi, and Drakkari. After defeating the aqir, they could claim the fertile new lands for themselves, without any competition.

The ambitious tribes readily agreed. The Drakkari pushed into the frigid north against a colony of aqir, but the trolls faced a weapon they had never expected: corrupted tol'vir. A small group of the titan-forged who dwelled outside Ulduar had been captured and enthralled by the aqir. These ferocious stone tol'vir, known as "obsidian destroyers," almost overpowered the Drakkari. But years of battle had shaped the tribe into cunning fighters, and they devised brilliant ways to topple and shatter their foes.

The Gurubashi also encountered corrupted titan-forged. These trolls had ventured southwest, where the aqir had overrun Ahn'Qiraj, the prison complex housing the Old God C'Thun. Upon infiltrating the stronghold, the insectoids had enslaved the anubisath giants who guarded the prison.

Early engagements between the Gurubashi and the aqir proved disastrous for the trolls. The insectoids and their mighty anubisaths slaughtered several large Gurubashi encampments. Thereafter, the Zandalari instructed Gurubashi priests to separate their tribe into smaller, more mobile raiding groups instead of large armies. This new tactic allowed them to constantly harass the aqir, bleeding the insectoid armies dry over a period of many years. Though they were never able to completely wipe out the aqir, the Gurubashi eventually won uncontested control of the surrounding territory.

Meanwhile, the Amani had set out to destroy Kith'ix. They tracked the C'Thrax's trail far to the northeastern woodlands, cutting through an unending mass of aqiri guardians. In a final savage battle, the entire tribe flung itself in a suicidal attack against Kith'ix and its remaining insectoid minions. Only a tiny fraction of the troll army survived. Even so, the C'Thrax succumbed to its tireless hunters.

Though the cost was high, the fearsome reputation of the Amani became legend among the other tribes. Atop the site where they had killed Kith'ix, the trolls established a new settlement. It would one day grow into a sprawling temple city known as Zul'Aman.

With the C'Thrax gone, the aqir no longer fought with as much ferocity or purpose. The war between the trolls and the aqir shifted dramatically. Extermination of the aqir became the trolls' new imperative.

After many centuries of brutal fighting, the trolls shattered the aqir empire, containing the insectoids in the far northern and far southern reaches of the continent. Central Kalimdor was permanently scoured of their presence. The surviving aqir fortified their underground colonies against further troll aggression. They showed no more interest in fighting. In time, the trolls proclaimed themselves victorious.

THE NERUBIANS, QIRAJI, AND MANTID

Three distinct cultures would arise from the aqir empire. The insectoids in the north gathered near the underground prison of Yogg-Saron. Due to their proximity to the Old God, these aqir would gradually evolve into a race called the nerubians. Their kingdom would become known as Azjol-Nerub.

The aqir in the southwest made their home in Ahn'Qiraj, the conquered prison complex of C'Thun. The captive Old God's foul presence would slowly warp the aqir's forms over time, molding them into a race known as the qiraji.

The aqir in the southeast congregated where Y'Shaarj's essence still polluted the land. These insectoids would eventually transform into a race called the mantid. Even before the aqir empire fell, they would establish the great colony of Manti'vess near the Vale of Eternal Blossoms.

Without war to bind them together, the troll factions grew ever more distant and insular. The far-flung strongholds of the different tribes blossomed into vibrant homes, temple cities, and eventually empires in their own right. The Zandalari withdrew to their mountain plateaus to pursue spiritual knowledge, but they would always maintain an immense influence over the disparate troll societies.

THE MANTID CYCLE

In the later stages of the war with the trolls, one enclave of aqir gathered at the southern edge of Kalimdor. Below the roots of the great kypari trees, they established a new empire. These insectoids, known thereafter as the mantid, saw no purpose in continuing a battle they knew they were not strong enough to win.

Such restraint was unusual among the insectoids, but then, so was the mantid's reasoning. They still fervently worshipped the Old Gods, believing that their ancient masters would one day rise from their prisons and reestablish their dominion over Azeroth. The best way to serve the entities was not to expend the mantid's strength, but to conserve it, refine it, and sharpen it. The mantid would grow stronger without jeopardizing their survival.

Though a revered empress ruled over the day-to-day activities of the mantid, another group controlled the insectoids' destiny. The members of this group called themselves the Klaxxi—meaning "priest" in their native tongue. They guided the actions of the empress and the mantid swarms in the hopes of preserving and strengthening their race. Rather than seek retribution on the trolls, the Klaxxi turned their gaze on another enemy.

Nearby dwelled the mogu, mighty titan-forged who had guarded the Vale of Eternal Blossoms for untold ages. The mantid found themselves drawn to the mystical valley. They were not aware of it at the time, but they were attracted to the lingering presence of the slain Old God Y'Shaarj, whose festering heart had been locked away beneath the vale by Highkeeper Ra.

To seek out the dark essence beneath the vale, the mantid launched a surprise attack against the mogu. The titan-forged narrowly withstood the swarm and drove them back to the kypari forests.

The Klaxxi did not consider their defeat a failure. The surviving mantid warriors had matured, grown more powerful and cunning. The Klaxxi patiently waited one hundred years before assaulting the mogu again. They dispatched a new generation of young mantid to besiege the titan-forged. Once again, the survivors returned stronger.

Thus began the mantid cycle. Every century, a new mantid clutch made war upon the mogu. The ferocious battles removed the weak from the swarm, and only the strongest returned to the kypari trees. Within only a few cycles, mantid civilization had become tightly honed and rigid, utterly focused on eradicating weakness and empowering the mightiest of their kind.

The mogu marked the change with concern. They launched a campaign into Manti'vess itself to ensure that the cycle would not come again.

The attack came at an inauspicious time for the mantid. It was decades before the next clutch of warriors would hatch. The mantid were few, and the mogu were many. Initially, the titan-forged devastated the insectoid ranks, even the strongest survivors of past swarms. Only one mantid, Korven, emerged to turn the tide of battle. Armed with blades forged of kypari amber, the warrior eviscerated the mogu ranks, thwarting their attack and sending them into retreat. So great was Korven's skill that many mantid came to believe that he was capable of cheating death itself.

The high elders of the Klaxxi proclaimed Korven a "paragon" and promised his deeds would become legend among their kind. But the honored warrior was still not satisfied. He knew it was only chance that he arose in his race's greatest hour of need. He did not want to leave the mantid's defense to chance alone. The Klaxxi agreed and tasked him with finding a solution.

After years of experimenting with kypari sap, Korven discovered that a living creature could be preserved within an amber cocoon, potentially for thousands of years. If the Klaxxi placed their greatest warriors in these cocoons, they could be awakened whenever they were needed to avert disaster. Korven became the first to undergo this preservation. In honor of his deeds, the Klaxxi named him "Korven the Prime"—the first of many paragons to come. As he lay undisturbed in his amber tomb, the great cycle he had almost single-handedly saved continued on, remaining unbroken for countless generations.

OVERLEAF: MAP OF AZEROTH AFTER THE WAR BETWEEN THE TROLLS AND THE AQIR

Aftermath of the Aqir and Troll War

Ulduar

Azjol-Nerub

Mount Hyjal

DARK TROLLS

Well of Eternity

Tribes under Drakkari control:
Frostmane
Winterax

Tribes under Amani control:
Firetree
Mossflayer
Revantusk
Smolderthorn
Vilebranch
Witherbark

Tribes under Gurubashi control:
Bloodscalp
Darkspear
Razorbranch
Shatterspear
Skullsplitter

ZANDALAR

Zul'Farrak

Zuldazar

Ahn'Qiraj

Thundering Mountain

Uldum

Mogu'shan Vaults

Vale of Eternal Blossoms

Manti'vess

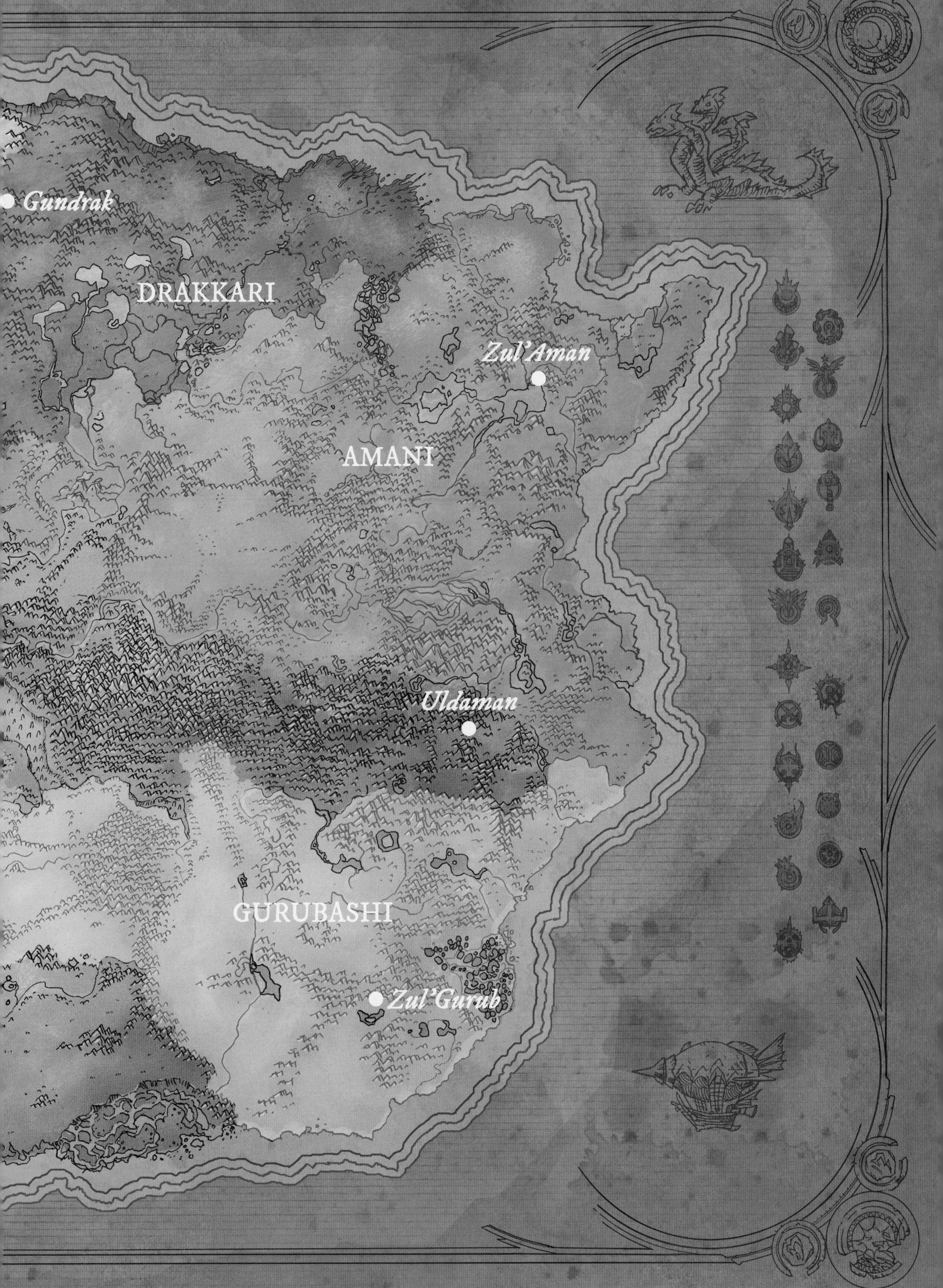

Gundrak
DRAKKARI
Zul'Aman
AMANI
Uldaman
GURUBASHI
Zul'Gurub

THE AGE OF A HUNDRED KINGS
15,000 YEARS BEFORE THE DARK PORTAL

Though Highkeeper Ra had not been seen in millennia, his loyal mogu maintained their vigil over the Vale of Eternal Blossoms, bravely fighting off each successive mantid swarm. Their faith that the highkeeper would one day return endured through century after century of hardships.

Yet that faith vanished once the curse of flesh manifested within the mogu ranks.

For the first time, the mogu faced mortality. Fear and uncertainty took root in their hearts. Small disagreements spiraled into conflict, violence, and bloodshed. Packs of mogu banded together. Clans and warlords emerged by the score and engaged in brutal power struggles. Those who triumphed were quickly toppled by rivals. Through it all, their culture and language—even their sense of purpose and identity—began to change. This period of turmoil and conflict became known as the Age of a Hundred Kings, and the mogu edged perilously close to destroying themselves from within.

Only their basest instincts prevented annihilation. At the beginning of each new mantid swarm, the mogu's petty conflicts would die down. The various clans would reluctantly band together to stand against the mantid. But once the swarm had retreated, internal hostilities would surface once again.

As the mogu battled the mantid, a number of other races arose in the region. Many of these creatures were drawn to the latent powers emanating from the Vale of Eternal Blossoms. Among these wondrous new races were the jinyu, fish-like mystics who dwelled in the rivers and lakes. A bold and mischievous race of monkeys, known as the hozen, also came to inhabit the dense jungles that encircled much of the vale. But by far, the most intelligent of these newcomers were the wise pandaren.

The emergence of so much life around the vale piqued the interest of four Wild Gods. Their names were Xuen, the White Tiger; Yu'lon, the Jade Serpent; Chi-Ji, the Red Crane; and Niuzao, the Black Ox.

Xuen and his fellow Wild Gods gathered at the vale to watch over and guide the myriad life-forms that dwelled in the area. Though the warlike activities of the mogu often troubled them, the Wild Gods delighted in watching the other races flourish. In particular, Xuen and the other demigods developed close ties with the pandaren, in large part due to their penchant for peace.

The pandaren considered the Wild Gods, whom they called the "August Celestials," to be benevolent deities. They formed a system of worship devoted to the extraordinary beings. In return, the Wild Gods bestowed knowledge on the pandaren, nurturing their ties to philosophy and the natural world. At the behest of the August Celestials, the pandaren formed a culture that sought peace and harmony with the surrounding environment.

Yet soon a new mogu leader would arise to challenge these philosophies. His name was Lei Shen, and his rule would threaten not only the mortal races of the vale, but the August Celestials as well.

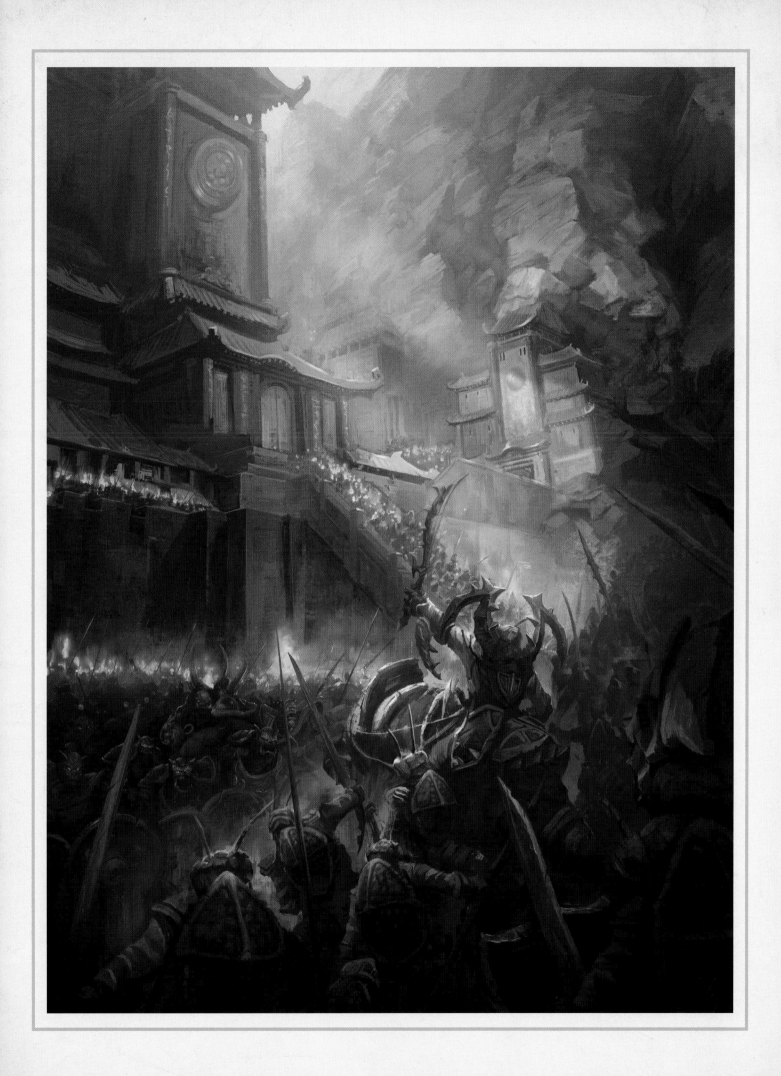

MOGU DEFENDING THEIR LANDS FROM THE MANTID

THE THUNDER KING
15,000–12,200 YEARS BEFORE THE DARK PORTAL

As the pandaren and other races prospered around the Vale of Eternal Blossoms, the mogu continued their endless squabbling. It was during this cycle of violence that a warrior named Lei Shen came to power.

A descendant of a minor warlord, young Lei Shen was thoroughly accustomed to the brutality of clan warfare. Despite his skill and success in battle, he saw the incessant conflicts and political maneuvering as a betrayal of the mogu's potential. Nevertheless, he remained stalwart as a vassal for his father.

A close advisor eventually betrayed and murdered Lei Shen's father. Almost all of the fallen warlord's clansmen sought refuge in the ranks of other clans, abandoning Lei Shen. Only a few loyal armsmen refused to leave his side. Rather than seek retribution and perpetuate the violence, Lei Shen chose to go into exile. He wandered the land, meditating on what he saw as the failures of his kind.

Soon Lei Shen desired answers his intellect and reason could no longer provide. He set off in search of the mogu's long-absent master, Highkeeper Ra.

In recent centuries, the highkeeper had become known as *Ra-den*, meaning "Master Ra" in the new mogu tongue. Few of Lei Shen's kind even believed he still lived. Why would their ancient creator have allowed them to suffer from the curse of flesh? Lei Shen believed Ra-den had a plan, a master purpose, and that the current trials of the mogu were merely a test. Perhaps it was even the will of the titans themselves. After all, Ra-den was their living instrument.

After years of searching, Lei Shen located the entrance to the hidden vaults beneath the land north of the vale, sacred chambers that the mogu had all but forgotten due to their ceaseless warring. There he found the highkeeper, sitting quietly in the stillness beneath the earth. Ra-den showed no reaction to the young mogu's intrusion. The highkeeper said nothing, even as Lei Shen began to ask him questions about the mogu's true purpose.

THE MADNESS OF LEI SHEN

The decision to abandon any claim to his father's power had spared Lei Shen's life. When a clan's leader was killed, it was customary for rivals to immediately murder his family and thus exterminate the clan lineage forever. Lei Shen's meditations were seen as a sign of despair and madness. Most assumed he would never be a threat to any mogu ever again.

Days and weeks passed, and Lei Shen grew frustrated with his master's silence. Finally the mogu realized that Ra was not contemplating some subtle plan, was not engrossed in the work of the titans ... The highkeeper had simply given up. The suffering of the mogu had been the result of an absentee master and nothing more.

Lei Shen unleashed his anger on Ra, accusing him of abandoning the titans and their purpose. His harsh words roused the highkeeper from his stupor. Ra took Lei Shen to the nearby Thundering Mountain, where unending storms roared and split the heavens. No mogu had dared scale its slopes before, for the mountain was believed to be a forbidden place. Inside a massive, ornate vault, Ra-den summoned the lingering power of Aman'Thul and showed Lei Shen the answers he wanted: the titans of the Pantheon were dead, murdered by one of their own. Their final hope was the world of Azeroth itself, but it was already infested with creatures of the Void.

The highkeeper had assumed that this knowledge would shatter Lei Shen's soul as it had his own. Yet the mogu reacted in a way Ra-den never expected.

Lei Shen decided that if his master had no interest in continuing the titans' purpose, he would do it himself. Without warning, he struck out and incapacitated Ra-den. Lei Shen then bound the mighty being in enchanted iron bands. He stole not only Ra-den's incredible power, but also the contained power of *Aman'Thul*.

Might beyond understanding flooded through Lei Shen's soul. He imprisoned Ra-den within the Thundering Mountain, ignoring the highkeeper's rage and confusion at the betrayal. When Lei Shen descended the mountain and met with his remaining armsmen, they were in awe of him. Rumors of Lei Shen's newfound might spread among the mogu clans. Some believed he had torn out the heart of a god and eaten it. A few claimed he had harnessed the ancient powers of the vale itself. Still others whispered that he was a titan reborn.

Yet all of the stories had one fact in common: this "Thunder King" had demanded that all mogu bow before him. He claimed the birthright of the titans, and he would destroy all those who refused to yield to his will.

Thereafter, Lei Shen set out to unify the mogu and forge them a new destiny as the masters of Azeroth and guardians of its world-soul. The petty squabbling and warfare that had plagued their kind would no longer be tolerated. With lightning and thunder at his command, Lei Shen crushed all opposition. The fortunate ones were killed quickly; the unfortunate ones were kept in chains for centuries.

Initially, most of the mogu rallied to him out of fear, but his "miracles" soon inspired devotion. The Thunder King had mastered the enchanted tools of the keepers. One of these was the Engine of Nalak'sha, a powerful device that Lei Shen had discovered beneath the land north of the vale. Using this extraordinary machine, the mogu began shaping flesh and stone into new living creatures. They even found a way to reverse the curse of flesh among themselves.

Under Lei Shen, a period of prosperity *and* brutality gripped the vale. For the mogu, it was the beginning of a glorious new empire. Yet for the region's other races, it marked the start of an age of tyranny.

THE TWO EMPIRES

As Lei Shen's empire expanded in scope and power, he soon regarded all living creatures within his domain as his servants. The curse of flesh was a weakness, he reasoned, and although not all of the mogu might ever be fully cleansed of the flaw, other beings of flesh would always be beneath them.

The Thunder King began a campaign of enslavement in the lands surrounding the vale. The wise jinyu had established a small empire of their own. Though they fought valiantly, the jinyu ultimately crumbled before the might of Lei Shen. The mogu sacked their towns and left their entire civilization in ruins.

Upon learning of the jinyu's fate, the pandaren fled to Kun-Lai Summit, north of the vale. There, they sought the protection of Xuen, the White Tiger. When Lei Shen brought his armies to the foothills, he challenged Xuen to a duel that would decide the fate of the pandaren. Xuen accepted, and for many days the great battle between the White Tiger and the Thunder King shook the skies over Kun-Lai. In the end, Xuen could not match Lei Shen's stolen titan power. Lei Shen chained Xuen near the peak of the mount, forcing the August Celestial to watch as the mogu bound the pandaren to slavery. Fearing that the pandaren's peaceful philosophies would undermine his rule, Lei Shen forbade them from learning how to read or write, or even how to speak any language other than the mogu tongue. To disobey was to be killed in slow, brutal fashion.

The mogu forged their greatest palaces and monuments with the blood and sweat of their subjugated races. Soon, the empire boasted a unified language, an established system of weights and measurements, and the first set of written laws in Azeroth—brutal codes that enshrined the mogu's place above the other creatures. Lei Shen also forced his slaves to act as soldiers or to expand the crude fortifications once used to defend the vale from the mantid. Thus was born the Serpent's Spine, a massive stone wall separating the mogu from the insectoid lands. When existing slaves perished or proved inefficient, Lei Shen shaped new ones with the power of the

THE HOZEN BETRAYAL

At the height of their empire, the jinyu held close ties with the hozen. Both agreed to help the other withstand the onslaught of the mogu. Yet on the eve of the jinyu's final stand against Lei Shen, the hozen betrayed them. The jinyu's so-called allies had secretly pledged their loyalties to the Thunder King in exchange for preferential treatment (a promise that was never kept). This act of treachery ensured the jinyu's defeat and ignited a bitter racial feud between them and the hozen that would last for generations.

FATE OF THE AUGUST CELESTIALS

After Lei Shen imprisoned the White Tiger, the other celestials came to the aid of the pandaren. Yet like Xuen, they all succumbed to the Thunder King. Thereafter, Lei Shen prohibited worship of the celestials on pain of death. The pandaren lost many of their ties to the Wild Gods, but not all. A few fearless slaves, in secret, carried on the teachings of the celestials.

Engine of Nalak'sha. This led to the creation of myriad beings, such as the diminutive yet resilient grummles and the barbaric, reptilian saurok.

The mogu empire quickly drew notice from other civilizations on Azeroth. The Zandalari trolls, in particular, were amazed at the otherworldly powers wielded by the Thunder King. One of the Zandalari's leaders, a revered high priest named Zulathra, saw in the mogu a golden opportunity. He and a retinue of trolls journeyed to the Thunder King's domain with a simple proposition: the mogu might hold the power of this world, but the trolls held the knowledge of the land. The two empires would make each other great and teach each other their secrets. Once they were allied, nothing on Azeroth would dare oppose them.

The offer intrigued Lei Shen. For the first time, he had met other living creatures who sought to master their environment rather than live in peace with it. The mogu rarely ventured far from their lands; superstitions and the deep-seated duty of protecting the vale still influenced their actions. They could explore the world from a position of ignorance, or they could ally with the trolls and learn its mysteries quickly.

In truth, both leaders plotted betrayal. Zulathra believed the Zandalari could steal Lei Shen's godlike powers once they learned the mogu's secrets, and the Thunder King schemed to enslave the Zandalari the moment they ceased being useful. Yet they kept their plans concealed, even from their own people, and publicly brokered an agreement. In exchange for the Zandalari's knowledge, the mogu would train them in the ways of arcane magic. They also promised the Zandalari a swath of fertile land near the vale.

Lei Shen even made a secret agreement with Zulathra. The Thunder King had devised a method to fully revive his spirit if he was ever killed, but he did not trust his own servants with such knowledge. The mogu were a power-hungry people, and they would likely try to claim the empire for themselves if Lei Shen fell. Only the Zandalari would hold the key to resurrecting Lei Shen. Without him, the trolls knew they would never fully learn the secrets of the arcane—nor would they be able to claim his awesome power.

Though both leaders continued scheming, their betrayals would never come to fruition. Indeed, they found each other to be invaluable allies, and their pact endured for many years.

THE THUNDER KING BATTLES XUEN, THE WHITE TIGER

THUNDER FALLS

While Lei Shen consolidated his empire, the tol'vir guarding Uldum struggled to endure the curse of flesh. The malady had spread throughout their ranks, slowly weakening the titan-forged. All the while, the tol'vir waited patiently for word from Highkeeper Ra or his mogu servants in the east.

Eventually the tol'vir received a summons from a mogu leader calling himself the Thunder King. They had heard nothing about the rise of the mogu empire. Curious, the tol'vir dispatched ambassadors to the east. When they reached the edges of the Thunder King's domain, they were stunned to see how advanced their mogu cousins had become. In some instances, the mogu had even managed to reverse the curse of flesh.

Lei Shen warmly greeted the tol'vir and showed them the wonders of his empire, from the immense Serpent's Spine wall to the gilded imperial palaces of the vale. The tol'vir were shocked at the deplorable treatment of the mortal races that had been enslaved by the mogu. Even so, the tol'vir were not stirred to action. Their prime concern was the protection of the keeper-wrought machineries in Uldum.

The Thunder King wholeheartedly agreed. The works of the keepers, such as the Forge of Origination in Uldum, were of utmost importance . . . and so Lei Shen announced he was claiming them as part of his empire.

He revealed that he had defeated Ra-den and taken his power. Therefore, Lei Shen claimed that he now held dominion over the keepers' instruments. With the Engine of Nalak'sha and the Forge of Origination at his command, he could remake Azeroth as he saw fit. As fellow titan-forged, the tol'vir would ascend to a place of honor in the mogu empire, but Lei Shen would be at its head, now and forever.

Upon learning that Lei Shen had betrayed Highkeeper Ra, the tol'vir grew furious. They refused the Thunder King's offer, vowing never to serve a traitor, and stormed out of his tyrannical empire. Lei Shen allowed the ambassadors to leave but warned them he would take what he wanted by force. Their armies could not possibly stand against his.

So confident was the Thunder King that he invited Zulathra to witness what he claimed would be the mogu empire's greatest victory yet. The elderly Zandalari leader agreed—Lei Shen had artificially extended the troll's life, but once all of the keepers' works were under mogu control, they would unlock the secrets of immortality. Almost all of the highest-ranking Zandalari leaders accompanied Zulathra as an honor guard, also expecting to return to their capital of Zuldazar with the gift of eternal life.

Lei Shen led his mogu host and the trolls to the west. The Zandalari had heard tales of the lands near Uldum, but they had never seen them with their own eyes. Pristine lakes and waterfalls dotted the region's lush jungles. It was a paradise, teeming with undiscovered life and wonders as far as the eye could see.

The full might of Lei Shen's empire trampled over the land, stopping just short of the monolithic pyramids that composed the keepers' bastion of Uldum. Only a small group of tol'vir emerged from the fortress to resist the mogu. Lei Shen mocked their numbers, for he knew that he alone could crush them.

Indeed, the tol'vir had known that defeating the Thunder King's forces in battle was impossible. As Lei Shen had marched toward Uldum, the titan-forged had prepared a final

THE TITAN-FORGED STRONGHOLD OF ULDUM

defense: the Forge of Origination locked beneath the fortress. Rather than using it to its full potential—which would eradicate all life on Azeroth—the tol'vir had configured the Forge of Origination to scour only the nearby land.

As Lei Shen led the charge, gloating in his impending victory, the tol'vir activated the weapon. Deep within the earth, the device rumbled to life. The earth heaved and buckled as waves of force erupted from Uldum, bathing the surrounding land in the energies of uncreation. The tol'vir defenders and nearly every other creature on the surface of Uldum that day died instantly.

Creatures all across Kalimdor witnessed the flash on the southern horizon. When it subsided, Lei Shen and his allies were no more. The unleashed power had also purged the area around Uldum of almost all life, leaving only a cracked and barren desert behind. Pockets of plant and animal life would slowly return over the millennia, but the vast jungle would never fully regain its vibrancy.

The surviving tol'vir within Uldum worked to ensure that no one would ever again attempt to claim such power. They shrouded the few mountain passes that led into the region with magic. In doing so, the tol'vir effectively sealed Uldum off from the eyes of mortals.

The tol'vir's noble sacrifice had kept the Forge of Origination out of Lei Shen's hands and prevented any other mogu emperor from daring to follow in his footsteps. The deaths of Lei Shen and the upper caste of the Zandalari left massive power vacuums in both empires. Before the tol'vir shrouded Uldum in their grand illusion, a handful of Thunder King loyalists recovered Lei Shen's corpse from the region. They brought it back to the empire and enshrined it within the Tomb of Conquerors. Yet with most of the Zandalari leadership dead, there was no one to revive the Thunder King.

A succession of emperors followed Lei Shen, but none would ever wield as much power as he had. The Zandalari, too, spent generations attempting to recover from the losses at Uldum. The catastrophic event had struck a mortal blow to both empires. Neither would ever regain its former glory.

And in time, both would crumble and fall.

THE PANDAREN REVOLUTION
12,000 YEARS BEFORE THE DARK PORTAL

The Thunder King's death weakened the mogu, but their civilization continued lording over the vale. The empire's slaves suffered greatly under Lei Shen's barbarous successors, each ruler seemingly crueler than the last.

The final mogu emperor, Lao-Fe, earned the title "Slavebinder" early in his tenure. He lived a life of decadence, confident that his supply of cowed slaves would never diminish. To earn their compliance, Lao-Fe would tear apart slave families for even mild transgressions. Parents were separated; children were dispatched to the Serpent's Spine to die as fodder before the mantid swarm.

It was this very fate that befell the family of a pandaren brewmaster named Kang—his son was sent to the mantid, and his wife died trying to stop it. After the mogu left his home and his life in ruins, Kang nearly succumbed to despair. But soon his thoughts circled around a particular question: why? Why did the mogu inflict such pain?

Kang meditated on the slavery of his people, and he reached a radical conclusion. The extreme cruelty toward slaves was not a sign of the mogu's strength. It was a symptom of their weakness. They had grown dependent on their servants; without them, they were nothing.

Kang devoted his life to exposing the mogu's vulnerability. Apart from those who were sent to defend the Serpent's Spine, no slave was permitted to touch a weapon (a crime punishable by death). Thus Kang taught himself to use his own body as one. To elude the ever-watchful eyes of the mogu, he learned to disguise his attacks as an artistic dance.

When he had finally mastered his techniques, he challenged his fellow slaves to strike him. None could. His "dancing," his flowing movements, kept him free of harm. The slaves begged Kang to teach them how to fight unarmed. Kang did, and word of this strange new combat method spread quickly among the oppressed peoples of the mogu empire.

Hundreds of slaves adopted Kang's teachings and devoted themselves to learning this newfound art, known thereafter as the way of the monk. When rumors of the movement reached mogu ears, Kang relocated his followers to Kun-Lai Summit, fully aware that his apprentices were not yet strong enough to topple their oppressors. In secret, the pandaren rebels built a monastery among the wind-lashed peaks and began to further train themselves as instruments of justice.

It was at Kun-Lai Summit that Kang found something utterly unexpected: the prison of Xuen, the White Tiger. Kang communed often with the August Celestial, learning the secrets of inner strength that lay within every heart. The pandaren master passed along Xuen's wisdom to his followers. At last, the pandaren monks were ready to fight.

Their first major victory came at the Mogu'shan Vaults, the sacred chambers that housed the Engine of Nalak'sha. There, the rebels successfully drove the mogu away from the source of their flesh-shaping power. The pandaren's devastating attack prevented the mogu from creating any new twisted soldiers.

This single victory not only heartened the pandaren but also drew other races to the rebellion. The hozen, the jinyu, the grummles, and a burly race of bovine creatures (called the yaungol) all joined the effort to topple the mogu empire.

Bit by bit, the revolution grew. Kang was right: the mogu had grown too reliant on their slaves, and as more rebelled, the empire fell into chaos. The grummles, masters of communication and trade, disrupted mogu supply lines. The mighty yaungol led raiding parties to wreak havoc in the northwest. The wily hozen dug tunnels to infiltrate the mightiest mogu strongholds. The mystic jinyu communed with the waters of the land to glean the future, telling Kang's forces where to strike and when to run.

Eventually Lao-Fe's forces retreated to the Vale of Eternal Blossoms, the royal seat of the mogu empire. Kang knew the enchanted land could sustain them for as long as they desired. Thus, to defeat the mogu, the rebels needed to expose themselves and launch an attack.

Kang did not hesitate to do so. He personally led the charge, striking deep into the vale. He fought Lao-Fe hand to hand and defeated him, but the pandaren sustained mortal wounds in return.

The Slavebinder and the former slave died together.

Flushed with victory, some of the freed slaves considered seeking revenge against the surviving mogu, butchering them as they had butchered their vassals for millennia. Yet one of Kang's most promising students calmed their bloodlust. As a secretive keeper of pandaren history, the pupil Song had memorized many of Master Kang's philosophies and tales. Song retold Kang's stories again and again to the liberated slaves, reminding them about his commitment to true justice, not

THE SHA

When Y'Shaarj died, its blighted remains scattered across the Vale of Eternal Blossoms and the surrounding regions. In time, the Old God's evil seeped into the land itself.

During his journeys, Song became keenly aware of this dark power that lurked in the earth. Y'Shaarj's lingering essence latched onto and amplified negative emotions, giving rise to malevolent spirits known as the sha. By spreading Kang's teachings, Song hoped that he could help the pandaren and other races negate the Old God's influence and nullify the sha.

revenge. He walked from one end of the fallen empire to the other for the rest of his life, sharing Kang's wisdom and urging all creatures to find emotional balance within themselves.

As Song's stories spread, others began to follow in his footsteps. More and more pandaren traveled the land, telling stories and encouraging inner peace in all they met. These "Lorewalkers," as they would eventually be named, became not only skilled storytellers but also conflict mediators, defusing tense situations with allegories and parables that would help all sides see reason and find a middle ground.

So began a time of peace and prosperity in and around the Vale of Eternal Blossoms. The pandaren, along with the other races that called the region home, flourished. A new empire—one built on the principles of justice, wisdom, and benevolence—emerged to watch over the war-torn land.

YAUNGOL MIGRATION

When the mogu empire was at its height, an intelligent bovine race known as the yaungol roamed the grassy plains of central Kalimdor. These burly creatures lived in harmony with nature, following the guidance of the wise demigod Cenarius.

Unlike many of the other Wild Gods, Cenarius was more humanoid in appearance. The majestic half-stag, draped in a cloak of flowers and vines, often walked among the nomadic yaungol. He taught these creatures the secrets of the wilds, and he delighted in watching them flourish.

Eventually, the yaungol grew weary of sharing hunting grounds with nearby trolls and decided to seek new lands. Although their beloved demigod Cenarius urged them to stay and make peace, they set out to the south. They hunted and foraged for food all the way to the edge of the mogu empire.

The emperor of the time, Qiang the Merciless, found the yaungol and their immense physical strength fascinating. He ordered his flesh-shapers to capture the nomads and transform them into even mightier and more intelligent servants, while at the same time tempering their more savage instincts. The yaungol suffered under the tyranny of mogu oppression for generations until they rose up alongside the other slaves to overthrow their cruel masters.

Although the yaungol gained their freedom, they had lost much. Their strong oral storytelling tradition had all but vanished due to strict mogu laws that forbade them from discussing their heritage. Much of their rich history had faded away. Some yaungol clung to the faint memories and incomplete myths of a benevolent demigod who had once watched over them. Others insisted that the yaungol should abandon all tradition and forge a new destiny by force. The disagreements grew heated and, on certain occasions, even led to bloodshed. Most yaungol despised the violence and set out to the north, determined to return to a life of hunting and living among the spirits of nature.

Some of the more nomadic tribes traveled all the way across the continent, only stopping when they reached the frigid climes near the Storm Peaks. Other tribes settled in the balmy areas of central Kalimdor and reunited with their ancient benefactor, Cenarius. Returning to their ancestral hunting grounds allowed them to rediscover their old traditions. Those who studied with Cenarius learned the druidic magic of the natural world, while others mastered the arts of wielding shamanic powers.

Yet not all yaungol left the vale. Those who stayed behind quickly found themselves at odds with the pandaren and other liberated slaves. The mogu flesh-shaping had not completely subdued the yaungol's bold nature, and conflict after conflict ignited over matters of land and resources.

Fearing an open war with their former allies, the yaungol moved west, settling outside the Serpent's Spine. That left them exposed to the mantid, and every one hundred years, the swarm would threaten to exterminate their people. The mantid cycle and constant infighting among these yaungol led to a strong warrior tradition, one that would make them far more savage than the tribes that had gone north.

Over the passing of generations, the energies emanating from the Well of Eternity and keeper-wrought machineries around Kalimdor changed the yaungol in unique ways. Those near the vale would keep the name "yaungol," though they grew more warlike than their distant cousins. Those in central Kalimdor, close to the Well of Eternity, would take the name "tauren." The tribes that ventured to the north, near the Forge of Wills, would be called "taunka," and they would adapt to the region's icy terrain.

These far-flung groups maintained contact with one another for many years, but when the Great Sundering eventually shattered the world, all connection between the tribes was lost.

ZANDALARI INVASION
11,900 YEARS BEFORE THE DARK PORTAL

The Zandalari had always maintained a distant relationship with the mogu following Lei Shen's death. Though the trolls found the mogu's knowledge of arcane magic useful, they loathed the constant intra-clan strife and tense political maneuvering. When it became clear that no mogu clan would establish total dominance, the Zandalari refrained from pledging their loyalties to any one faction in particular.

But they never forgot the promise Lei Shen had made to them: a large plot of land near the Vale of Eternal Blossoms would forever belong to the trolls. When at long last the mogu empire crumbled, the Zandalari saw an opportunity to take what they believed was rightfully theirs. They did not move immediately. Internal debate raged in the Zandalari capital of Zuldazar about whether the territory should be taken by diplomacy or force.

In the end, it was a descendant of the great high priest Zulathra who made the strongest case. His name was Mengazi, and he knew that the pandaren would be unlikely to honor the Zandalari's agreement with the mogu. The former slaves had also overthrown their masters, and as such, they could be strong enough to mount a fierce resistance against the trolls if given time to prepare. To succeed in claiming their land, the trolls would need to strike without warning and with enough force to shatter the pandaren's will.

To this end, the trolls marched south, intent on seizing a fertile region north of Kun-Lai Summit. The Zandalari stormed the main settlement in the area—a tranquil pandaren farming village. Imbued with mystic powers and riding atop colossal saurian war mounts, the trolls slaughtered almost every single resident of the settlement. The Zandalari ranks then pushed into the Jade Forest, a dense jungle that had become the heart of the newly established pandaren empire.

When word of the invasion reached other pandaren settlements, panic seized them. No standing army existed to thwart the trolls. In the decades since the slave revolution, few had seen the need to carry on the militaristic ways of the mogu, preferring instead to let all residents live in peace, without an overarching authority. The only real fighting force was an order of monks, charged by the pandaren emperor to patrol the Serpent's Spine and stand against the periodic mantid swarm.

Though the monks raced from the Serpent's Spine to defend their lands against the trolls, they found themselves hopelessly outnumbered and outmaneuvered. The trolls were employing a form of warfare none had ever seen, descending into battle on the backs of reptilian pterrorwings and giant bats. The pandaren had no means to counter these ferocious aerial attacks.

Ultimately, salvation came from a young pandaren named Jiang. When she was but a child, she had found a cloud serpent hatchling, alone and badly injured after a terrible storm had destroyed his nest. At the time, the pandaren regarded the flying cloud serpents as untamable and violent beasts, but Jiang nursed him back to health and befriended him. Those in her village often saw them flying the skies together.

As the monks fought a losing battle atop the cliffs of the Jade Forest, Jiang and her serpentine companion, Lo, swooped down from the clouds. Lo's fury and fire broke the Zandalari ranks, forcing them to retreat. News of the victory spread throughout the empire, and others followed in Jiang's footsteps. They tamed the powerful cloud serpents, and soon a small army arose to fly into battle at Jiang's side. These brave pandaren became known as the Order of the Cloud Serpent.

CHAPTER III: ANCIENT KALIMDOR

PANDAREN SERPENT RIDERS STRIKE AT THE ZANDALARI TROLLS

The tide of the war had turned. The trolls knew there was little they could do to win by conventional means, so Mengazi turned to a final tactic: resurrecting the Thunder King, Lei Shen.

Lei Shen had granted the Zandalari the secret to his revival, not trusting any of his mogu underlings to do it for him if he were ever killed. The trolls knew the Thunder King would have the power to purge the troublesome serpent riders and destroy any army on the ground. A pitched battle erupted near the Tomb of Conquerors, where Lei Shen's corpse was enshrined. Jiang sacrificed herself in a final, desperate attack, killing Mengazi. The other Zandalari soon broke ranks and fled back to their homeland in shame. Through her heroic act, Jiang had prevented the trolls from resurrecting the terrible Thunder King.

There was great celebration throughout the empire, but also mourning over the lives lost, especially Jiang's. For decades after the conflict, Lo was seen circling the skies above the Jade Forest, as though searching for his old friend and rider. The other serpent riders honored Jiang's memory by codifying her teachings. Within the Order of the Cloud Serpent, her tradition of training and befriending the majestic creatures would survive for millennia to come.

The Well of Eternity and the Rise of the Night Elves
15,000–10,000 Years Before the Dark Portal

Before their war with the aqir, the troll tribes claimed large swaths of Kalimdor. Many of these groups, such as the Gurubashi and the Amani, clashed with each other over hunting grounds and territory. Yet one tribe was unconcerned with these battles for land and power. Known as dark trolls, they lived in a network of deep caverns that stretched beneath Mount Hyjal. They abhorred daylight, only emerging from their underground burrows at night. The dark trolls' nocturnal habits changed them over time, turning their blue-hued skin into shades of gray.

The dark trolls cherished their independence from greater troll society, and they largely ignored the activities of other tribes. Unlike their Gurubashi and Amani cousins, they longed for a peaceful connection to the natural world. Dark troll mystics often sought ways to commune with the land and live in harmony with it. Many of these trolls gradually migrated toward the center of Kalimdor. They explored the labyrinthine groves at the heart of the continent, crossing paths with the elusive faerie dragons, chimaeras, and dryads. In time, the dark trolls also discovered an enormous lake of scintillating energies, a lake they would later know as the Well of Eternity.

Mesmerized by their discovery, the dark trolls settled along the Well of Eternity's shores. Over generations, the energies radiating from the lake suffused the trolls' flesh and bones, elevating their forms to match their graceful spirits. They transformed into highly intelligent and virtually immortal beings. These former trolls gradually abandoned their ancient heritage and traditions. The tribe's mystics began worshipping the moon goddess, Elune, who they believed was bound to the Well of Eternity itself. They claimed that the deity slumbered within the fount's depths during daylight hours.

The former trolls also discovered the name "Kalimdor" and other titan-forged words from communing with Elune and investigating strange artifacts scattered around the Well's periphery.

Sisterhood of Elune

The city of Suramar became the center of night elf worship and home to the Sisterhood of Elune. This order, composed of female night elves, dedicated itself to venerating the moon goddess. The Sisterhood's priestesses had a hand in nearly all aspects of early night elf civilization, from acting as spiritual leaders to helping defend their burgeoning territories from outside threats.

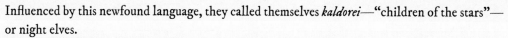

Influenced by this newfound language, they called themselves *kaldorei*—"children of the stars"—or night elves.

The trees, flowers, and woodland creatures silently watched the night elves flourish, whispering news of them to the Wild Gods of Hyjal. Among them, the demigod Cenarius took a keen interest in these newcomers at the Well of Eternity's shores. The night elves would claim he was the son of the great White Stag, Malorne, and Elune herself. Cenarius adored the night elves and believed they had the potential to become great caretakers of nature. He befriended the fledgling race and taught them about the natural world. It was Cenarius's hope that the night elves would strive to live in harmony with the wilds.

For many centuries, the night elves did. They built a graceful society around the Well of Eternity. The capital of their small nation was called *Elun'dris*, or "the Eye of Elune," and it was founded on the shores of the fount of power. The night elves also honed their ties with the surrounding woodlands and their myriad inhabitants. Cenarius guided the night elves when necessary, pleased by the wisdom and benevolence that thrummed in their hearts.

But in time, many of the night elves yearned for a different life. These individuals became obsessed with unlocking the Well of Eternity's secrets. They rigorously studied the fount's arcane energies, becoming learned sorcerers. They harnessed the powers of the arcane lake and constructed wondrous temples and roadways around it. Magic became an inseparable part of life as the night elves reveled in the power at their fingertips. Pushing the boundaries of their intellect became the driving force of their culture.

It was during this era of unprecedented growth that the night elves' most prolific leader came to power. Her name was Queen Azshara. Through her unbridled ambition, she would elevate her people to extraordinary new heights . . . and sow the seeds of their destruction.

QUEEN AZSHARA

Beautiful and wise beyond her years, Queen Azshara embodied the most coveted traits of her people. She indulged in sorcerous pursuits and constructed a breathtaking, bejeweled palace on the shores of the Well of Eternity. There, the most powerful nobles—who became known as the *quel'dorei*, or "Highborne"—answered to her every beck and call.

The Highborne were incredibly gifted and ambitious sorcerers. Some, such as Lady Vashj, served as the queen's adoring and loyal handmaidens. Others, like Lord Xavius, were consulted by Azshara in matters of governance and acted as trusted advisors. But no matter what specific role these Highborne played at the queen's side, all of them occupied the upper echelon of night elf society. They believed themselves to be superior to the rest of their race, a fact that drew the ire of the "lower born" night elves.

But such contempt did not extend to Azshara. Although the queen was born of the highest noble pedigree, night elves of every social standing adored her. The elves were so enamored with their queen that they renamed their wondrous capital *Zin-Azshari*, or "the Glory of Azshara," in her honor.

Under Azshara, night elf civilization blossomed into a sprawling empire, a dreamscape of gilded spires, vast cities, and other marvels that would not be seen again even in the modern age. Networks of luminescent causeways, limned by the silver light of Elune, radiated out to the far corners of Kalimdor.

At Azshara's behest, expeditionary forces set out to explore the world and also spread the empire's borders. They often returned to Zin-Azshari with samples of exotic flora and fauna, and tales of the mythical dragonflights that ruled the roof of the world. The expeditionary forces also founded dozens of outposts and repositories, such as Shandaral in the icy northern forest of Moonsong, Then'Ralore in the lush central wilds (later known as the Barrens), and Eldre'Thalas in the southern jungles of Feralas. The queen herself oversaw the building of a wondrous new temple to Elune, a sprawling expanse of gem-encrusted bridges and effervescent lakes at the western edge of Kalimdor. Upon its completion, she named the mesmerizing grounds *Lathar'Lazal*, or "Seat of the Sky."

Not since the Black Empire in ages past had a territory grown so vast in size and scope. The immense influence Azshara held over the world and its denizens eclipsed even Lei Shen's wildest dreams of power.

There was, however, one location Azshara and her forces avoided: Mount Hyjal. The spirits and demigods who roamed the sylvan forests unsettled the queen. She knew in her bones that Hyjal was somehow beyond even her influence. It was a place steeped in ancient magic, a wild, untamable, and unchangeable land that stood in stark contrast to her vision of a new Kalimdor. Publicly, Azshara prohibited expansion into Hyjal out of respect for the night elves' ancient kinship with the forests. In truth, she despised the mountain and the harmony it represented.

Azshara's views on Hyjal were well known to Cenarius. With growing unease, he had watched the night elf empire expand. Year by year, he became increasingly frustrated with the hubris and thoughtless actions of the sorcerous Highborne. The majority of night elf society continued honoring the old ways of revering the wilds. The fact that these folk still lived in harmony with the land warmed Cenarius's heart, but he knew that they had no influence over Azshara and her arrogant followers.

As time passed, the night elves began eschewing diplomacy and largely ignored Azeroth's other cultures. Azshara's dogmatic beliefs regarding racial purity seeped into the night elves' psyche, creating an atmosphere rife with xenophobia.

THE NIGHT ELF EMPIRE

Uldum

Shandaral

Azjol-Nerub

Mount Hyjal

Lathar'Lazal

Then'Ralore

Well of Eternity
Zin-Azshari

Eldre'Thalas

Zul'Farrak

Zuldazar

Ahn'Qiraj

Uldum

Mogu'shan Vaults

Vale of Eternal Blossoms

Manti'vess

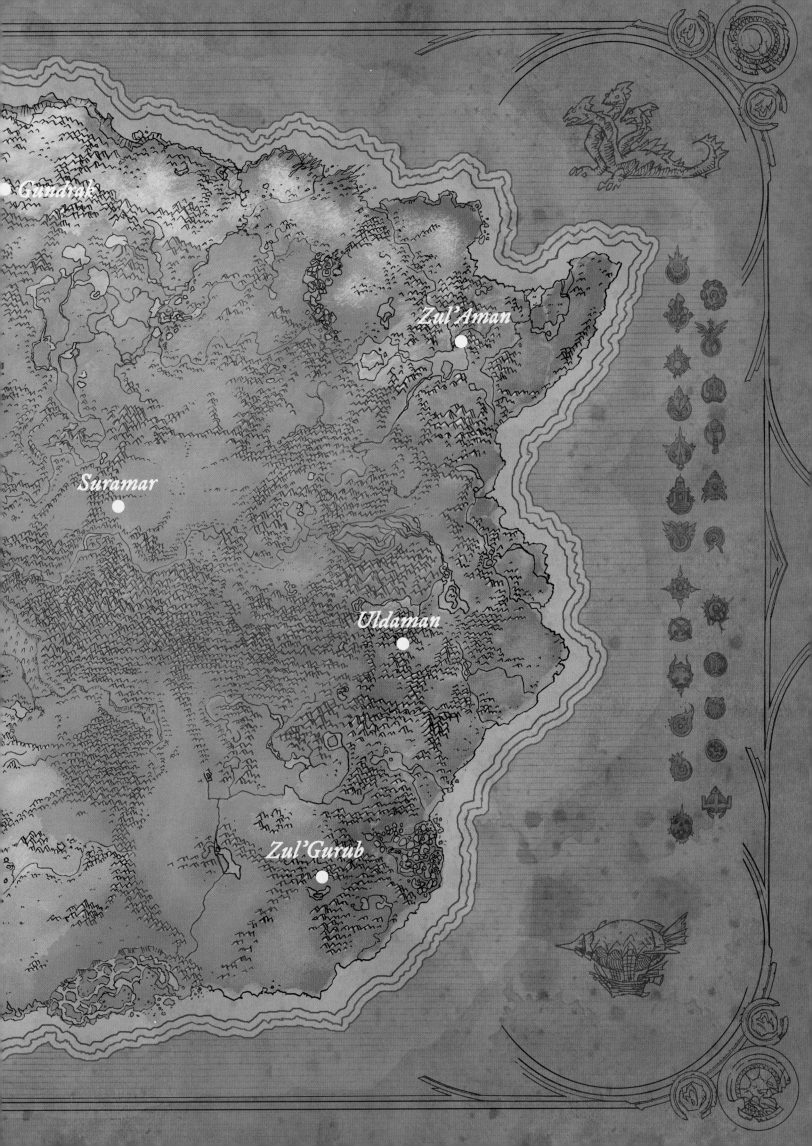

Gundrak

Zul'Aman

Suramar

Uldaman

Zul'Gurub

Only the openly hostile troll nations drew the full attention of the elves. Small, sporadic battles ignited between the two sides. On every occasion, the trolls buckled before the devastating magics wielded by the night elves. Azshara, however, was not interested in conquest. In her eyes, the trolls were a minor nuisance, their battle lust a symptom of primitive and unenlightened minds. Ultimately, the queen struck an accord with the Zandalar tribe, which held immense influence over all other trolls. In exchange for ending troll incursions into night elf territory, the Zandalari would be allowed—by Azshara's grace—to keep the sacred Zandalar Mountains south of the Well of Eternity.

The trolls begrudgingly agreed, fully aware that they stood no chance against their enemies' arcane powers. This shameful acquiescence fostered the trolls' deep resentment toward night elves, a bitter hatred that would carry on for generations to come.

With the trolls no longer a threat, Azshara continued expanding her dominion. Yet even as she did so, she spent more time in the confines of her palace, obsessing over the Well of Eternity and the arcane secrets held within it. She believed that the night elves had thus far only tapped a small portion of the fount's power. She pushed the Highborne to plumb the Well of Eternity's depths, to expand their knowledge and reach for new heights of cultural and technological advancement.

Their reckless experiments sent torrents of magic crashing through the Twisting Nether. Like moths to the flame, the Nether's demonic inhabitants were drawn toward the irresistible source of power.

It was only a matter of time before Sargeras and the Burning Legion also took notice.

At long last, Sargeras had discovered the location of Azeroth. The fabled world-soul. Without delay, he gathered all of his rage, all of his terrible demonic legions, and turned his baleful gaze upon the distant world. All that remained was for Sargeras to find a way to reach Azeroth.

WAR OF THE ANCIENTS
10,000 YEARS BEFORE THE DARK PORTAL

As the Highborne continued experimenting on the Well of Eternity, a young night elf named Malfurion Stormrage honed his ties to nature. Under the tutelage of the wise Cenarius, he had become the first mortal druid on Azeroth. Malfurion excelled in his studies, and he often spent his days wandering the forests of Hyjal.

Cenarius was greatly pleased by Malfurion's progress. He had sensed something special in his student from the very first time the night elf's spirit explored the Emerald Dream. Cenarius hoped that Malfurion would spread druidism among the night elves and help them return to their harmonious roots.

Yet this change would not come to Azshara and her followers. Unbeknownst to greater night elf society, the Highborne had begun communing with Sargeras. The fallen titan hoped to use the sorcerers and their great magic to expedite the Legion's journey to Azeroth. Without a suitable gateway, he knew that traveling to the world would take ages.

Much as he had done with the eredar on Argus, Sargeras reached out to the Highborne and capitalized on their hubris. Lord Xavius was the first of the Highborne to hear Sargeras's call. The

CENARIUS AND MANNOROTH DURING THE WAR OF THE ANCIENTS

power-hungry Xavius quickly brought Sargeras to Azshara's attention. The fallen titan promised to grant the night elf queen and her servitors unfathomable power, thereby allowing them to remake Kalimdor into a paradise. Sargeras requested only that Azshara and her followers summon his agents into the world of Azeroth so that they could give the Highborne this power.

Enthralled by Sargeras's might, Azshara and her Highborne used the Well of Eternity's energies to bring the Legion's minions into Azeroth. Waves of demonic warriors flooded out from the queen's palace, murdering every night elf in their path save for their Highborne allies.

Led by the likes of Mannoroth the Destructor, Hakkar the Houndmaster, and Archimonde the Defiler, the Legion stormed across the night elf empire in a tide of death and destruction. Blazing infernals tore through the skies, shattering night elf cities, while thousands of bloodthirsty doomguard and ravenous felhounds reduced Kalimdor's tranquil woodlands to smoldering green embers.

War, the likes of which no mortal empire had ever witnessed, had come to Azeroth.

A night elf resistance force, led by a noble named Lord Kur'talos Ravencrest, formed to stand against the Legion's furious onslaught. Among these brave defenders were Malfurion, his sorcerous twin, Illidan, and the beautiful priestess whom both brothers loved dearly, Tyrande Whisperwind. Ultimately, these three unlikely heroes would change the fate of Kalimdor forever.

Though Ravencrest's forces initially suffered many defeats against the demons, the night elves did make gains. Malfurion himself delivered one of the most decisive early blows against the Legion and its Highborne allies. From the depths of the Emerald Dream, he unleashed his druidic magics upon Azshara's trusted servant Xavius, striking him down. Not only did this act destroy one of the Highborne's most powerful sorcerers, but it also proved the incredible potential of druidic magic to Malfurion's allies.

Illidan also became invaluable to the resistance. During one engagement, his courage and mastery of arcane magic allowed him to save Ravencrest's life. For this selfless act, Illidan was appointed the commander's personal sorcerer. He would later go on to lead the host of sorcerers that fought for the night elf resistance.

For her part, the priestess Tyrande emerged as one of the greatest members of the Sisterhood of Elune. Through her unbreakable faith in the benevolent Elune, she saved countless innocents from the marauding Legion. In time, Tyrande would become the high priestess of Elune, the revered leader of her sacred Sisterhood.

Yet despite the bravery with which the resistance fought, more and more demons spilled into Azeroth through the Highborne's portals. The Legion also bolstered its numbers with a new breed of demon, born from denizens of Azeroth itself.

The first of these abominations was Xavius. Sargeras had warped the defeated Highborne's body into a twisted demonic visage of jagged horns and cloven hooves. This new form became known as a satyr, and it would mark Xavius as an eternal servant of the Legion. At Sargeras's bidding, he set out to curse many of his fellow Highborne, transforming them into satyrs as well.

As the Legion's numbers swelled and the war progressed, Malfurion realized that the night elves could not prevail alone. He convinced Tyrande and Illidan to accompany him to the tranquil Moonglade near Mount Hyjal, where they beseeched Cenarius for aid. The great demigod agreed to rally the mighty Wild Gods against the Legion, but they were unpredictable beings, unaccustomed to fighting as one.

Spurring them to action would take time . . . a luxury the night elves did not have.

DEATHWING AND THE DRAGON SOUL

While Cenarius gathered the Wild Gods, Malfurion called on the mighty Dragon Aspects to defend Azeroth. Led by Alexstrasza the Life-Binder, the dragons convened at their ancient meeting ground of Wyrmrest Temple to discuss how best to hold back the Legion's invasion.

It was during one of these gatherings that Neltharion the Earth-Warder proposed a solution. He convinced his fellow Aspects to sacrifice a portion of their power and infuse it into the Dragon Soul, a singular artifact of his own design. The weapon, he claimed, would focus their powers and scour the Legion from the face of Azeroth.

Unbeknownst to the other Aspects, Neltharion had fallen prey to the whispers of the Old Gods. Over the ages, the vile entities' influence had tainted the bedrock surrounding their underground prisons. Neltharion's innate ties to the earth made him uniquely susceptible to this evil. Darkness had gradually pervaded the Aspect's once-great heart. His descent into torment and madness led him to create the Dragon Soul, although it would later be called by another, more fitting, name: the Demon Soul.

Amid a furious battle between the Legion and the night elf resistance, the five dragonflights made their final assault against the Legion. Working in unison with his comrades, Neltharion unleashed the full might of the empowered Dragon Soul and utterly decimated the Legion. Yet just as hope began to swell among the defenders, Neltharion turned the weapon against his own allies, night elf and dragon alike.

Neltharion's brutal attack murdered nearly all of the blue dragonflight. Though the other dragons attempted to stop him, they were forced to flee. The night elves were also horrified and awestruck by the sudden betrayal. Eventually they, too, retreated from the battlefield to escape Neltharion's wrath.

As the Dragon Soul's energies flooded through him, Neltharion's body began tearing apart. A raw power like the seething heart of a volcano engulfed his soul. Smoldering fissures wrenched open across Neltharion's scaly hide. From these wounds, geysers of white-hot fire and magma burst forth. With a howl of rage, Neltharion finally withdrew from the engagement and disappeared into the skies.

Though Neltharion's assault was short lived, it had changed the world forever. Single-handedly, he had shattered the unity and power of the great dragonflights. They would never be the same again. Malygos, leader of the blue dragonflight, would suffer far more than any other Aspect. On seeing his followers die, he was driven mad with a grief that would linger for thousands and thousands of years.

Henceforth, Neltharion would be known as Deathwing. His treachery would curse his own black dragonflight to a life of fear and seclusion. In the coming ages, they would find themselves hunted to the brink of extinction by the other flights due to Deathwing's unforgivable betrayal.

ILLIDAN'S BETRAYAL

Deathwing's betrayal struck a terrible blow to the night elves' morale. And worse, Illidan had mysteriously vanished from their ranks. Many night elves feared for his life, but none of them could have imagined that the talented sorcerer had actually abandoned the resistance.

Illidan's decision to strike out on his own stemmed from his relationship with Malfurion. The sorcerer had always lived in his brother's shadow. Although Illidan had also studied under Cenarius, he had lacked the patience to master druidism and instead had pursued arcane magic. Throughout the war, Illidan was driven by a fervent determination to rise above his brother and become a hero for his people.

Yet time and again, Malfurion's deeds eclipsed Illidan's own. This was no more apparent—and no more painful—than in the sorcerer's desire to win the heart of Tyrande Whisperwind. When Illidan finally summoned the courage to profess his love for her, the priestess rejected him. Illidan took this as a sign that Tyrande intended to choose Malfurion as her mate.

In the wake of this bitter rejection, dark thoughts plagued Illidan. Unbeknownst to the sorcerer, the satyr Xavius was subtly twisting his mind and fanning the flames of his despair.

Illidan's mounting discontent ultimately led him to break from the night elf resistance. He set out to join the Legion, hoping to gain power unimaginable to any night elf. Once he did so, Illidan believed he would finally transcend Malfurion and prove to the world that he was capable of greatness.

Against all odds, Illidan secured an audience with Sargeras himself. His plan, to steal the potent Dragon Soul, intrigued the fallen titan. So pleased was Sargeras that he granted Illidan exceptional power. He scarred the night elf's body with fel tattoos and burned out his eyes, setting the hollows alight with otherworldly fire. Although excruciatingly painful, this final act gave Illidan the ability to see myriad forms of magic.

The newly empowered Illidan immediately set out to steal the Dragon Soul. During the course of this perilous quest, the wayward night elf would stumble across Deathwing and witness the Aspect's ravaged and tormented form. To hold his broken body together, Deathwing had resorted to bolting adamantium plates to his spine.

THE DEFEAT OF XAVIUS

Malfurion finally vanquished Xavius during one of the later engagements of the war. With the aid of a brave young night elf named Shandris Feathermoon, Malfurion trapped the satyr lord and warped his body and spirit into a gnarled oak tree. Xavius's legacy, however, would persist on Azeroth. To this day, satyrs still roam the world, polluting nature with their foul magics.

Ultimately, Illidan secured the Dragon Soul and delivered the artifact to the waiting Highborne. They immediately used the weapon for the next phase of their plans. The Dragon Soul would prove vital to creating a massive gateway within the heart of the Well of Eternity.

A gateway through which Sargeras himself could enter the world of Azeroth.

Illidan would later claim that his actions were for a noble cause, that he had joined the Legion to learn more about the demons and find a means to destroy them. Nonetheless, his foolhardy quest for greatness would haunt him like a specter, tarnishing his reputation forever after.

SURAMAR AND THE PILLARS OF CREATION

As battles raged across central Kalimdor, one group of Azshara's servants grew increasingly concerned for their own future. This small sect of Highborne sorcerers acted as an extension of the queen's will. From their headquarters in Suramar, they engaged in covert activities aimed at securing Azshara's rule and strengthening the empire.

Of the many duties that these Highborne performed, they excelled at hunting down and acquiring artifacts of great power. Most of these relics were stored in the Vault of Antiquities, a vast repository located in Suramar. Among the greatest archaeological discoveries made by this group of Highborne were the long-lost Pillars of Creation, an extraordinary set of relics that the ancient keepers had used to shape and order Azeroth in ages past.

Though Suramar's elite Highborne had pledged their undying loyalty to Azshara, their views on the queen began to shift as the war dragged on. The group's leader, Grand Magistrix Elisande, feared that the Legion did not have the Highborne's best interests in mind. The monstrous demons had already destroyed much of the night elves' glorious empire and poisoned the surrounding land with their fel magics.

Elisande's distrust of the Legion only deepened when she discovered that demons were planning to transform Suramar into a new staging ground for the war. Legion agents had begun forming a gateway to the Twisting Nether within the city's most prominent structure, the Temple of Elune. Once open, this portal would allow the Legion's reinforcements to storm into Azeroth and crush the night elf resistance on a second front.

Yet Elisande thought that such a portal would likely destroy Suramar and everyone who dwelled within. Thus the grand magistrix and her followers formed a plan to sabotage the Legion's efforts. They severed their ties with the other Highborne and moved to seal the demons' new portal. To do so, Elisande and her allies sought out the potent artifacts they had gathered over the years. In particular, they knew that the Pillars of Creation possessed the raw power that they would need to neutralize the Legion's portal.

With these artifacts in hand, Elisande and her Highborne led an assault against the demons in Suramar. Just as the Legion's new portal began roaring to life, the sorcerers channeled their magic through the Pillars of Creation. They wove a great spell that closed the howling gateway and locked it with a set of unbreakable seals.

Though they had thwarted the attempt to create a new portal, the rebellious Highborne had no plans to join the night elf resistance and continue fighting the Legion. Fearing calamity, Elisande and her followers worked to fortify their holdings in Suramar. They harnessed the Eye of Aman'Thul, one of the Pillars of Creation, to create an immense fount of arcane magic. Known as the Nightwell, this source of power would nourish the sorcerers and protect them from future threats. In the millennia to come, the fount would also change Elisande and her allies, transforming them into a new race called the nightborne.

THE FALL OF ZIN-AZSHARI AND THE SUNDERING OF THE WORLD

Despite a series of crushing defeats, hope yet lingered among the night elf resistance. A brave new leader, Jarod Shadowsong, had assumed the mantle of command. Unlike his predecessors, he was not born of noble blood. A fierce combatant and a brilliant strategist, Jarod went to great lengths to strengthen the resistance. He stripped away the night elves' inherent xenophobia and invited many of Azeroth's other races—such as the earthen, tauren, and mighty furbolgs—into the night elf army.

The resistance also found allies among their Highborne enemies. A group of the sorcerers, led by Dath'Remar Sunstrider, had come to realize that their allegiance to demons would bring ruin to Azeroth. These Highborne abandoned Azshara and pledged their lives to the resistance.

Even the Wild Gods finally emerged from the forests at Cenarius's goading, prepared to fight tooth and claw for the resistance. The forests trembled as these gargantuan beings marched down from the slopes of Hyjal. Each of the Wild Gods possessed strength and power unlike anything the demons had yet faced. Some, such as the white wolf Goldrinn, dwarfed even the largest demons in size.

With the Wild Gods came a host of other fay creatures, including the woodland dryads and the many-headed chimaeras. Even the elusive treants, mighty tree-folk imbued with great wisdom and strength, emerged to fight the demons.

Under Shadowsong, the combined army launched a desperate assault against Zin-Azshari itself. The resistance stormed the broken capital and clashed with the Legion's seemingly numberless ranks. The cost was horrific. Thousands upon thousands of demons fell, but so, too, did many of Azeroth's mighty defenders. The Legion's bloodletting warriors even overwhelmed a number of the Wild Gods. One by one, these primordial creatures succumbed to the poisoned black blades and fel powers wielded by the demons. With each death, the forests atop Hyjal shivered, and the winds howled in sorrow.

As the battle continued, Malfurion and Tyrande journeyed to the Well of Eternity's shores with a small, elite force. They hoped to reclaim the Dragon Soul and prevent the Legion from using its powers. Malfurion and his allies were soon joined by Illidan, who claimed his previous allegiance to the Highborne and the Legion had merely been a ruse to learn of their ways.

Although Malfurion remained deeply suspicious of his brother, a much greater threat consumed his attention. He discovered that the Well of Eternity had become a colossal portal—a direct gateway for Sargeras himself to enter Azeroth.

Malfurion then realized that no standing army, no matter how vast, could withstand the terrible might of Sargeras. Victory, he determined, could only be achieved by destroying the Well of Eternity itself. While such an act was unthinkable, the Well of Eternity was the Legion's umbilical link to the physical world. Malfurion knew that destroying the fount of power would spell the end of night elf civilization as he knew it, but it was the only chance of saving the world.

After reclaiming the Dragon Soul, Malfurion and his companions infiltrated Azshara's palace. They discovered that many of the Highborne were in the midst of weaving a spell to strengthen the portal within the Well of Eternity. In a desperate attempt to throw their magic out of alignment, Malfurion drew on the potent energies of the Dragon Soul and lashed out at his enemies. The great druid conjured a colossal thunderstorm that devoured the skies over the broken palace. The tempest battered Zin-Azshari with ferocious winds and a barrage of lightning strikes, decimating the demons and Highborne within the city.

Just as Malfurion had hoped, his efforts to disrupt the Highborne and their enormous gateway worked. As Sargeras prepared to emerge from the portal, the Highborne's spellwork unraveled and an unstable vortex of arcane energies ignited within the Well of Eternity. The fount buckled in upon itself. In that moment, Sargeras was ripped back into the Twisting Nether. Volatile energies whipped out from the collapsing Well of Eternity, hurling most of the Legion's ranks into the Nether as well. As their roars of fury echoed across the Nether, massive earthquakes began rupturing the crust of Azeroth.

Malfurion and the night elf resistance had won, but they had no time to savor victory. The world itself was coming apart beneath their feet.

En masse, the night elves scrambled to put distance between themselves and the crumbling Well of Eternity. The fount completed its collapse, igniting a cataclysmic explosion that blotted out the skies. The howling ocean surged in to fill the void left by the explosion, devouring the ruins of Zin-Azshari.

When the apocalyptic earthquakes finally ceased, the surviving night elves saw that their world had been torn asunder. The Well of Eternity's destruction had shattered nearly eighty percent of Kalimdor's landmass, leaving only a handful of separate continents and small archipelagoes. A tumultuous storm of energies—known as the Maelstrom—had engulfed the Well of Eternity itself. Ever after, the constantly spinning vortex would stand as a reminder of the terrible cost of the war.

For the night elves and all other living creatures on Azeroth, the world had changed forever.

THE FATE OF AZSHARA AND HER HIGHBORNE

Queen Azshara and many of her loyal Highborne survived the Sundering, but not without consequences. The imploding Well of Eternity sucked them into the fathomless depths of the Maelstrom. Some were cursed and irrevocably warped into a new and hateful serpentine race called the naga. One of the most powerful among these twisted abominations was the queen's former handmaiden, Lady Vashj. Hidden from the world, she and Azshara would quietly build the naga capital of Nazjatar in the cold darkness at the bottom of the sea.

CHAPTER III: ANCIENT KALIMDOR

THE BURDENS OF SHAOHAO
10,000 YEARS BEFORE THE DARK PORTAL

The Sundering decimated life across the face of Azeroth, but one secluded region of southern Kalimdor miraculously escaped destruction: Pandaria. For centuries, a succession of peaceful emperors had ruled over the mysterious land. Prior to the Burning Legion's invasion, a new pandaren ruler had taken the throne, brimming with confidence and hope about his future.

His name was Shaohao, and although he did not know it at the time, his reign would mark the beginning of a new chapter in Pandaria's history.

As was tradition among new emperors, Shaohao consulted a mystic jinyu waterspeaker to glean knowledge of what the future held. The news he heard was dire: the jinyu foresaw a horrific invasion of ravenous demons, kingdoms engulfed in sickly green fire, and the land itself howling in pain and torment.

Plagued with uncertainty, Shaohao went to see the legendary August Celestials and his great friend the Monkey King in order to make sense of the terrible vision. With their help, the emperor expelled the dark emotions that troubled his heart: his doubt, despair, fear, anger, hatred, and violence. As he did so, these negative traits took on physical form. They manifested into powerful spiritual entities known as the sha.

One by one, Shaohao used his wisdom to battle these sha and lock them away deep beneath Pandaria. There they would remain, festering beneath the earth. To stand watch over these imprisoned sha, Shaohao also founded the Shado-pan—an elite order of highly trained pandaren soldiers.

Brimming with newfound confidence and purpose, Shaohao set out to spare Pandaria from the Sundering that was to come. He planned to do so by separating his land from the rest of Kalimdor. The emperor would perform his grand task in the heart of Pandaria: the sacred Vale of Eternal Blossoms.

In the vale, Shaohao focused his powers to sever his empire from Kalimdor. Yet try as he might, he could not succeed. His doubts and fears returned. Across Pandaria, the imprisoned sha stirred to life and feasted on the emperor's uncertainties.

As the Legion's fel magics set the heavens alight, Shaohao desperately called upon the aid of the wisest August Celestial, the Jade Serpent. She appeared in the roiling skies and told Shaohao that Pandaria was more than just *his* empire. Everything in Pandaria was connected. Everything in Pandaria was one.

It was then that Shaohao understood the Jade Serpent's advice: to save his land, he would need to become one with it. Despite his dream of living a long and prosperous life, he knew it was not to be.

With his mind clear and his heart set on the task ahead, Shaohao merged his spirit with the land itself and forced it to break away from the rest of Kalimdor. His very essence shrouded Pandaria in a thick mist that would hide it from the outside world and protect it from the terrible Sundering.

For the next ten thousand years, Pandaria would remain hidden, and it faded into legend.

THE SHA OF PRIDE

There was one negative emotion that Shaohao never purged from himself: pride. It would silently lurk in Pandaria in the millennia after the emperor spared his people and his land from the Sundering.

OVERLEAF: MAP OF AZEROTH AFTER THE SUNDERING

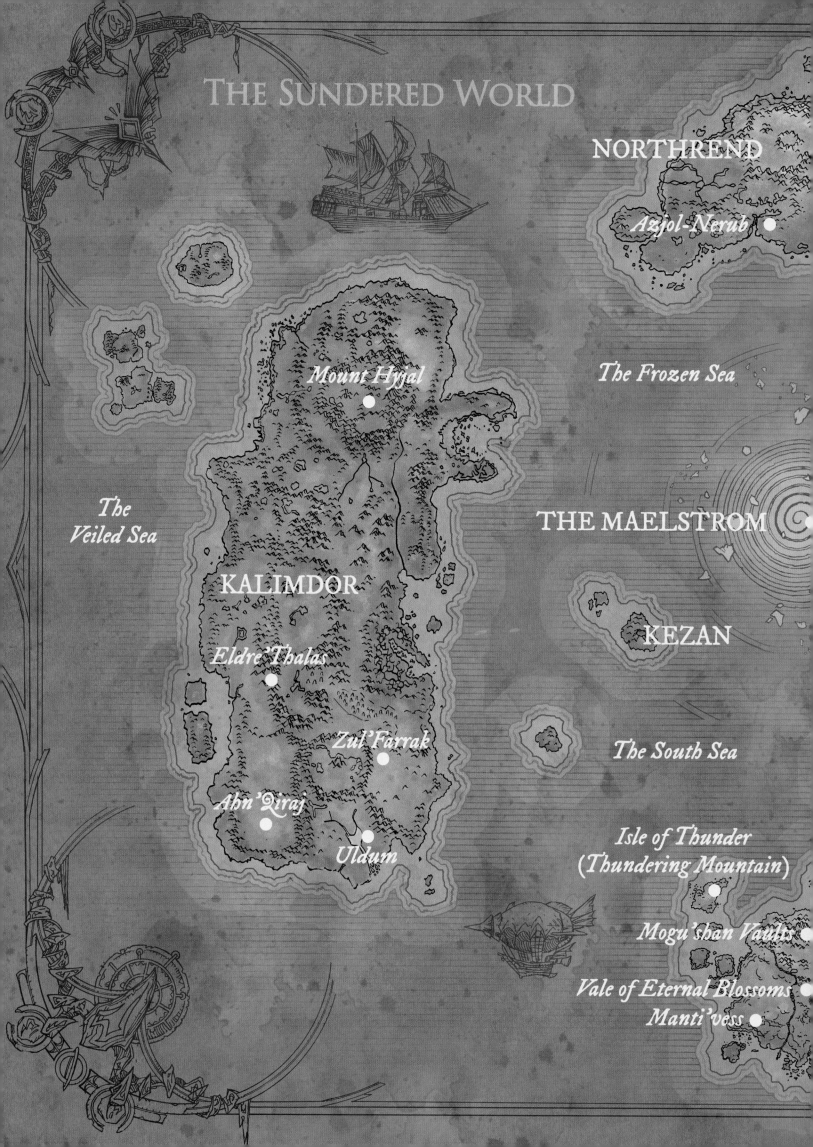

The Sundered World

NORTHREND

Azjol-Nerub •

The Frozen Sea

The Veiled Sea

Mount Hyjal

KALIMDOR

Eldre'Thalas

Zul'Farrak

Ahn'Qiraj

Uldum

THE MAELSTROM

KEZAN

The South Sea

*Isle of Thunder
(Thundering Mountain)*

Mogu'shan Vaults

Vale of Eternal Blossoms

Manti'vess •

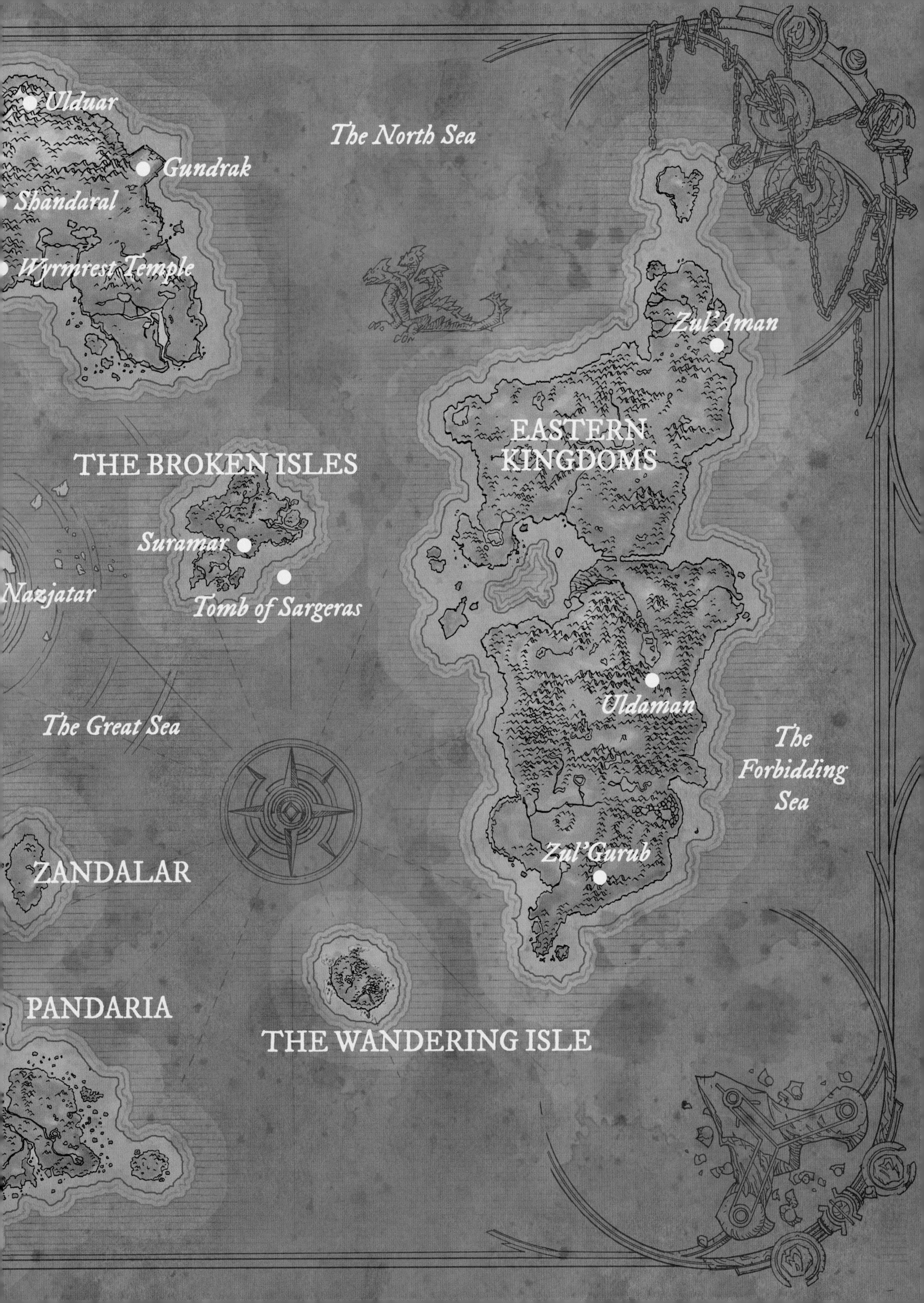

Ulduar
The North Sea
Gundrak
Shandaral
Wyrmrest Temple
Zul'Aman
EASTERN KINGDOMS
THE BROKEN ISLES
Suramar
Nazjatar
Tomb of Sargeras
Uldaman
The Great Sea
The Forbidding Sea
ZANDALAR
Zul'Gurub
PANDARIA
THE WANDERING ISLE

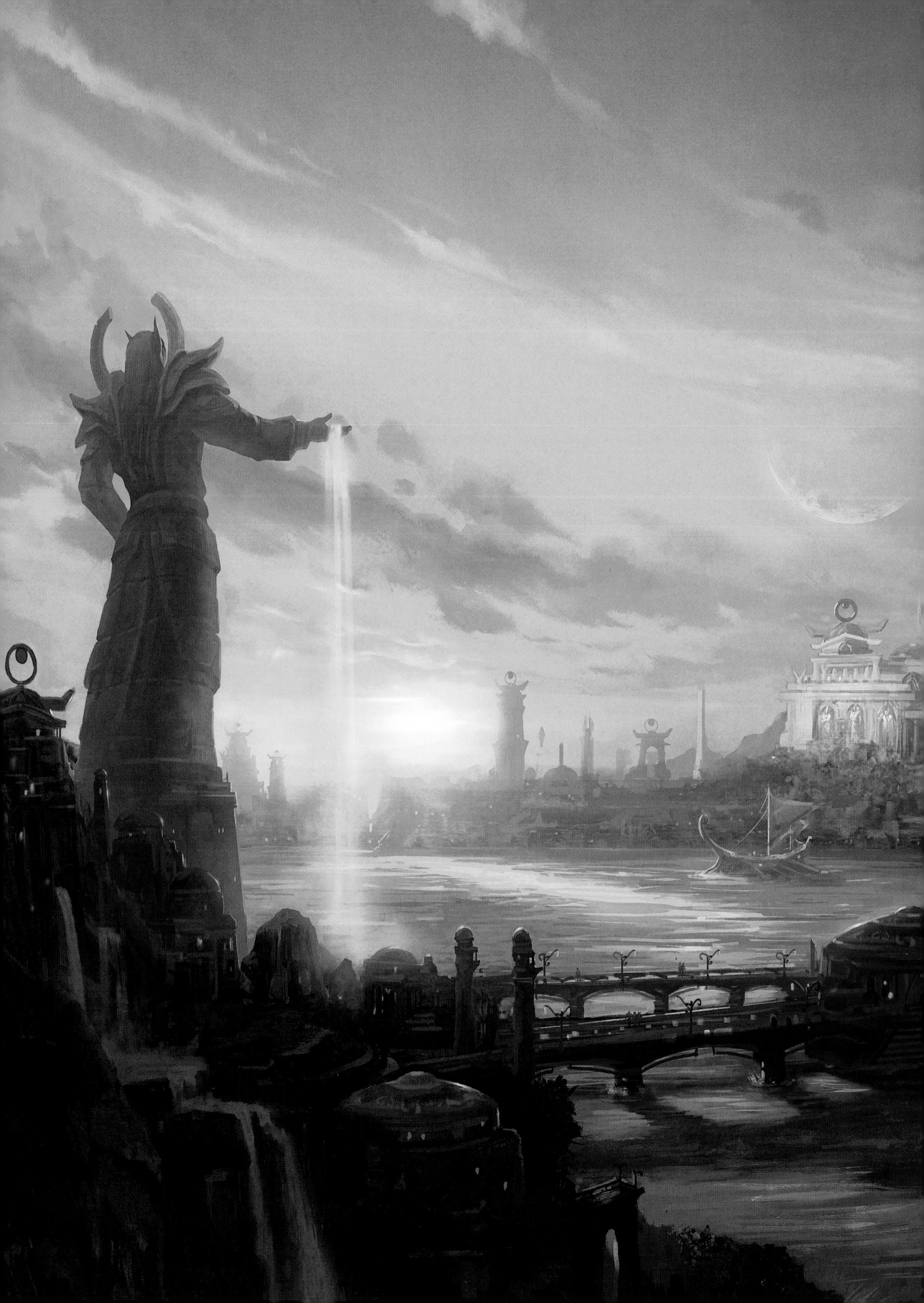

CHAPTER IV
A NEW WORLD

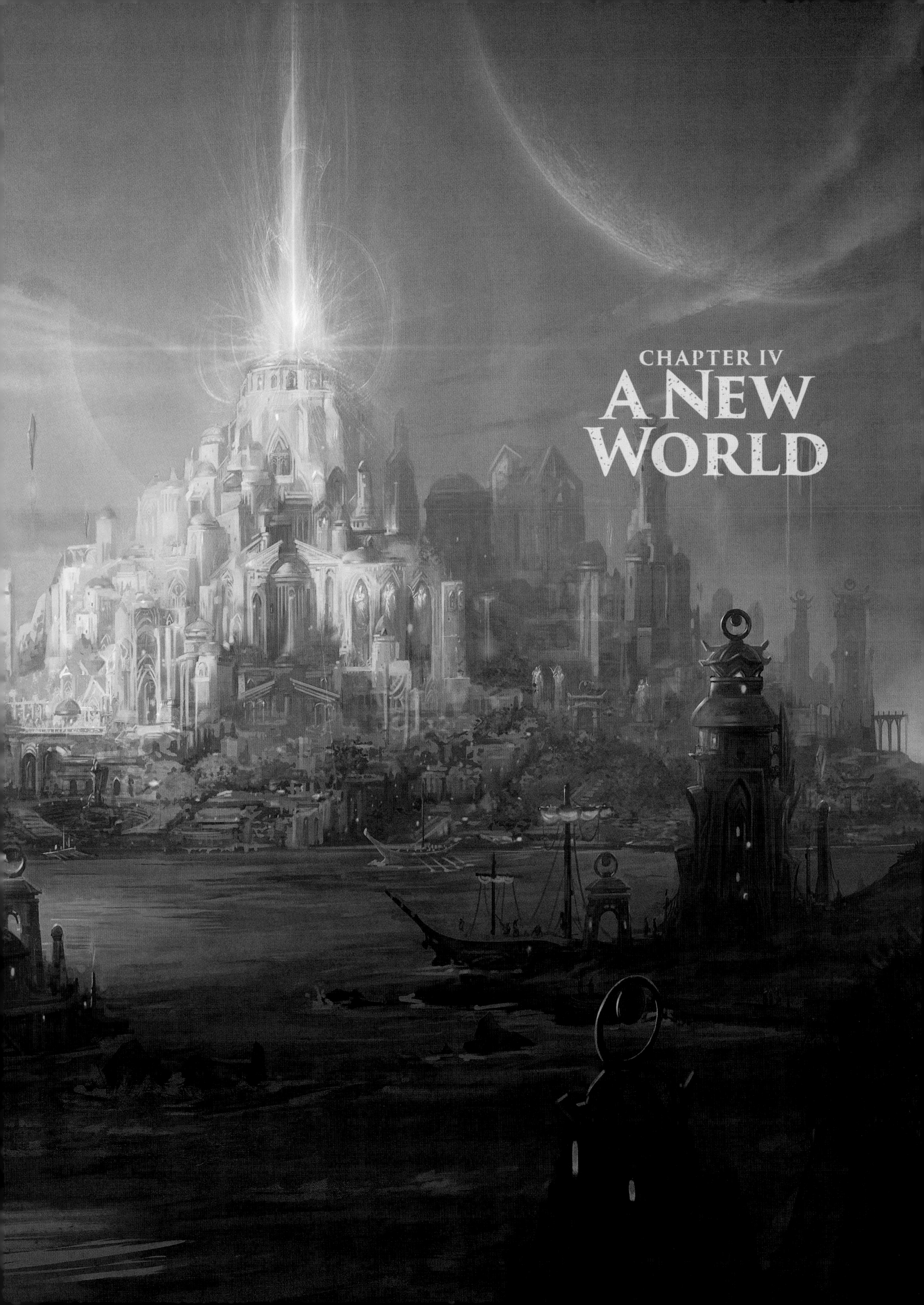

CHAPTER IV
A NEW WORLD

MOUNT HYJAL AND THE WORLD TREE
10,000 YEARS BEFORE THE DARK PORTAL

The Sundering had left the world broken. The Well of Eternity was gone, and so, too, was the once-coveted source of the night elves' arcane power. Desperate for refuge, the surviving night elves fled northwest to Mount Hyjal, one of the few places on Azeroth untouched by the destruction.

En route to Hyjal, Malfurion Stormrage and the other night elves concluded that arcane magic was not safe. They agreed to prohibit its use to avoid another catastrophe like the War of the Ancients. Yet as they reached the summit of Hyjal, they were horrified to discover a second, smaller Well of Eternity. Equally shocking was the figure whom the night elves found standing at the fount's shores: Illidan.

Before the Sundering, Illidan had filled several vials with enchanted liquid from the original Well of Eternity. He had poured some of them into the lake atop Hyjal, transforming the idyllic waters into another fount of arcane power.

Violence erupted when a group of night elves confronted Illidan, and his brother Malfurion was forced to restrain him. Yet Illidan insisted that a new Well of Eternity was necessary. With it, the night elves would have the arcane power they needed to fight off the Burning Legion when—not *if*, but *when*—it returned.

Though some of the surviving Highborne agreed with Illidan, the majority of the night elves did not. They chastised him for his brash and selfish act, claiming that a new Well of Eternity could be used as a gateway for the Legion. Even then, Illidan remained unapologetic.

Seeing no other recourse, the night elves decided to deal with Illidan once and for all. Ultimately, the decision was made to imprison the sorcerer. Malfurion himself would see to enacting this punishment. With the help of Cenarius, he chained Illidan deep within a barrow prison. Malfurion then charged the priestess Maiev Shadowsong to stand guard over the wayward sorcerer. She would later take on the mantle of warden, founding an order of elite and secretive night elf jailors.

OVERLEAF: THE HIGH ELF KINGDOM OF QUEL'THALAS

THE DRAGON ASPECTS BLESS THE WORLD TREE NORDRASSIL

Upon learning of the second Well, three of the great Dragon Aspects converged on Hyjal. Like the night elves, they knew that so long as the fount of power existed, the Legion would have a means to invade Azeroth once again. Thus the Aspect of Life, Alexstrasza, used an enchanted seed to sprout a mighty tree over the Well of Eternity. The tree's boughs soon towered over the lake, scraping the belly of the heavens. Its roots grew deep into the earth, spreading life-giving energies across the war-torn world. Thereafter, the great tree would act as a seal over the new Well of Eternity, preventing the Legion or anyone else from abusing its powers.

Malfurion and the other night elves looked upon this colossal World Tree and named it *Nordrassil*, meaning "Crown of the Heavens." They vowed to keep it safe and protect the Well of Eternity at any cost.

To honor this decision, the Dragon Aspects agreed to bless the night elves so that they could perform their guardianship successfully. Alexstrasza infused Nordrassil with renewed strength and vitality, which would also extend to the night elves.

The Aspect of Dreams, Ysera, then blessed the tree, binding it and all night elf druids to the Emerald Dream. Prior to this, Malfurion and his followers had wandered Ysera's realm, but doing so required difficult meditation. The new enchantment placed on Nordrassil would allow these druids to journey into the Dream whenever they so wished.

Lastly, Nozdormu, the Aspect of Time, wove his energies through the boughs and roots of Nordrassil, assuring that as long as the colossal tree stood, the night elves would possess immortality.

With that, the Aspects ventured back to their hidden lairs. Due to their enchantments, the second Well of Eternity would no longer act as a beacon to demons, nor could the Legion easily use it as a gateway into Azeroth. It would become a symbol of the night elves' connection to the natural world, a sacred monument that empowered their race with immunity to sickness, disease, and aging.

THE SENTINELS
9,400 YEARS BEFORE THE DARK PORTAL

As the centuries passed, the burgeoning night elf society expanded into the dense forests of Ashenvale, south of Mount Hyjal. Tyrande Whisperwind, high priestess of the Sisterhood of Elune, led the night elves in rebuilding their society. Her order was uniquely positioned to fill the power vacuum among the night elves, for it had emerged from the War of the Ancients relatively unscathed.

Tyrande deftly positioned the Sisterhood as the leaders of both the night elf government and the military. She also forged a new fighting force: the Sentinels. Composed of devout and highly trained warrior women, this order dedicated itself to protecting the emergent night elf society. The Sentinels set out to patrol their misty forest home, befriending the native creatures of the land and standing guard against any threat.

Meanwhile, Malfurion continued fostering a culture of druidism among his people. Having abandoned arcane magic, many former sorcerers embraced Malfurion's teachings and devoted themselves to living in harmony with nature. These early druids lacked the stringent militaristic codes and hierarchy of the Sentinels. Malfurion's followers were free to explore the depths of the Emerald Dream at will. They also experimented with the art of shapeshifting, taking on the forms

Shandris Feathermoon

The Sentinels included a number of night elves who had fought bravely during the War of the Ancients. Chief among them was Shandris Feathermoon. Orphaned during the Legion's invasion, she was taken under Tyrande's care. Young Shandris distinguished herself in combat time and again throughout the conflict. Her heroics earned her a place at Tyrande's side thereafter, and when the Sentinels were forged, Shandris was named captain of the fledgling order.

of mighty bears, lithe nightsabers, swift-winged crows, and many other animals that roamed the woodland deeps.

The druids regularly entered long periods of hibernation as they journeyed through the Dream. This aloofness frustrated Tyrande and her Sentinels. Though they often sought the druids' help to safeguard night elf lands, few of Malfurion's followers were ever awake to answer the call.

As these changes in night elf society took shape, an old foe was gathering strength in Kalimdor. Following the War of the Ancients, the remaining satyrs stayed hidden in the dark corners of the world, waiting to strike back at the night elves. Eventually one of the horned aberrations, Xalan the Feared, gave his brethren this chance. He rallied the satyrs and girded them for war.

Xalan's rise also drew the attention of the Burning Legion remnants trapped on Azeroth after the Sundering. Doomguard and other wicked beings emerged from dark warrens, drawn to the satyr's call. As one, this demonic army launched its first brutal assault on the night elf stronghold of Night Run, plunging the fragile society into war once again.

The War of the Satyr
9,300 Years Before the Dark Portal

Initially, the night elves suffered terrible losses from the satyrs' assaults. Yet the tide of battle soon changed when Tyrande's adopted daughter, the captain of the Sentinels, Shandris Feathermoon, proposed a new strategy to fight the demons. She suggested that the druids be called from their sojourns in the Emerald Dream so they could be used as a fighting force.

Upon seeing how Xalan had corrupted the night elves' forests, Malfurion agreed to Shandris's request and summoned the most powerful druids of Kalimdor to his side. As one, the druids and Sentinels struck into the heart of satyr territory. Shandris's brilliant guerrilla maneuvers led the night elves to overcome many of their enemies, including Xalan himself.

But while the night elves made gains in the war, a new threat emerged from within their ranks. A group of wayward druids seeking to harness the fury of the Wild God Goldrinn had adopted

WORGEN, SATYRS, AND NIGHT ELVES CLASH DURING THE WAR OF THE SATYR savage wolf forms. Led by Ralaar Fangfire, these druids became known as worgen. Ralaar and his ferocious companions were slaves to their own rage, and they tore through friend and foe alike amid battle. Night elves bitten by the wolf-beasts contracted a virulent curse that transformed them into worgen as well.

The worgen catastrophe forced Malfurion to reflect on the state of druidism. Without some form of regulation, he concluded that individuals like Ralaar would inevitably go too far in their application of druidic power. Malfurion and his followers therefore created the Cenarion Circle, a harmonious order that would guide and keep watch over the world's druids and their practices.

The Cenarion Circle's first great task was to deal with the worgen threat. Seeing no other recourse, Malfurion reluctantly banished Ralaar and his worgen to the Emerald Dream. There, Malfurion believed that they would enter a peaceful eternal slumber beneath the enchanted tree known as Daral'nir.

After the worgen's banishment, any hope the satyrs had of achieving victory was lost. The night elves cut deep into their enemy's domain until most of the forests had been cleansed of corruption. The few remaining satyrs retreated into the shadows. Never again would they pose so great a threat to night elf society.

EXILE OF THE HIGH ELVES
7,300 YEARS BEFORE THE DARK PORTAL

In the centuries after the Sundering, the surviving Highborne attempted to assimilate in the new night elf society. Yet many of them struggled to do so. They found the temptation to delve into arcane magic irresistible, despite the strict laws banning sorcery.

Over time, these Highborne were warned again and again to stop meddling with the otherworldly powers—the penalty for repeat offenders was death. Despite this extreme punishment, the Highborne could not stop. The call of arcane energy was simply too strong to ignore.

A revered Highborne elf named Dath'Remar Sunstrider chafed at the restrictions and punishments that weighed on his kind. He eventually proclaimed that arcane power was the birthright of the Highborne and that anyone who feared it was a coward. He and his followers began to practice the arcane arts without fear or restraint, daring the other night elves to act.

For Dath'Remar and the other Highborne, using arcane magic was more than just an act of rebellion. They had always believed that night elves were destined for greatness. Though these Highborne did not wholly condone the evils of Azshara, they knew in their bones that night elf society could once again flourish into a mighty empire. Yet to do so, they would need to revive the study and use of arcane power.

The Highborne's reckless defiance was as sudden as it was startling. In the end, the other night elves could not bring themselves to sentence so many of their brothers and sisters to death. Instead, they barred the Highborne from setting foot on Hyjal ever again. Dath'Remar and his followers were exiled, cut off from the Well of Eternity's energies.

Most of the Highborne happily accepted their banishment. They were finally free of the other night elves' constraints. Under Dath'Remar's guidance, the Highborne built a fleet of mighty ships.

THE SUNSTRIDER DYNASTY

Dath'Remar Sunstrider hailed from a long line of illustrious Highborne, all of whom had served the night elf throne. Their namesake was something of an oddity among their moon-worshipping race. Dath'Remar's ancestors had chosen "Sunstrider" to symbolize their penchant for delving into the unknown, for breaking expectations and throwing caution to the wind in their search for greatness. Like his bold progenitors, Dath'Remar carried on this tradition with pride.

They then set sail, leaving Kalimdor for whatever lands might lie beyond the churning Maelstrom. The Highborne's determination was rewarded when they made landfall on a new continent some years later. This region, filled with lush wildlife and woodlands, would one day become known as the Eastern Kingdoms.

The Highborne traveled on foot for months before finally settling in a place marked by a strange silver hand—a land called Tirisfal by tribes of primitive humans that inhabited the area. Initially, these humans rarely interacted with the Highborne. Yet as time passed, they began to tell legends of a brave metal-skinned guardian named Tyr, who had sacrificed himself to kill a monstrous foe in Tirisfal.

Indeed, the Highborne detected potent ley energies in the land—energies that the primitive humans could not detect. It was no Well of Eternity, but the lingering supernatural presence intrigued the experienced arcane practitioners. Some elves speculated that, in time, they could unlock its secrets and restore themselves to their former glory.

They were desperate to succeed quickly. After being exiled from the Well of Eternity, the Highborne began to feel the effects of aging and disease. Their skin had even lost its violet hue, and they had begun to shrink in stature. The Highborne feared that the effects would only worsen over time.

Led by Dath'Remar, the Highborne made a new life in Tirisfal Glades. For a time, they dwelled in peace and reveled in their independence. Yet as they tapped into the area's latent magic, they found shades of dark energy. These shadowy powers drove some of the Highborne to madness. They began to argue that the humans had built their settlements atop the most potent ley lines in the region. Therefore, the Highborne should force them to relocate . . . or even conquer the primitive beings outright.

Dath'Remar did not agree. He had no wish to war against a people who posed no threat to his kind. The wise leader had also sensed the dark energies radiating from the land. He theorized that they might be responsible for the sudden rise of belligerence and madness that was afflicting the Highborne.

Ultimately, Dath'Remar chose to lead his people away from Tirisfal to avert violence and spare them from further calamity. He decided that they would try to make a new home in the north. There, Dath'Remar's scouts had discovered a region rife with lush forests and powerful ley energies. Intent on reaching this land, the beleaguered Highborne struck out north and into the unknown.

THE LONG VIGIL
7,300 YEARS BEFORE THE DARK PORTAL

The exile of the Highborne ended a tenuous chapter in night elf history. Yet even so, Tyrande and Malfurion found no time to rest.

Malfurion and the Cenarion Circle busied themselves with upholding the balance of nature and healing lands still polluted with demonic corruption. Much of this they did in unison with Ysera and her green dragonflight, deep within the twisting pathways of the Emerald Dream. Malfurion and the other druids slumbered for decades at a time, their dreamforms wandering Ysera's realm.

Tyrande, Shandris, and the Sentinels maintained their guardianship over the night elf domain. They patrolled the forests without rest, ever wary of another demonic resurgence. Their efforts resulted in a long-sought period of peace and tranquility. Life in the forests and thickets of Hyjal thrived.

In time, the enchanted keepers of the grove and woodland dryads emerged from the secluded Moonglade. The night elves revered these creatures, for they were Cenarius's own sons and daughters. Their presence in the wilds of Ashenvale was seen as an omen of better times to come.

Along with the keepers of the grove and the dryads, other creatures appeared in the open with greater frequency. The wise treants, the elusive faerie dragons, and the mythical chimaeras all began roaming the forests near night elf holdings. In the centuries to come, the night elves would foster strong bonds with these fay creatures and call on them in times of need.

With Malfurion in the Dream, the task of governing the daily activities of the night elves fell to Tyrande. The mantle of leadership was demanding, but she enjoyed it. Yet despite the hope and optimism that blossomed among the night elves, Tyrande could not shake the feeling that dire times were ahead. They had banished the Burning Legion, but they had not killed Sargeras. Tyrande believed with all her heart that the fallen titan was somewhere out in the darkness between the stars, plotting another attack. Perhaps it was only a matter of time before Sargeras renewed his Burning Crusade to decimate all life.

And if that day did come, Tyrande hoped she and her people would be ready for it.

CHAPTER IV: A NEW WORLD

THE FOUNDING
OF QUEL'THALAS
6,800 YEARS BEFORE THE DARK PORTAL

Far from the dense woodlands of Ashenvale, Dath'Remar Sunstrider and the Highborne continued their quest to find a home in the Eastern Kingdoms. They followed the trails of magical essence, seeking the confluence of ley lines that their scouts had spied in the north. The Highborne's journey proved unexpectedly brutal. A ferocious blizzard stopped the elves dead in their tracks for nearly a month as they traveled, with no way to move forward or escape from the mountain passes.

The Highborne quickly realized just how vulnerable they had become without the Well of Eternity. For the first time in memory, they began to die of starvation. Only the compassion of some primitive humans living in the mountains kept the entire expedition from perishing in the winter's fury.

Once the storm lifted, the Highborne forged ahead, shaken but determined to find a new home. As they drew closer to the land that the scouts had found, hope warmed their weary hearts. Verdant woodlands blanketed the terrain, and the ground beneath the Highborne's feet crackled with potent lines of magic. But the elves soon discovered that another race also called this region home: the barbaric Amani trolls.

The arrival of the Highborne infuriated the trolls, who harbored a bitter hatred of elves from the days of Queen Azshara. The Amani sent out raiding parties immediately, and the Highborne soon learned to fear troll ambushes in the dense forests. Yet the elves stubbornly pressed forward, using their magical prowess to decimate any Amani who dared cross their path. Soon the trolls also learned to tread cautiously. The continuous skirmishes fostered a mutual enmity between the Amani and the Highborne.

Despite the trolls' ferocity, the elves finally reached the nexus of ley lines they had been seeking. Powerful torrents of arcane energy converged in the vibrant forests. Dath'Remar proclaimed that this was where they would begin their civilization anew.

Before the eyes of his followers, Dath'Remar revealed something he had kept hidden over the long and torturous journey to the north: a vial filled with the enchanted waters from the original Well of Eternity. Just before the Highborne had been exiled from Mount Hyjal, Dath'Remar had secretly taken one of Illidan Stormrage's remaining vials from the custody of the night elves.

Dath'Remar poured the vial into a small lake at the center of the nexus, and a brilliant fount of energy tore through the skies of Azeroth. The Highborne dubbed this glorious cradle of power "the Sunwell," a name chosen in honor of Dath'Remar and his bold quest to reignite their culture.

Thereafter, the Highborne abandoned their traditional worship of the moon, instead taking their strength from the sun. In time, they would even be known by a new name: high elves. The amount of arcane power available to the elves increased by an astonishing degree. Many of them proclaimed that Dath'Remar had brought them salvation. They called their new land *Quel'Thalas*, or "High Home," and declared that it would dwarf the night elves' civilization and stand as a monument for the ages.

The trolls did not agree. The high elves had built their new kingdom atop ancient Amani ruins—ruins still considered hallowed ground by the trolls. Outnumbering the elves by more than ten to one, the Amani struggled ferociously to drive the invaders from their sacred land.

The high elves drew on the full might of their newfound power, barely holding off the trolls' assaults. Dath'Remar himself led almost every battle against the fierce Amani. Bit by bit, the elves carved out the borders of their kingdom, securing a new home, paid for in the blood of their brothers and sisters.

Yet many of the high elves grew wary of their rampant use of arcane magic, fearing that it could draw the Burning Legion to Azeroth once again. Dath'Remar sent his most powerful arcanists to find a solution. Over several decades, they built a series of monolithic Runestones around Quel'Thalas's borders. This barrier was called *Ban'dinoriel*, or "the Gatekeeper" in the high elven tongue. It would prevent others from detecting the elves' usage of arcane magic, and it would also frighten away the superstitious Amani.

The trolls eventually retreated back to their temple city of Zul'Aman. They decided it was safer to ambush elven convoys that strayed beyond the magic barrier than to launch a full-scale assault on Quel'Thalas. An elite group of high elf rangers soon arose to combat this threat.

Inside the borders of Quel'Thalas, civilization thrived. No longer fearful of using magic, the high elves created marvelous works and bathed their land in eternal springtime. Never again would they experience another winter as brutal as the one they had suffered en route to this land. Their capital, Silvermoon City, became a shining monument to the memory of the elves' ancient empire.

With the new empire established, Dath'Remar stepped down as leader. His bloodline would go on to inherit a kingdom of peace and prosperity. Yet this era would come to an end when Dath'Remar's great-grandson, Anasterian, donned the mantle of leadership. He would come to power at a time when his people faced war with the trolls once again.

THE CURSE OF CRYSTALSONG
6,000 YEARS BEFORE THE DARK PORTAL

As Quel'Thalas flourished, other Highborne communities across the world struggled to survive. One such community dwelled in the city of Shandaral, a repository of arcane relics and artifacts. At the apex of the night elf empire, this outpost had been established in the northern reaches of Kalimdor. Following the Sundering, Azeroth's main continent had fractured into multiple landmasses. Now, Shandaral and its Highborne dwelled in the frigid heart of a new and harsh continent known as Northrend.

The Shandaral Highborne remained in total isolation, cut off from their cousins in Kalimdor and the Eastern Kingdoms. Their distance from the second Well of Eternity left them vulnerable to disease and other ailments. Yet unlike Dath'Remar's followers, the Shandaral Highborne did not possess any vials of the Well of Eternity's waters. They had no way to create a surrogate source of power. For centuries, these Highborne scoured the surrounding forest of Moonsong for a means to sustain themselves.

During this time, the Highborne witnessed members of the blue dragonflight using spells to crystallize living things and draw power from them. Although the dragons performed these acts out of mere curiosity, the elves saw the technique as a means to end their suffering forever.

Attempts by the Highborne to interact with the dragons were ignored or, in some cases, met with open hostility. Out of desperation, a group of Highborne sorcerers infiltrated the blue flight's wondrous lair, the Nexus. The Highborne succeeded in learning the dragons' techniques, but greed also drove them to take more than they had come for. The elves pilfered some of the powerful relics stored in the Nexus. In doing so, they triggered magical wards, sending the blue dragons into a frenzy. Although the Highborne thieves escaped with their lives, they knew full well that the dragons would seek retribution.

That day soon arrived. Dozens of blue dragons descended on Shandaral, seething with indignation at the theft of their precious relics by the "lesser" Highborne. The elven sorcerers, desperate to drive away their enemies, gathered on an icy cliff overlooking Moonsong. There, they agreed to use the techniques they had acquired from the Nexus. As one, the Highborne sorcerers focused their power, hoping to crystallize a small portion of the forest and use its energies as a weapon to annihilate the dragons.

The spell proved disastrous. The Highborne's reckless casting set off a blinding explosion visible from as far away as Kalimdor and the Eastern Kingdoms. The roaring torrent of energy instantly crystallized the entire forest of Moonsong. The blue dragons, sensing the impending spellwork, escaped before disaster struck. The physical forms of every other living creature in the region were shattered by the release of energy. Their spirits, although warped by the powerful spell, were left intact, cursed to mindlessly wander the haunted land that would become known as Crystalsong Forest.

THE FELLING OF ANDRASSIL
4,500 YEARS BEFORE THE DARK PORTAL

When the Sundering tore through Azeroth, the tectonic devastation rattled the captive Old Gods and weakened their keeper-wrought prisons. The apocalyptic event also stirred the malign entities to new degrees of deadly awareness. Over the millennia that followed, great tendrils of corruption spilled from the Old Gods' damaged prisons and gradually seeped to the world's surface. Northrend, where Yogg-Saron was imprisoned, saw some of the most severe effects. Festering blooms of a strange new mineral, saronite, spread throughout the crust of the land and sapped the life of native flora and fauna.

Upon discovering saronite, a small group of druids from the Cenarion Circle decided to eradicate it. They reasoned that if the life-giving energies of the World Tree could heal the lands around Mount Hyjal, another great tree could do the same in Northrend. The group's leader, Fandral Staghelm, soon became obsessed with the idea.

Some druids advised him to seek the guidance of the Dragon Aspects. Their knowledge and blessings had allowed Nordrassil to flourish; without them, planting another great tree could

BLUE DRAGONS DESCEND ON THE HIGHBORNE IN THE FOREST OF MOONSONG have unforeseen consequences. Yet Staghelm believed there was no time to wait. Saronite was spreading unchecked throughout Northrend and even in other parts of the world. Rather than waste time in endless debates, Staghelm moved to act—without consulting the Aspects or the rest of the Cenarion Circle.

Fandral and his closest followers secretly cut six enchanted branches from the boughs of Nordrassil. With the branches in hand, they traveled the world to locations where saronite blooms had sprung to life. One by one, the druids planted the branches in these regions, hoping to thwart the corruption. The areas where Fandral and his allies left their mark included Ashenvale, Crystalsong Forest, Feralas, and two remote regions in the Eastern Kingdoms that would later be known as Duskwood and the Hinterlands.

The branches quickly took root and became new trees. Together, they acted like conduits, channeling the powers of the Emerald Dream into the waking world, strengthening the nearby wildlife, and scouring the saronite deposits. Heartened by their success, the druids planted the last and greatest of the branches in the mountains of Northrend, over the largest growth of saronite. This new World Tree—named *Andrassil*, or "Crown of the Snow"—grew with astonishing speed, and the benefits were almost immediate. The spread of saronite ceased, and wildlife flourished anew.

Malfurion and the rest of the Cenarion Circle became furious upon learning that these branches had been planted without their approval. They did, however, agree that the plan seemed to have worked. For several decades, Andrassil towered over Northrend, and all seemed well.

Yet in time, circumstances changed. Bloody battles erupted between the taunka and the forest nymphs of Northrend, two races not known for their warring ways. The fighting was sudden and shockingly vicious, filled with barbarism and unspeakably vile acts. Word slowly reached the druids, and the Cenarion Circle launched an expedition to investigate the source of the violence.

What the druids found chilled them to their marrow. Andrassil's roots had reached so deep into the earth that they had touched Yogg-Saron's subterranean prison. The Old God had infused the tree with its foul energies, and thus all living creatures in the area were slowly being driven to madness.

The Cenarion Circle knew that, without the blessing of the Aspects, Andrassil was vulnerable to corruption. They were also aware that there was no way to spare the World Tree or ease its suffering. The Cenarion Circle sorrowfully decided that the only recourse was to destroy Andrassil. With heavy hearts, they felled the great tree. It slammed down onto the icy surface of Northrend with a deafening boom that echoed even through the ethereal forests of the Emerald Dream. Forever after, the druids would refer to the fallen World Tree as *Vordrassil*, or "Broken Crown."

Although killing Andrassil had been a heartbreaking task, the Cenarion Circle was pleased it had stopped the growth of saronite. Yet unbeknownst to the druids, something dark had taken root in the Emerald Dream.

Yogg-Saron had used the trees planted by Fandral as a doorway into the Dream—a doorway through which the other Old Gods could grasp the ethereal domain as well. Small seeds of corruption were spread throughout Ysera's realm. In time, these seeds polluted the dreamways. This marked the beginning of what would become known as the Emerald Nightmare.

Exodus of the Gnomes
3,000 YEARS BEFORE THE DARK PORTAL

As wars raged and new civilizations arose across the surface of Azeroth, the earthen largely kept to themselves. They were unconcerned with the activities of the world's other races. Some earthen remained isolated underneath the icy mountains of Northrend. Others, who came south with Keeper Archaedas and the giantess Ironaya in an earlier age, slumbered within the catacomb vaults of Uldaman. Only a small number of these earthen had chosen not to be placed in stasis, deciding that they would watch over and maintain the facility alongside their mechagnome companions.

During this period, Archaedas and Ironaya grew distant from their servants. They became ever more obsessed with trying to cure the curse of flesh. Archaedas and Ironaya often retreated into the lowest chambers of Uldaman, spending years in quiet contemplation. Eventually the two colossal titan-forged would disappear from sight and settle into a long period of hibernation. Centuries passed without word from either of them, and the mechagnomes and earthen were left to manage Uldaman on their own.

When the Sundering tore through Azeroth, many of the active earthen reeled from the catastrophe. They felt the pain of the broken world as their own. They tunneled deep within Uldaman and locked themselves away within the hibernation chambers alongside their sleeping brethren.

Only the mechagnomes remained to watch over the facility. Yet they, too, eventually succumbed to the curse of flesh. The affliction caused many of them to degenerate into fleshy beings later known simply as gnomes. Physically and mentally debilitated, these creatures lost all sense of purpose and abandoned the halls of Uldaman. They fled into the surrounding mountain peaks and caverns. Only a handful of mechagnomes stayed in the facility, still driven by their titan-forged imperative.

The first generation of gnomes carved out an existence in the snowy mountains to the west of Uldaman. Lacking natural strength and defenses, the frail gnomes struggled to survive amid the harsh elements, barbaric ice trolls, and other threats that roamed the land. They did, however, retain their natural intellect and ingenuity. As generations passed, the gnomes dedicated themselves to technological advancement and discovery; these would be their only means of sustaining themselves in the savage new world. To this end, the gnomes eschewed record keeping and oral storytelling, considering them immaterial to survival.

In only a few generations, the gnomes lost all knowledge of their titan-forged heritage. What they gained, however, was a new society. Their ingenious engineering and sciences had helped them overcome hardship after hardship. The gnomes carved out a series of highly fortified dwellings deep within the cold mountains of what would become known as Dun Morogh.

THE RISE OF ARATHOR
2,800 YEARS BEFORE THE DARK PORTAL

Over thousands of years, humanity flourished in the Eastern Kingdoms. This young race had originated from a group of vrykul who had settled in Tirisfal Glades. Although humans were diminished in size and strength from their progenitors, they possessed incredibly strong willpower and survival instincts.

Groups of hunter-gatherer humans proliferated throughout the forests and hillocks of the continent. As their society evolved and advanced, humans gathered in an array of different tribes. Each one practiced animistic beliefs—mainly crude forms of druidism and elemental shamanism. Despite the existence of Amani trolls, high elves, and other potential threats, humanity's greatest adversary proved to be itself. The early tribes constantly warred with one another for land and, by extension, power.

One tribe, the Arathi, came to realize the error of its ways. Over the span of a few decades, troll incursions into human territories had become more pronounced and ruthless. Something was changing among the brutish Amani to the north. The Arathi knew that if humankind remained divided, it would stand little chance against a true war with its moss-skinned foes. Led by Warlord Thoradin, the tribe embarked on a campaign to bring its rivals under a single banner, whether by force or diplomacy.

The Arathi lived on the northeastern borders of human lands and had a long history of skirmishes with the trolls. This experience had honed Thoradin into a master tactician and strategist. In the span of just six years, the warlord brought the other tribes to heel. He won a few of his adversaries to his side through political marriages. In other cases, Thoradin pitted his rivals against each other. On rare occasions, the canny warlord was forced to outright conquer some of the more belligerent tribes.

Much to the surprise of those he had defeated, Thoradin did not reign as a tyrant. He offered his former enemies peace and equality in what he claimed would be a glorious new human nation—a united kingdom of limitless potential. The tribal leaders would not fade into obscurity. They would serve as honored generals. With these acts, Thoradin won the loyalty of his adversaries and was crowned king.

King Thoradin named his new kingdom Arathor. He tasked his most gifted builders with constructing a mighty capital called Strom southeast of Tirisfal Glades. The semiarid terrain around the city acted as the ideal buffer zone between humanity and the Amani, prohibiting the trolls from launching their much feared forest ambushes. Thoradin also ordered his people to build a great wall near the capital to further shield them from Amani incursions. Word of Strom's might quickly spread among other disparate human tribes throughout the continent. Many flocked to the fortress for safety.

Just as Thoradin had expected, Amani trolls soon began encroaching on outlying lands controlled by the humans. The king dispatched two of his most prominent generals to gather intelligence on their enemies and waylay any of the brutes who strayed too deep into Arathor's borders.

One of these generals was named Ignaeus. He and his people originally dwelled among the rugged slopes around the Alterac Mountains. Though considered uncouth and savage by many of

LEGEND OF THE SILVER HAND

No one knows what became of Tyr's fabled silver hand, left behind in ages past at the heart of Tirisfal Glades. The silver hand was a common symbol for the human tribes that inhabited the region. It appeared on clothing and pendants, worn to ward away evil spirits, protect warriors in battle, and cure disease. Many centuries later, it would come to represent a great order of paladins: Light-wielding warriors who placed self-sacrifice above all else.

the humans from other regions, Ignaeus and his northlanders were unmatched in their bravery and strength. They stalked well beyond Arathor's borders, slaughtering any trolls whom they found skulking in the woodlands. Ignaeus would garner the name "Trollbane" for the amount of Amani blood he spilled.

Thoradin's other favored general was Lordain, who hailed from the heart of Tirisfal Glades. He and his regimented warriors were considered more refined than Ignaeus and the other mountain folk. Knightly in appearance and mindset, Lordain's forces thoroughly patrolled the edges of Arathor's northern borders. On the rare occasion that Amani raiding parties approached the kingdom, Lordain put them to the blade.

Both Lordain and Ignaeus often returned to Strom with tales of a horrific conflict brewing between the Amani and the high elves far to the north. There were also whispers of something else stirring in the darkened forests—tales of strange voodoo rituals and supernatural beings prowling the wilds in the dead of night.

Though the reports unsettled them, Thoradin and his generals agreed that they would not risk their own kind or send any aid to the reclusive high elves. For the time being, they kept the bulk of their forces behind Strom's massive ramparts, confident they could withstand any foe.

THE TROLL WARS

The Sunwell

Silvermoon City

QUEL'THALAS

EASTERN
KINGDOMS

Zul'Aman

AMANI EMPIRE

Alterac Fortress

ARATHOR

Strom

THE TROLL WARS, PART I:
THE SIEGE OF QUEL'THALAS
2,800 YEARS BEFORE THE DARK PORTAL

Millennia after being defeated by the high elves, the Amani trolls plotted revenge within their temple city of Zul'Aman. Yet though they were fierce warriors, the trolls lacked a strong leader who could bring them victory. Infighting had also spread throughout the tribe, threatening to destroy it from within. The Amani's fortunes soon changed when they received aid from the revered Zandalar tribe.

The Zandalari saw themselves as the protectors and spiritual leaders of all trolls. They were eager to strengthen troll societies across Azeroth, many of which had languished since the time of the Great Sundering. Even the Zandalari had suffered from that catastrophic event. Their once-glorious mountain home of Zandalar had been swallowed by the sea, leaving nothing more than a small island behind.

In the Amani, the Zandalari saw an opportunity to revitalize one of their race's most powerful tribes and reassert troll dominance in the Eastern Kingdoms. Overwhelming the high elves would be no easy task, but the Zandalari were confident of victory. Quel'Thalas was not as powerful as the ancient night elf empire that had decimated the trolls so long ago. In addition, the Zandalari had honed and perfected their own voodoo arts over recent millennia.

A handful of wise Zandalari emissaries made the journey from their island home to Zul'Aman. There, they promised to help the Amani plan for their impending conflict. More importantly, the Zandalari would ensure that the mighty loa demigods would aid the trolls in battle. To settle matters of leadership, the Zandalari also made one of the Amani's most fearless warriors, Jintha, the ruler of his people.

Small Amani warbands began emerging from the forests and attacking Quel'Thalas's borders, testing the high elves' strength. Always, the cunning trolls hid their true numbers and capabilities. After a series of successful skirmishes, the Amani decided that the time for all-out war had finally come.

Without warning, tens of thousands of troll fighters exploded from the shadowy forests. Monstrous loa demigods marched alongside the Amani, infusing their troll adherents with supernatural might. The high elves struggled desperately to hold back their foes, but they were forced to give ground. With astonishing speed and ferocity, the Amani laid waste to the outer reaches of Quel'Thalas.

From Zul'Aman, the Zandalari emissaries observed the unfolding war with pleasure. Even the elves and their potent arcane powers could not withstand the might of the Amani—*the might of the troll race.*

The trolls' ultimate victory was only a matter of time.

THE TROLL WARS, PART II: FIRE FROM THE HEAVENS

King Thoradin kept a careful watch over the intensifying war between the high elves and the trolls. Scouts returned to Strom with tales of smoke rising along Quel'Thalas's borders, of brutalized elven corpses littering the once-tranquil grottos of the northlands. Clearly, the trolls were winning, but Thoradin clung to his stubborn belief that intervening in the conflict would put his people at unnecessary risk.

However, Thoradin's opinion changed when a group of high elven ambassadors sent by King Anasterian Sunstrider suddenly arrived at Strom. With growing horror, Thoradin listened as the messengers related firsthand accounts of the Amani's stark brutality and the otherworldly demigods who fought by their side.

The Amani threat was far greater than Thoradin or his advisors could have ever imagined. The high elves argued that without assistance from Arathor, the trolls would soon destroy Quel'Thalas. After that, the Amani would launch the full might of their blood-crazed warbands against Strom itself.

Following the meeting, Thoradin consulted with his advisors. They agreed that allying with the elves was prudent, but they also knew that Arathor did not have the forces required to fight an open conflict with the trolls. Thoradin and his advisors debated well into the night before coming to a conclusion. If humans were taught magic, it might give them the edge they needed to truly make an impact in the war.

Elven magic was legendary among humans, but they had never learned its secrets. Although Thoradin harbored a deep suspicion of sorcery in all its forms, he knew that his forces would require it in order to vanquish the Amani. The next day, Thoradin returned to the ambassadors with an offer: in exchange for military aid, the high elves would teach humans magic.

The high elves dispatched messengers to consult with King Anasterian. Like all of his kind, he knew well the dangers of unchecked magic. Teaching the arcane arts to humans could easily lead to disaster. Yet as much as this possibility troubled Anasterian, his own people were facing extinction. Knowing he had little choice, he agreed that the high elves would tutor one hundred humans in the rudimentary ways of magic.

Before long, elven magi journeyed to Strom and hastily began their mentorship of humans. Over the course of many months, the tutors observed something remarkable in their students. Although the humans lacked grace and subtlety in their castings, they possessed a startling natural affinity to magic.

Meanwhile, Thoradin ordered his generals to establish a stronghold at the base of the Alterac Mountains. This would act as a staging point for their future offensive against the trolls. Thoradin's generals also erected other crude forts in the Eastweald, a large stretch of fertile foothills east of Tirisfal Glades. However, Alterac Fortress would remain the humans' most important northern holding.

Once the elves had finished tutoring the human magi, Arathor began its offensive. Over twenty thousand human soldiers gathered at Alterac Fortress. From there, Thoradin himself led his forces toward Quel'Thalas. He did not, however, bring the human magi with him. They would remain behind the walls of Alterac. If things progressed as Thoradin hoped, the magi would play a part later in the war . . .

Generals Ignaeus and Lordain acted as the vanguard of Arathor's armies. Riding days ahead of the advancing Arathi host, they cleared the way north and slaughtered any troll scouts and raiding parties they could find. After weeks of hard marching, the full might of Arathor's armies finally reached the outskirts of Quel'Thalas and smashed into the southern flank of the Amani. In coordination with the Arathi, the high elves launched a counterattack from the north and laid waste to the trolls' front lines.

The Amani now found themselves fighting a war on two fronts. Yet Jintha remained confident the trolls would emerge victorious. The elves' decision to ally with the primitive humans reeked of desperation. The Arathi had a reputation as fierce warriors, but they lacked the magic powers and battle discipline of the elves. The crude humans were a minor nuisance—one that Jintha would quickly eradicate. Intent on destroying Arathor's armies, he turned his warbands south to crush the humans. Once he had slaughtered them, Jintha would refocus his forces on Quel'Thalas and exterminate the elves for good.

On Thoradin's orders, the humans began a slow retreat back toward Alterac. Weeks of brutal and bloody fighting followed as the overconfident Amani chased Arathor's armies to the mountains. As the humans moved south, the high elves emerged from Quel'Thalas and marched for Alterac as well. They constantly harried the northern flank of the Amani, slowly whittling down the trolls' rear guard.

Upon finally reaching Alterac Fortress, Thoradin was pleased to find that the Amani were still in pursuit. He readied his forces for the attack that he knew was soon to come. One morning, as a thick fog enveloped the Alterac foothills, the Amani fell upon the human army. Although outnumbered, the Arathi fought back with unexpected tenacity. The battle raged on for days with neither side giving ground. Before long, the high elves arrived from the north and assailed the Amani on a second front.

When the humans and elves were confident they had worn down the Amani ranks, they unleashed their secret weapon: the one hundred human magi. Throughout the recent days of fighting, Thoradin had kept them hidden within Alterac Fortress. Now, it was time to test their mettle in battle.

Alongside the elven sorcerers, the human magi called upon their vast newfound powers. Instead of attacking individually, the magi did something unprecedented: they pooled their power and wove a single terrible spell. The Alterac Mountains heaved and trembled as torrents of fire lashed down from the blood-red sky. The energies engulfed the Amani ranks in a searing conflagration. These sorcerous flames burned loa and troll alike from the inside out.

Among the first of the Amani to be consumed in the enchanted flames was Jintha. Without their leader, the surviving trolls broke ranks and retreated north. The elves and humans hunted them down like game, slaughtering every Amani combatant they could find.

The disastrous battle floored the Zandalari emissaries. Once so confident of victory, they skulked back to their island home in disbelief and shame. For them, the defeat marked a dark turning point in troll history, one from which their beleaguered race might never recover.

Yet for Quel'Thalas and Arathor, the war was the beginning of a glorious new era. For months after the cessation of the conflict, celebrations graced the streets of Strom and Silvermoon City. The grateful elves pledged their undying loyalty to Arathor and to Thoradin's descendants.

HUMAN MAGI UNLEASH THEIR POWERS ON THE AMANI TROLLS

THE SACRIFICE OF LORDAIN

During the retreat to Alterac, the Amani began gaining on the humans too fast, threatening to flank and overwhelm Arathor's armies. To avert disaster, General Lordain volunteered to waylay the trolls, knowing full well he would not survive. He and five hundred of his bravest warriors held off the Amani host in a narrow valley while the rest of the Arathi army continued retreating south. Lordain and his warriors paid the ultimate price, but their valiant stand helped secure victory for humans and elves alike. Lordain's legacy of pure selflessness and sacrifice would live on among his people in the coming millennia.

THE EXPANSION OF ARATHOR
2,700 YEARS BEFORE THE DARK PORTAL

After King Thoradin's reign had ended, new generations of humans expanded the nation of Arathor in size and power. Many of the first human magi tutored pupils in the ways of the arcane. Within a few decades, the number of spellcasters within Arathor had increased dramatically.

Protected from natural threats by these powerful magi, enterprising humans founded new Arathi settlements in the frontier lands. Some claimed the verdant pastures of the Eastweald, territories once lorded over by the trolls. Others migrated to Alterac Fortress as well as to the smaller forts that had been built during the Troll Wars. These fortified holdings soon flourished into bustling trading outposts.

The most coveted and fertile lands were located in Tirisfal Glades. There, the Arathi established a stronghold to protect their farmsteads from gnolls, kobolds, and other dangerous wildlife. Many former soldiers settled in this region, which they renamed Lordaeron in honor of the late general Lordain.

Other Arathi expanded to the coastal region known as Gilneas, where they constructed a series of robust harbors. The settlers fished the waters and engaged in rigorous trade with other parts of Arathor. The boldest of these sailors ventured into the open waters around Gilneas. In time, they discovered a large island to the south that was rich with metal ores and other valuable natural resources. Some of the sailors stayed on this island and founded a mighty maritime outpost named Kul Tiras.

Over the decades, these new cities continued to grow and develop their own unique customs. The ruling powers in Arathor's capital, Strom, were ever wary that these settlements would become too independent. Despite these rulers' attempts to retain control over the kingdom, many cities did eventually gain more autonomy. The first and most notable example of this was the trading outpost of Dalaran.

Established in the heart of Arathor, Dalaran quickly became a trading center of great import and influence. Citizens from across Arathor flocked to the city in a quest for wealth and new opportunity. One of these immigrants was a brilliant and eccentric mage named Ardogan. He won the admiration of Dalaran's populace and was elected as its ruler.

Under Ardogan's governance, Dalaran would continue expanding in power and would ultimately evolve into an autonomous city-state. It would also become a much needed haven for Arathor's magi—a population that the kingdom's citizenry increasingly viewed with suspicion and wariness.

THE COUNCIL OF TIRISFAL
2,680 YEARS BEFORE THE DARK PORTAL

The growth and prosperity experienced by Arathor was due in large part to magi and the protection they offered settlers. Even so, private distrust of sorcerers festered among the general populace. Over time, dissent and superstition grew, igniting tensions between magic users and the rest of society. Most magi withdrew from cities and towns, angry at being subjected to what they saw as baseless paranoia.

Dalaran's ruler, Ardogan, invited many of these disgruntled magi to his city. There, he proclaimed, they could live free of prejudice. Many of these magi answered Ardogan's call and settled in Dalaran. When the first group of these sorcerers arrived, they decided to remake the city into a glorious center of knowledge. Using their great powers, the magi expanded Dalaran in size and scope. They raised gleaming spires throughout the city and constructed vast libraries and repositories of arcane wonders.

Ardogan and the most powerful of these newly arrived magi formed a magocracy to govern the burgeoning city. This ruling body encouraged the study and practice of arcane arts. As word of Dalaran spread, magi from across Arathor began to see it as a symbol of hope and freedom.

Within a few years, Dalaran exploded in population. Though only a small percentage of residents could wield the arcane, the protection they offered allowed trade and industry to grow unimpeded. Crime was virtually nonexistent. The dangers of the wild were largely forgotten.

But this unchecked spellcasting had disastrous consequences.

The reckless use of magic began tearing through the fabric of reality in the region. Dalaran's magi were unaware that waves of arcane energy billowed out from the city and into the Twisting Nether. These tides of power drew the attention of scattered demons belonging to the Burning Legion. A small number of these demons slipped into the physical world, infiltrating Dalaran itself. Though these creatures were weak and usually alone, they succeeded in sowing chaos and terrorizing the peaceful city.

The magocracy struggled to deal with these demonic intrusions while also keeping them a secret from the public. More and more, the city's rulers feared that if the superstitious populace learned the truth, they would panic and riot. Eventually, the magocracy sought help from beyond the city's walls. The ruling magi sent an urgent request to the high elves of Quel'Thalas. The humans hoped that the elves, in their infinite wisdom, might understand how to deal with the sudden influx of demons.

The ruling body in Quel'Thalas, the Council of Silvermoon, immediately dispatched the high elves' greatest magi to investigate. They determined that only a few demons had crossed into the physical world, but the magi knew that this was merely the beginning. The problem would grow worse unless the magocracy placed limits on humans' use of magic.

Many of Dalaran's leaders rejected the high elves' recommendation. Magi had come to the city because they could freely practice their arcane arts. Restricting them would result in a number of detrimental effects. At best, most of the brightest magi would leave and continue their arcane studies elsewhere. At worst, Dalaran's entire economy would collapse, sparking a revolt and scattering the magi to the far corners of the land. One way or another, the use of arcane magic would continue, be it within Dalaran's walls or without. No matter what happened, the threat posed by the Burning Legion would always exist.

Having agreed that they could not prohibit the use of magic, the Council of Silvermoon and the magocracy of Dalaran decided on another solution. Together, they formed a clandestine order to deal with the demonic invaders. This new group met within a secret grove in Tirisfal Glades to discuss its work, and it became known as the Council of Tirisfal. The order's gifted members would be responsible for tracking and banishing the Legion's agents wherever they might be found across the land. The magi would also quietly educate other magi about the dangers of reckless spell-weaving.

THE FIRST GUARDIAN
2,610 YEARS BEFORE THE DARK PORTAL

For decades, the first members of the Council of Tirisfal discreetly tracked down and banished any demons they could find. When facing extraordinarily powerful foes, the council's members would channel their abilities into a single individual, who would act as a solitary vessel of their power for a short time.

Empowering a single champion was a dangerous ritual. As such, it was only done in rare and dire circumstances. The council members would have to be in close proximity to perform the ritual, leaving them vulnerable. The massive influx of energies also had the potential to destroy the appointed champions. Yet if they survived, they could overwhelm even the Burning Legion's mightiest agents. Despite the risks, the Council of Tirisfal used this empowering technique to great effect for many years.

But everything changed when a dreadlord named Kathra'natir infiltrated Dalaran. This cunning demon stalked the city's beautiful spires, spreading his poison through the hearts and minds of the populace. Terrible plagues gripped Dalaran. As the affliction spread, a veil of paranoia enveloped the city.

Upon investigating these phenomena, the Council of Tirisfal discovered and confronted Kathra'natir. The gifted magi found themselves outmatched by the demon. Seeing no other recourse, they moved to empower a high elf named Aertin Brighthand as their champion. Aertin hurled himself against Kathra'natir, wielding the council's combined might as his own.

It was here that Kathra'natir turned the council's greatest strength to his own advantage. Rather than face the champion directly, the demon struck out at the order's members. With their energies in Brighthand's control, they could not defend themselves. Kathra'natir's shadowy assault disrupted the connection between the council members and Aertin. This in turn weakened the champion's powers, until eventually he fell to the demon. Only the desperate intervention of a young half-elf named Alodi spared the council from total annihilation.

The wary council rallied for another battle, but this time as individual magi with no champion to focus their strength. Kathra'natir reveled in the council's disarray, easily thwarting his adversaries.

The defeat shattered the Council of Tirisfal's confidence and hope. The magi knew that they could not overcome Kathra'natir as individuals, nor could they rely on their empowerment ritual.

In this dark moment, Alodi and his allies discovered a new way to wield their power. No longer would the council members need to be present for the battle. Through a complex ritual, they could *permanently* grant someone a portion of their power. Alodi was the first to undergo this experimental technique. When the ritual proved successful, he declared himself not the council's champion but its Guardian.

The newly empowered Alodi faced and struck down Kathra'natir, banishing the dreadlord back to the roaring depths of the Twisting Nether. Hailed as a hero, Alodi would serve as the first Guardian of Tirisfal. He used his great powers to prolong his life, and for a hundred years he hunted down the Legion's minions. At the end of his century of service, Alodi gave up his power voluntarily, choosing to live out the remainder of his days in peace and tranquility.

So began the tradition of the Guardian. Every century, a new mage would arise to dedicate his or her life to safeguarding Azeroth. The magi chosen to wield the council's might would demonstrate their humility and commitment to peace by giving up their tremendous power after a hundred years.

For more than a millennium, an unprecedented era of prosperity reigned across the whole of Azeroth. Though conflict and suffering could not be entirely eradicated, the Guardians ensured that no demonic intruders would harm the world. As these noble individuals waged their lonely secret war against the Legion, Dalaran continued to serve as one of the world's foremost centers of arcane knowledge and research.

Ironforge and the Awakening of the Dwarves
2,500 Years Before the Dark Portal

Far to the south of Dalaran, the ancient vault of Uldaman lay darkened and silent. Ages ago, Ironaya and Keeper Archaedas had gone into hibernation. Many of the mechagnomes who had once watched over Uldaman's machineries had departed as well after being afflicted by the curse of flesh. But a handful of these faithful clockwork servants had remained. Their once-resilient forms gradually succumbed to the degradations of time. They broke down and died out until only one was left.

Although this lone mechagnome did her best to maintain Uldaman, much of the stronghold fell into disrepair. Soon, the curse of flesh began to chip away at her metallic form. The affliction eventually transformed her into a gnome, and she grew old and close to death. Aware that she did not have much time left, the gnome worked to free the earthen hibernating deep within Uldaman. She could not bear the thought that when she passed, they would be abandoned forever in the vault's deadened halls.

With her dying breath, the gnome activated the earthen's hibernation chambers. The chambers stirred to life. The titan-forged slumbering within awoke to a new world . . . and a new destiny.

These awakened earthen discovered that they had changed dramatically. The curse of flesh had taken its toll, transforming them into creatures of flesh and blood—creatures who would call themselves dwarves.

Still groggy from their years of slumber, the dwarves stumbled from the broken halls of Uldaman and emerged onto the surface of the world. They found themselves drawn to the west, where a range of majestic stone mountains towered into the clouds. Much like the gnomes who had left Uldaman centuries ago, the dwarves were forced to contend with the savage beasts that prowled the land. Yet whereas the gnomes had used their ingenuity to overcome these threats, the dwarves relied on their resilience and natural physical strength. Eventually, they reached the mountains they had seen on the western horizon, and they settled in the snowy region of Dun Morogh.

Although the curse of flesh had diminished their memories, the dwarves still held faint ties to their titan-forged heritage. Inspired by these recollections of the past, they named their new home *Khaz Modan*, or "Mountain of Khaz," in honor of the titan shaper Khaz'goroth. The dwarves retained a natural affinity to stoneworking and mining as well. They delved into the heart of Khaz Modan's tallest mountain and crafted an immense forge. Around it, the dwarves built a proud city called Ironforge. This would become the seat of their new home, a great and mighty nation that would stretch deep under the mountains.

As the dwarves set out to mine Khaz Modan's mountains and expand their holdings, they discovered the gnomes dwelling in the nearby caverns. The people of Ironforge were enthralled by the ingenuity and techno-savvy of their diminutive neighbors. The dwarves also sensed a natural kinship with the gnomes, due in large part to their shared titan-forged ancestry.

The dwarves imparted their knowledge of stoneworking and construction to the gnomes, helping them lay the foundations of a wondrous city that would later be called Gnomeregan. In turn, the gnomes taught the dwarves engineering and science, introducing much needed efficiency and advancements to Ironforge. Although the gnomes and dwarves would largely keep to themselves in the centuries that followed, they had formed an unbreakable bond and would aid each other in times of need.

THE GURUBASHI CIVIL WAR
1,500 YEARS BEFORE THE DARK PORTAL

In the southern reaches of the Eastern Kingdoms, the Gurubashi jungle trolls languished in poverty and hardship. They had never fully recovered from the destruction wrought by the Sundering. Many hunting and farming grounds were forever lost, and famine was a constant companion for the empire.

Desperate to reclaim their former glory, the Gurubashi of Stranglethorn Vale eventually turned to the powerful loa spirits whom the trolls worshipped. One such creature answered their call: Hakkar the Soulflayer, the Loa of Blood. The malevolent spirit promised to help the Gurubashi extend their empire across the lower half of the Eastern Kingdoms. In return, he demanded large numbers of living sacrifices.

The Gurubashi who pledged their loyalties to Hakkar became known as the Hakkari. They soundly defeated nearby packs of gnolls and tribes of murlocs, as well as other trolls who opposed Hakkar. Those taken prisoner soon wished they had died in battle; Hakkar's disembodied spirit gorged on the blood of the captives for years. Under the Hakkari's control, the Gurubashi had achieved all they had hoped, conquering vast swaths of land and even many of the islands that dotted the coasts of the South Seas.

The Zandalari, observing these events from afar, were pleased at first with the Gurubashi's return to conquest and traditional worship. Yet once it became clear that Hakkar's bloodlust would *never* be sated, they knew that the fiendish god would drive not only the troll race to destruction, but the entire world.

The Zandalari rallied their forces and set sail for the Eastern Kingdoms. There, they met with Gurubashi trolls who had kept their dissent hidden from the Hakkari. The Zandalari and their new allies learned that a faction of Hakkar's most zealous priests, the Atal'ai, were attempting to summon the loa's spirit into a living form. This in turn would awaken terrible new dimensions of his power and spell certain doom for the troll race.

Horrified by the Atal'ai's plans, the Zandalari host stormed the Gurubashi capital of Zul'Gurub. Battles raged among the vine-covered ziggurats of the temple city day and night. Finally, atop Hakkar's bloodstained shrine, the Zandalari defeated Hakkar and most of his crazed followers.

Despite this victory, the Zandalari and their allies agreed to remain vigilant for any sign of Hakkar's reappearance. The loa was not truly dead—his spirit had merely been banished from the physical world.

A number of his fanatical Atal'ai priests had also escaped into the jungles surrounding Zul'Gurub. These trolls finally settled in the Swamp of Sorrows, north of the Gurubashi capital. In the heart of the wild marshland, they secretly constructed a great temple to their bloodthirsty loa: the Temple of Atal'Hakkar.

Deep within the temple, the Atal'ai continued their worship of Hakkar. They practiced grisly rituals and ceremonies, hoping to once again summon the loa into the physical world. Dark magics twisted the flora and fauna surrounding the temple. This in turn drew the attention of the green Dragon Aspect, Ysera.

Upon learning of the Atal'ai's plans to summon Hakkar, Ysera unleashed her powers on the temple and its inhabitants. The Dragon Aspect's attack buckled the temple's walls and blasted its foundations apart. The immense ziggurat began sinking beneath the land. As the swampy mire engulfed the temple, the terrified Atal'ai abandoned their rituals and scattered into the marshlands.

Though Ysera had thwarted Hakkar's return, she knew that the Atal'ai might someday attempt to summon the loa again. Thus, she commanded a number of her loyal green dragons to watch over the ruined temple and ensure it would never again be used to bring such evil into the world.

ELDRE'THALAS AND THE BINDING OF IMMOL'THAR
1,200 YEARS BEFORE THE DARK PORTAL

Far across the sea from the Gurubashi empire, a secretive society of Highborne who had survived the Great Sundering grappled with an uncertain future. They were known as the *Shen'dralar*, meaning "Those Who Remain Hidden." Nearly ten thousand years before, Queen Azshara had charged them with the storage and safekeeping of her most precious tomes. Led by Prince Tortheldrin, the Shen'dralar dutifully obeyed their queen. They journeyed into the misty heart of Kalimdor's southern jungles and established a grand city called Eldre'Thalas.

When the Great Sundering later decimated the world, Eldre'Thalas narrowly escaped destruction. Only the efforts of Tortheldrin and his followers spared the city. Together, they wove a great spell to shield Eldre'Thalas from the destructive forces of the Sundering.

Although they had saved their city, the Shen'dralar soon discovered that the Well of Eternity had been consumed in the Sundering. Without the fount of power to draw on, Tortheldrin and his followers saw their immortality greatly diminished. The Shen'dralar soon fell into a deep lethargy and languished in their isolated sanctuary.

Tortheldrin eventually formulated a plan to revitalize the Shen'dralar. He forged pylons in one of the damaged wings of Eldre'Thalas, constructing a prison to house a new source of power: a demon named Immol'thar. To the shock of the other Shen'dralar, Tortheldrin had covertly summoned and bound the terrifying creature to siphon the demon's power and give it to his followers. Any objections were quickly settled once the other Shen'dralar experienced the demon's energy for themselves. Though dark and volatile, Immol'thar's power was invigorating and addictive, more so than even the Well of Eternity had been.

The Shen'dralar reveled in their newfound source of power, but they knew that keeping Immol'thar in their midst was dangerous. Thus, they developed a means to use the demon's power to keep him imprisoned. For thousands of years, all seemed well.

Yet the cost of keeping Immol'thar restrained required more and more power. Nearly nine thousand years after the Sundering, the demon's prison crossed a dangerous threshold. It began consuming so much energy that the Shen'dralar were left with none to siphon for themselves. Almost overnight, Tortheldrin's seemingly ingenious plan unraveled, and his access to the demon's magic was gone.

THE HIGHBORNE CITY OF ELDRE'THALAS (LATER KNOWN AS DIRE MAUL)

Not only had the Shen'dralar lost their immortality once again, but they had also grown hopelessly addicted to Immol'thar's potent energies. Desperate to regain his power, Tortheldrin plotted with his closest allies and murdered the other Shen'dralar in cold blood.

Tortheldrin's treacherous plan worked. Having thinned the population, the remaining elves could draw on Immol'thar's power indefinitely.

With the Shen'dralar's numbers diminished, Tortheldrin and his followers abandoned much of their once-glorious city. The greater part of Eldre'Thalas fell into darkness and disrepair. Soon, other creatures from the surrounding jungles moved in to stake their claim to the crumbling elven refuge.

THE FRACTURING OF ARATHOR
1,200 YEARS BEFORE THE DARK PORTAL

As Tortheldrin and his followers retreated deeper into Eldre'Thalas, the kingdom of Arathor began to split apart. The once-small trading outposts and cities that had been established after the Troll Wars had grown into mighty city-states of their own. Eventually, Strom saw its influence over these regions slip away.

The island bastion of Kul Tiras continued its traditions of trading and shipping. The city-state boasted a massive navy—the greatest in all of Arathor. Its most daring captains explored the coasts of the Eastern Kingdoms, returning with exotic goods and tales of strange lands in the remote corners of the continent.

Kul Tiras's shipping and fishing economy eclipsed the maritime power of its northern neighbor: Gilneas. Unable to compete with Kul Tiras's burgeoning navy, Gilneas focused on bolstering its land-based armies and mercantile capabilities. The military of Gilneas became one of the most powerful in Arathor, equaled only by the city-state of Alterac, which held dominion over much of the northlands.

Gilneas and Alterac often combined their forces and led grand expeditions to secure the borders of Arathor. South of Strom, in Khaz Modan, they discovered the dwarves and the gnomes. The expeditionary forces marveled at the wondrous feats of construction and engineering that were Ironforge and Gnomeregan. The humans became quick friends with both races, especially the dwarves, who also shared their love of battle, storytelling, and strong ale. The three cultures engaged in rigorous trade, exchanging knowledge of smithing, mining, engineering, and even arcane magic.

Over the years, Strom's power continued to wane. Bound by rocky, mountainous terrain and lacking natural resources, Strom could not compete with the economies of the other city-states. Eventually, many of Strom's noble families departed to the fertile valleys and pastures of the north. There, they founded a city-state and named it after the surrounding region: Lordaeron. The nobles used their wealth to buy up large plots of land, some of which had been developed by earlier settlers. These areas included the Agamand Mills and the farmsteads owned by the Balnir and Solliden families.

LORDAERON AND THE HOLY LIGHT

After the Troll Wars, a number of human priests began having faint visions and dreams of angelic beings, geometric forms that thrummed with living light. Although they did not know it, the priests had actually communed with the naaru in the Great Dark Beyond. Through this connection, the naaru guided the hearts of some humans and introduced them to the Holy Light.

From their tenuous encounters with the naaru, the priests learned to harness the extraordinary healing effects of the Light. They also formed a religious movement founded on the tenets of justice, peace, and altruistic works. Popular among common folk, this movement flourished.

Lordaeron was also home to deeply religious ascetics who believed in the Light, a cosmic power they claimed infused every living thing in existence. Many sick and elderly people traveled to religious communes in Lordaeron, hoping to find a cure for their ailments. Others made pilgrimages to the city-state in search of wisdom and enlightenment. Lordaeron's borders quickly expanded, and it matured into a proper kingdom. The noble families eventually renamed the heart of their flourishing nation Capital City.

Not long after the lords of Strom went north, the last living descendants of King Thoradin also left Arathor. Led by a member of Thoradin's line named Faldir, they set off by sea and ventured far to the south, enticed by rumors of a lush, unplumbed land where they could make a new beginning.

The stories proved true. Thoradin's descendants settled the land and founded the kingdom of Stormwind. Nestled among cliffs and boasting a natural protected harbor, this city-state established itself as a major power in the region.

Strom was left in the hands of a few ruling families too stubborn to abandon the old capital. Among them were the descendants of Ignaeus Trollbane, a general who had become a legend during the Troll Wars. Over the years, these families rebuilt Strom's crumbling infrastructure and renamed their capital Stromgarde. The city, however, would never regain its former glory.

Indeed, Thoradin's dream of a unified people was dying. Over generations, the various city-states became increasingly distant and insular. Rivalries emerged as these nations turned inward, concerned with their own well-being and less inclined to offer aid to each other.

OPPOSITE: MAP OF HUMAN TERRITORIES IN THE EASTERN KINGDOMS

CITY-STATES OF ARATHOR
(HUMAN KINGDOMS)

Lordaeron

Alterac

Dalaran

Gilneas

Strom

EASTERN
KINGDOMS

Kul Tiras

Stormwind

Maraudon and the Rise of the Centaur
1,100 YEARS BEFORE THE DARK PORTAL

For thousands of years, the nomadic tauren wandered Kalimdor's lush forests, living in harmony with nature and the elements. Of the many lands the tribes roamed, one in particular became sacred ground for all tauren shaman. It was called *Mashan'she*, or "the Loom of the Earth Mother," named in honor of the mythical deity who they believed had created the world. This verdant grassland sat along Kalimdor's western coast, wedged between the jungles of Feralas and the Stonetalon Mountains.

Drawn by faint elemental whisperings, the tauren shaman grew convinced that the Earth Mother herself dwelled somewhere beneath the meadows. They spent decades attempting to wake her by communing with the region's elementals and conducting celebratory rituals.

The shaman eventually succeeded, but they soon discovered that the whispers they had heard did not come from a benevolent Earth Mother. They were echoes of something far darker—something from Azeroth's violent elemental past. From the depths of a massive cavern below the grasslands emerged a colossal earth elemental: Princess Theradras, a descendant of the elemental ruler Therazane.

In ages past, the keepers had imprisoned most of the elementals in another plane of existence. Yet some, like Theradras, had eluded this banishment. She had hidden beneath the earth, eventually falling into a deep slumber. The millennia of sleep had slowly weakened Theradras's mighty form.

The newly awakened Theradras reached out to the verdant surroundings and consumed their energies. Invigorating power flooded through the elemental, regenerating her craggy form. Theradras's siphoning left enormous tracts of land desiccated. Plant life across Mashan'she withered and died. The horrified tauren, now forced to scavenge for sustenance, would later rename the barren plains Desolace.

The sudden and violent death of such vast intertwined ecosystems sent ripples throughout Azeroth and beyond. Many of the mortal druids and spirits in the Emerald Dream reeled from the staggering loss of life. One of Cenarius's woodland sons, Zaetar, emerged from the Dream to investigate.

Much like his father, Zaetar walked the physical world in the form of a majestic half-stag. Supple vines and verdant leaves circled his limbs and great antlers. Wherever his hooves touched the soil, dozens of saplings would sprout. In time, they would bloom into lush forest groves.

Zaetar's investigation led him into the damp caverns beneath Desolace, where he discovered Theradras. Though he set his mind to imprisoning the strange creature, he soon grew enchanted with the princess. The stolen life energies that radiated from Theradras enticed Zaetar, and he became enthralled by her beauty.

Theradras also found Zaetar beautiful, and she resolved to do whatever she could to win his undying love. The elemental princess was keenly aware of the influence she held over Zaetar, and she used this to her advantage. Theradras claimed that she had meant no harm to the land and that she was seeking ways to restore the region to its former beauty. Together, she urged, perhaps they could succeed.

Zaetar abandoned his earlier quest and became Theradras's mate. He knew it was against nature, but he could not deny the love that bloomed in his heart. From this forbidden union, an aberrant race was born. They were called the centaur, and their barbarism would come to terrorize the lands of Kalimdor.

What the centaur lacked in elegance and beauty, they made up for in strength. Their horse-like lower bodies afforded them great speed, while their burly humanoid torsos gave them incredible physical power. Yet the centaur's penchant for brutality overshadowed all of their other traits.

Upon seeing the centaur, Zaetar immediately recognized the depths of his sin. Though he tried to connect with his offspring, he could not bear their presence. The centaur recognized the loathing in their father's eyes, and it drove them into a blind rage. The savage horse-men lashed out, striking Zaetar down.

Zaetar's death shattered Theradras's heart. The elemental princess chastised the centaur for the senseless murder, and they grew forlorn at realizing they had hurt their beloved mother. They begged her forgiveness and promised that from that day forward, they would honor and revere their late father. Theradras later entombed Zaetar's spirit in the great cavern where she had once slumbered. The centaur would name this site Maraudon, and ever after they would treat it as holy ground.

The centaur quickly proliferated, and they fanned out across Desolace. They unleashed their wrath on the hapless tauren who inhabited the area, forcing them to abandon their homes. Yet Theradras's barbarous children did not stop in Desolace. In the centuries that followed, marauding bands of centaur would hunt down Kalimdor's tauren, igniting a long and dark period of war between the two races.

THE WAR OF THE SHIFTING SANDS
975 YEARS BEFORE THE DARK PORTAL

Since the last war against the troll empire, the descendants of the aqir had stayed hidden in their subterranean domains. Only the mantid of Pandaria remained an active threat. Nearly all of Azeroth's races had forgotten the ruthless potential of the insectoid colonies that lurked beneath the earth.

One of these colonies, the qiraji, had taken root in the ancient fortress of Ahn'Qiraj. The keepers had originally built the enormous stronghold to imprison the Old God C'Thun. There, within Ahn'Qiraj's lifeless sandstone corridors, the insectoids had lain dormant.

Though Azshara and her night elf empire had once known of the fortress, its existence had become lost to time. Few living creatures dwelled near Ahn'Qiraj. This was due in part to the vast and inhospitable desert of Silithus, which stretched out from the stronghold's towering obelisks.

Ahn'Qiraj wasn't rediscovered by the elves until Archdruid Fandral Staghelm initiated a quest to regrow the land of Silithus. He dispatched his warrior son, Valstann, and a group of his most trusted druids to perform this task. They trudged across the scalding dunes, searching for hidden water reservoirs that they could use to transform the region into a lush forest. Valstann and his comrades eventually stumbled across Ahn'Qiraj. Although some of the druids cautioned against entering the fortress, Fandral's son forged ahead. His presence in the cold, dead halls inadvertently roused the dormant qiraji back to life.

From its prison beneath Ahn'Qiraj, C'Thun also became aware of the awakened qiraji. The Old God drove the insectoids into a murderous frenzy. The highest castes of qiraji society began organizing their lesser minions, the most numerous of which were known as the silithid. These vicious insectoids came in many forms, and all obeyed the will of their qiraji overlords.

The discovery of the qiraji shocked Valstann and his druid companions. Upon retreating from Ahn'Qiraj, they established a small outpost in Silithus to keep watch over the insectoids. Before their eyes, the fortress swelled with greater and greater numbers of qiraji.

Then, without warning, a massive army spilled forth from the tunnels beneath Ahn'Qiraj. At the head of this swarming host were the qiraji. They directed their silithid minions to engulf the surrounding deserts and spread into other regions as well.

By this time, Valstann had called for help from his father. Fandral rallied a force of druids, Sentinels, priestesses, and keepers of the grove to deal with the qiraji threat. In the southern reaches of Kalimdor, the night elf host clashed with their vicious foes. At times they managed to drive the qiraji back toward the dunes of Silithus, only for the insectoids to mount a counterattack and regain the advantage. This ebb and flow continued for many months, leaving in its wake the broken corpses of elves and insectoids alike.

The War of the Shifting Sands had begun.

Fandral and his comrades established outposts across southern Kalimdor as they prosecuted their war. From these locations, they continued their brutal fight against the qiraji. Eventually, the tireless druids and their allies managed to push the qiraji back into the heart of Silithus itself.

Yet just as victory seemed within reach, the war took a dire turn. During a feint orchestrated by the qiraji, Valstann was captured and ripped apart before Fandral's eyes.

Valstann's death shattered the archdruid and sowed uncertainty throughout the night elves' ranks. The qiraji seized the opportunity and swarmed out of Silithus once again, pushing into the eastern deserts of Tanaris. In their fervor, they assaulted the sanctum of the bronze dragonflight: the Caverns of Time.

The qiraji's reckless attack spurred the bronze flight into action. Led by Anachronos, they enlisted the help of the red, green, and blue dragonflights. The mighty dragons joined the night elves and helped drive the qiraji armies back behind the walls of Ahn'Qiraj.

But even with the mighty dragons joining the war, the qiraji were too numerous to vanquish entirely. Fandral feared that the war would never end. Thousands of elves had already perished at the claws of the insectoids, and he was loath to sacrifice more of his people. Ultimately, he and the dragons devised a means to end the war immediately. They would lock the insectoids inside Ahn'Qiraj itself.

The night elves and dragons gathered before Ahn'Qiraj to complete this task. Fandral called on his druids to focus their powers as one. Along with Anachronos, the elves summoned a great barricade to close off Ahn'Qiraj. Outside the cursed city, the dry earth split wide, and a magical barrier of stone and colossal roots emerged. This impenetrable Scarab Wall towered high over the barren landscape, effectively sealing the qiraji within their city forever.

THE SCARAB WALL AND THE SCARAB GONG

As a final act, Anachronos forged two mystical artifacts: the Scarab Gong and the Scepter of the Shifting Sands. The dragon entrusted the scepter to Fandral. Should the need ever arise to enter Ahn'Qiraj again, he could use this artifact to open the Scarab Wall.

Fandral found no solace in ending the qiraji threat, for Valstann's death still tormented his heart. In his rage, he shattered the Scepter of the Shifting Sands, and the pieces became lost for the next thousand years.

THE GUARDIAN AEGWYNN
823 YEARS BEFORE THE DARK PORTAL

As the years passed in Dalaran, new Guardians of Tirisfal came and went. Some retired in peace; others fell during their tireless war against the Burning Legion's agents. Nevertheless, Dalaran remained safe under the Guardian's watchful eye.

One of the last Guardians to serve was a brilliant magus named Scavell. At the end of his century of commitment, he found no suitable candidate to take his place. The Council of Tirisfal, worried about what could happen in the years or decades it might take to find another Guardian, requested that Scavell remain in his position. The human mage was reluctant, but he ultimately agreed. After all, the century of service was only a tradition, not a law. The relationship between Scavell and the council was relatively strong; together, they continued to protect the world from the Legion's predations.

Years passed before Scavell finally found a group of apprentices who might succeed him. Among them was a human woman named Aegwynn, who quickly distinguished herself as the most skilled and dedicated of the prospects. The Council of Tirisfal eventually bestowed the honor of Guardianship upon her with Scavell's blessing. She immediately began banishing the forces of darkness.

Aegwynn was a brilliant Guardian, but she was also stubborn and bullheaded in her relations with the Council of Tirisfal. Her deep-seated mistrust of authority figures often put her at odds with the elder magi. Ignoring their recommendations and advice, Aegwynn forged her own path during her long years as Guardian. Yet the Council of Tirisfal was not troubled by her demeanor. The magi knew that Aegwynn was a sorceress without equal, a prodigy capable of wielding massive amounts of arcane energy. Her effectiveness as Guardian outweighed her unpredictability and penchant for disobedience.

Near the end of her century of stewardship, Aegwynn sensed something dark stirring in the icy lands of Northrend. She traveled to the distant continent and discovered a pack of demons that were hunting errant blue dragons, feeding on their potent arcane energies. Although mighty, the dragons could not withstand the Legion's cunning and power.

Aegwynn immediately journeyed to the tower of Wyrmrest Temple, the hallowed shrine of all dragons. She called on the majestic creatures to make good on their sacred pact to protect the world from evil. Led by Alexstrasza the Life-Binder, several of the dragonflights agreed to fight at the Guardian's side. Together, they staged an ambush near the gigantic skeletal remains of Galakrond.

AEGWYNN CLASHES WITH THE AVATAR OF SARGERAS IN NORTHREND

The demons fell into Aegwynn's trap. As a blizzard tore over the terrain, the Guardian and her winged allies overwhelmed the Legion's minions. Yet neither Aegwynn nor the dragons expected what came next.

The skies of Northrend churned and darkened. A monstrous demonic form emerged upon the battlefield: Sargeras, ruler of the Burning Legion. This was only an avatar of the demon lord, a tiny portion of Sargeras's vast cosmic power. Yet he nonetheless radiated great strength and fury. He unleashed his terrible might on Aegwynn, intending to destroy the Guardian who had thwarted his agents for so long.

Aegwynn did not hesitate to fight back. She summoned her powers and brought them to bear against Sargeras. The battle that followed was the most difficult Aegwynn had ever fought. In the shadow of Galakrond's gargantuan remains, Sargeras and the Guardian called down the fury of the heavens. Their attacks tore the darkened skies asunder and scarred the icy crust of Northrend. A storm of magic engulfed the region and held even the mighty dragons at bay. With a final relentless flurry of spellwork, Aegwynn defeated her foe. Though drained from the effort, she was victorious.

Or so it seemed.

When Aegwynn had struck Sargeras down, he had transferred his spirit into her weakened body. There, a sliver of Sargeras's undying malevolence would remain, lurking within the depths of her soul.

Unaware of the dark presence hidden deep within her, Aegwynn gathered Sargeras's colossal, broken form to seal it away where it could harm no one else. She considered many locations to serve as the demon lord's final resting place. In the end she chose the ancient night elven city of Suramar, some of which had been blasted to the bottom of the sea during the Sundering.

During the War of the Ancients, the Legion had attempted to open a gateway within Suramar itself. This plan was foiled by a sect of Highborne led by Grand Magistrix Elisande. These powerful sorcerers created a series of enchanted seals to close the demons' portal and also negate nearby fel energies. When the Sundering later tore through the world, the part of Suramar containing the Legion's failed gateway was sucked beneath the waves.

It was these lost ruins that drew Aegwynn's attention. Knowing that the Highborne's seals would nullify whatever evil still lingered in Sargeras's avatar, she buried the demon lord's broken body within the sunken portion of Suramar. Aegwynn hoped Sargeras's remains would lie undisturbed there until the end of time.

LIU LANG AND THE WANDERING ISLE
800 YEARS BEFORE THE DARK PORTAL

While Guardian Aegwynn kept watch over the world of Azeroth, the lonely pandaren continued their isolated existence. Life on their homeland of Pandaria progressed in relative peace, save for the mantid's periodic assaults against the Serpent's Spine. As a people, the pandaren were content to live out their days behind the thick mists that shrouded their domain. They all believed that the rest of Azeroth had been annihilated in the terrible Sundering.

But a young pandaren, Liu Lang, did not share this belief. He had been raised on a small ranch in the tranquil Valley of the Four Winds. He often wandered the cliffs that overlooked the sea, wondering if anything existed beyond the horizon. His curiosity led him to make a bold proclamation: he would embark on a great sea voyage and discover, once and for all, what had become of the outside world.

Ignoring the warnings and ridicule of his fellow pandaren, Liu Lang gathered a few meager supplies and began his journey. Atop a small turtle named Shen-zin Su, he sailed through the cloaking mists. Time passed without word from Liu Lang, and the other pandaren believed he must have died on his foolhardy venture.

Then, five years later, Liu Lang returned. He told incredible tales of mysterious lands and peoples on the other side of the sea. After gathering more supplies, Liu Lang set out once again.

This time, he would not endure his journey alone. Shen-zin Su had grown larger over the years, and Liu Lang's stories had inspired one pandaren to join him on the next leg of his voyage. Her name was Shinizi, and she later became Liu Lang's wife.

Every five years, Liu Lang returned. Each time, Shen-zin Su had become larger, and more pandaren decided to join the eccentric explorer for a life of adventure. This tradition continued for decades until the Great Turtle had grown to the size of a giant island. Misty mountains and lakes formed atop the turtle's shell. In time, villages sprang up across the landscape. These became home to a thriving community of pandaren who would eventually name their unique refuge the Wandering Isle.

On his final voyage from Pandaria, the elderly Liu Lang fell into a deep sleep from which he never awoke. In death, his spirit merged with the sea turtle himself. Liu Lang's tradition of bold exploration and daring to dream beyond the known did not die with him. The pandaren of the Wandering Isle would carry on his values for many centuries to come.

The Vanishing of Aegwynn
600 Years before the Dark Portal

After their battle in Northrend, Sargeras began twisting Aegwynn's thoughts. He pushed her to isolate herself from the Council of Tirisfal, drawing on concerns that she had always harbored about the order. Chief among these concerns was something Aegwynn had recently discovered: the Council of Tirisfal's members were interfering in the politics of human nations. The magi argued that what they were doing was necessary—their order had stayed in the shadows for too long. With their knowledge and wisdom, they had the power to prevent war and suffering in the mortal world.

Aegwynn, however, viewed the council's shadowy activities with skepticism and unease. She feared that if she stepped down, they would choose a weaker Guardian, someone they could use to pursue their political agendas. Thus Aegwynn decided to stay on as Guardian past her first century of service. She used her powers to extend her own life for decades longer than what would have been otherwise possible. Though some members of the council were displeased with Aegwynn's choice, they accepted her decision. After all, she had performed incredible feats during her time as the Guardian.

Over the next hundred years, Aegwynn's relationship with the council became more and more strained. Sargeras's subtle influence made her ever more paranoid about her fellow magi. Her growing unease led her to construct a refuge far from the eyes of the council. Within the barren and remote Deadwind Pass, she forged the grand tower known as Karazhan. Its whereabouts would remain a secret from the council for many years.

Aegwynn would often retreat to Karazhan to work in peace and quiet. Yet the tower also served another vital purpose. It acted as a conduit for the potent ley lines in the surrounding region, through which Aegwynn could siphon power when needed.

In time, the aging members of the council began passing away, their powers still held in Aegwynn's grasp. New sorcerers arose to join the order. They continued the council's practice of interfering with the nations of the Eastern Kingdoms. Many of these new members also pushed for a more hard-line approach to deal with the wayward Guardian and force her to relinquish her powers.

During one of Aegwynn's rare visits to Dalaran, the council demanded that she step down as Guardian or face immediate consequences. Aegwynn balked at their threat. Her distrust of the council had now shifted to outright hostility. She told the magi that putting the fate of Azeroth in their hands was tantamount to dooming the world.

Furious with Aegwynn's behavior, the council members agreed among themselves to take action. If the Guardian would not give up her powers voluntarily, they would force her to do so. The council long debated how best to accomplish this. Some members proposed empowering a new Guardian, but this idea presented too many dangerous possibilities. If Aegwynn and another Guardian were to do battle, the results could be disastrous for the world. Of even greater concern was that such a conflict would call public attention to their clandestine order.

Ultimately, the council agreed on a more subtle course of action. They formed the Tirisgarde, an order of magi girded with relics and armaments that could diminish the Guardian's incredible powers. After years of training, these resourceful and gifted hunters set out to find Aegwynn and bring her back to Dalaran.

The Guardian eluded many of the Tirisgarde with ease. However, the hunters did succeed in finding Karazhan and reporting its location back to the council.

With Karazhan no longer safe, Aegwynn magically sealed off the tower from outsiders. She then set out to locate a new refuge—one that neither the council nor the Tirisgarde would ever find. After much consideration, she decided to build this stronghold in the ruins of ancient Suramar, deep beneath the sea. Her dwelling, the Guardian Sanctum, would stay hidden from the Tirisgarde for centuries.

THE WAR OF THE THREE HAMMERS
230 YEARS BEFORE THE DARK PORTAL

Far from the hidden Guardian Sanctum, High King Modimus Anvilmar and his dwarves thrived in their mountain home of Ironforge. Over the centuries, trade partnerships with the human city-states had filled Ironforge's coffers with riches. Great architectural feats, such as the Stonewrought Dam, attracted curious visitors from as far away as the elven kingdom of Quel'Thalas.

Yet beneath the façade of prosperity, tensions simmered between Ironforge's three powerful clans: the Bronzebeards, the Wildhammers, and the Dark Irons.

Thane Madoran Bronzebeard was the head of the Bronzebeard clan, the largest of the three factions. The clan, which formed the bulk of Ironforge's military and mercantile classes, considered itself the backbone of the kingdom and claimed to share distant blood relations with High King Modimus.

The Wildhammers lived among the craggy hills and icy slopes outside Ironforge. Led by Thane Khardros Wildhammer, they gained notoriety as adept and incredibly resilient mountaineers. Considered uncouth by the Bronzebeard clan, the Wildhammers struggled to gain more sway with High King Modimus and to solidify their place among the ruling elite of Ironforge.

Sorcerer-Thane Thaurissan ruled the Dark Irons, who inhabited the deepest and darkest corners of the subterranean city. Their long-standing practice of dabbling in sorcery, along with a penchant for secrecy and political scheming, drew the ire of Ironforge's other inhabitants. Thaurissan held firm control over the kingdom's richest gem and mineral deposits, using his wealth as leverage to protect his people and secure a place in Ironforge's increasingly volatile political arena.

High King Modimus strived to treat each clan with fairness and respect, but his inability to ease tensions between the factions ultimately led to disaster. The high king passed away from old age, and before his eldest son could be crowned, the simmering cauldron of Ironforge boiled over.

No one knows exactly who struck the first blow. War ignited between the three clans as each vied for dominion of the mountain. Bloody battles raged in every corner of the kingdom for many long and terrible years. In the end, the Bronzebeard clan used its martial expertise to drive the Wildhammers and Dark Irons from the mountain and claim total victory.

Khardros conceded defeat and led his clan north. The Wildhammers eventually settled in a nearby region of marshlands. They carved out a great subterranean city named Grim Batol, one that soon rivaled even Ironforge in scope and prestige. The earlier defeat weighed heavy on Khardros's shoulders, but in time, he and his kin accepted their lot and prospered in their new home.

The Dark Irons ventured south to the tranquil Redridge Mountains. There, they founded the new kingdom of Thaurissan, named after their leader. Although his people prospered, Thaurissan himself wallowed in humiliation. He dreamed of one day exacting retribution upon his cousins in the north and claiming all of Khaz Modan as his own.

After years of secretly forging a new army, Thaurissan launched a brazen two-pronged assault against the Bronzebeard and Wildhammer clans. The sorcerer-thane himself led the attack on Ironforge. He had bolstered his formidable Dark Iron warriors with legions of immense war golems and siege engines. The invaders reached the very heart of the city before the Bronzebeards finally rallied and pushed the Dark Irons all the way back to Redridge.

Thaurissan's wife, the sorceress Modgud, led the second army against Grim Batol. The Dark Irons besieged the mighty fortress and called upon their dark magics to break the Wildhammers' will. They brought the shadows of Grim Batol to life, transforming the bustling city into a realm of nightmare and terror. Khardros led his Wildhammers in a daring counterattack and vanquished Modgud. With her death, the Dark Irons retreated south, only to find themselves face to face with the armies of Ironforge. Madoran had caught wind of the attack and brought his forces north. The Bronzebeard and Wildhammer armies crushed the Dark Irons from both sides, utterly annihilating them.

In the Dark Irons, Madoran and Khardros found a common enemy and a new purpose. They put aside their old rivalries and marched their mighty host southward, pledging they would not stop until they had purged Thaurissan and his treacherous Dark Irons from the face of the world.

As the Bronzebeard and Wildhammer armies drew near, Thaurissan scrambled for a way to defeat his enemies. He decided to draw the fiery power from deep within the world and use it as a weapon. Thus Thaurissan wove a great spell to save his kingdom. Yet amid his conjuration, his mind turned to the death of his wife and his recent defeats. Anger roiled through Thaurissan's heart. His rage grew so absolute that his spellwork breached the Elemental Plane and tapped into Ragnaros the Firelord.

Unwittingly, Thaurissan ripped Ragnaros from the Elemental Plane and summoned him to the surface of Azeroth. The earth buckled and wrenched apart. The Firelord's violent rebirth sparked a series of apocalyptic explosions that instantly killed the sorcerer-thane and shattered the surrounding mountains.

From afar, Madoran and Khardros watched in horror as the world was torn asunder and firestorms engulfed the area. They knew in that instant that Thaurissan had doomed himself and his people. Frightened for their own safety, the Wildhammers and Bronzebeards turned north and fled.

THAURISSAN SUMMONS RAGNAROS THE FIRELORD INTO THE WORLD

Aftermath and Reconstruction

In the years that followed the War of the Three Hammers, Madoran and his people rebuilt Ironforge. Khardros and the Wildhammers, however, chose to abandon Grim Batol. Modgud had cursed the great city upon her death, leaving it uninhabitable. The Bronzebeards offered the Wildhammers a place in Ironforge, but it was a conciliatory gesture at best. Madoran knew in his heart that Khardros was too proud to accept such an offer. As expected, the Wildhammer ruler set out to forge a new future for his clan.

Some of the Wildhammers settled in a region called Northeron. Yet Khardros led most of his clan even farther north, into the wooded Hinterlands. The memories of Grim Batol still haunted the Wildhammers, and so they decided to eschew the subterranean dwellings of the past. Upon reaching the Hinterlands, Khardros and his people built a majestic city, Aerie Peak, high in the mountains. The Wildhammers fostered their traditional ties with the natural world. They practiced shamanism and befriended the intelligent half-lion, half-eagle gryphons—creatures that called the nooks and crannies of the mountains home. The gryphons became emblematic of the Wildhammers, an inseparable part of their culture.

Madoran and Khardros established diplomatic ties between their two healing nations. The great arches of the Thandol Span were constructed as both an economic and a symbolic bridge between the dwarven territories. Although rivalries and ideological differences would persist, the two leaders vowed never to take up arms against each other again.

When Khardros and Madoran passed away, their sons commissioned masons to forge two great statues of the leaders. The craftsmen erected these at the entrance to the southlands, beyond which lay the Dark Iron territories. There, the statues would maintain a tireless vigil, their stony eyes ever watching over the broken domain of their nemeses.

Ragnaros's rebirth had decimated much of the Redridge Mountains. A raging volcano known as Blackrock Mountain now towered over the ruined Dark Iron kingdom. The smoldering wasteland south of the volcano was called the Burning Steppes. The yawning chasm to the north was dubbed the Searing Gorge.

Ragnaros himself retreated deep within the blistering heart of Blackrock Mountain. From his lair, the Molten Core, he enslaved the surviving Dark Irons. The dwarves obeyed their elemental master's every beck and call. They carved out a new fortress under the mountain and named it Shadowforge City. Within their fiery home, they would continue nursing their hatred of the Wildhammers and the Bronzebeards.

Reign of the Anvilmar Line

The Anvilmar family's control of Ironforge came to an end with the costly War of the Three Hammers. Madoran Bronzebeard assumed leadership of the dwarf nation, but he did not wish to make an enemy of its former rulers. Thus, Madoran offered the now-deposed prince of the Anvilmar family and his descendants a permanent seat on Ironforge's senate.

DWARVEN AND
GNOMISH LANDS

EASTERN
KINGDOMS

Aerie Peak

Thandol Span

Grim Batol

Ironforge

Gnomeregan

Uldaman

Shadowforge City

THE LIBERATION OF KEZAN
100 YEARS BEFORE THE DARK PORTAL

After the Sundering, the Zandalari set out to explore the numerous islands that dotted the newly formed sea between Kalimdor and the Eastern Kingdoms. It was during these voyages that the trolls discovered Kezan, an isle inhabited by goblins. These small green-skinned beings were clever but crude.

At first, the two races kept their distance from each other. The Zandalari had come to Kezan in search of a strange mineral called kaja'mite. The consumption of vaporized kaja'mite caused a range of effects, such as heightened senses, hallucinations, and increased intelligence. The trolls greatly valued the mineral and saw it as a sacred component in their rituals and ceremonies. For centuries they mined from the numerous kaja'mite veins running close to the surface of the island. Occasionally they employed goblins to work for them, paying with shiny but cheap trinkets that the small creatures prized.

The arrangement changed once the trolls discovered an unimaginable deposit of kaja'mite buried deep underground—more than the Zandalari would ever need. Rather than dig for it themselves, they enslaved the goblins and forced them to mine under abysmal conditions. For thousands of years, the goblins suffered under the yoke of troll oppression, too weak to resist.

In the end, it was the kaja'mite itself that led to the goblins' salvation.

A cloud of kaja'mite dust always blanketed the mines. Over time, breathing it in awakened the goblins' intelligence . . . and craftiness. Secretly, they plotted the overthrow of their slave masters, using what materials they could find to fashion traps, explosives, and other ingenious weaponry.

The troll overseers were caught off guard when the goblin masses stormed from the mines, armed with technology beyond even what the Zandalari possessed. The revolution shattered the trolls' hold over Kezan, laying waste to their mining operation and leaving behind untold destruction.

The surviving Zandalari fled, and the goblins celebrated their new liberation by turning on each other in a mad scramble to fill the void of power. Amid the chaos, countless factions and allegiances formed. The most powerful of these groups were known as cartels. When no clear winner emerged from the fighting, these cartels brokered an uneasy truce.

Conflict would never really end between the various goblin factions, but for decades, they waged most of their battles in the economic arena. The cartels ultimately turned to trade to sustain themselves and used their profits to amass ever more wealth and power.

Ancient Goblins

In ancient times, Keeper Mimiron had discovered kaja'mite and used it to experiment on various races, greatly enhancing their intellect. Some of these test subjects were members of a small, primitive race that roamed the forestlands near Ulduar. Consuming kaja'mite transformed the creatures into a highly intelligent, industrious breed known thereafter as goblins.

The destruction caused by the Sundering cut off the goblins' supply of kaja'mite. In just a few generations, their heightened intelligence vanished. Those goblins who had found refuge on the Isle of Kezan had already forgotten the role kaja'mite had played in their old society.

Stormwind and the Gnoll War
75 Years Before the Dark Portal

Throughout the Eastern Kingdoms, the disparate human nations flourished. The smallest and most isolated of these kingdoms was Stormwind. Over the years, it found prosperity through the farmsteads that dotted the surrounding fertile region. As Stormwind's population grew, small towns sprang up in nearby Elwynn Forest, the Redridge Mountains, Brightwood, and the breadbasket of the kingdom, Westfall.

Although the land was relatively peaceful, threats soon emerged. Packs of ferocious but simple-minded gnolls saw their human neighbors as easy prey. These brutish creatures launched raiding parties against Stormwind's convoys, farmsteads, and even small towns. In response, Stormwind sent its valiant knights and other soldiers to diligently patrol the land.

Stormwind City became a sanctuary for the beleaguered refugees driven from their homes. The fortified heart of the kingdom offered not just safety, but spiritual guidance. Over the decades, devout clerics from the emergent Church of the Holy Light had ventured south from Lordaeron to spread their faith. Upon reaching Stormwind, these pious individuals founded the Holy Order of Northshire Clerics. The kingdom looked to these clerics as a source of wisdom and comfort in hard times.

While the devout clerics used the powers of the Light to soothe the hearts and minds of Stormwind's citizens, military forces patrolled the kingdom's borders. Although their vigilance prevented major bloodshed in the outer territories, the gnolls would remain a danger.

During the reign of King Barathen Wrynn, this lurking threat spiraled out of control. The gnolls began launching brazen attacks on Stormwind City itself. It quickly became clear that these assaults were merely distractions—while soldiers defended the city, Westfall farmsteads would burn. The gnolls assailed the city in such numbers that few soldiers could be spared to protect the agricultural lands.

This was no ordinary tactic for the crude gnolls, and for good reason: never before had an intelligent leader emerged among their kind. Packlord Garfang, a cunning gnoll alpha of the Redridge pack, had spent years conquering other packs in the surrounding regions. Now he had an army of vicious raiders at his command and the tactical wherewithal to use them efficiently. Within a year of the first attack, his gnolls had raided almost a third of all human settlements outside of the city.

King Barathen sent envoys to beseech Lordaeron, Gilneas, and the other human kingdoms for aid. But they would not send assistance, seeing no advantage in helping the smaller, rural nation end the threat. Stormwind was self-sufficient, so trade with the other kingdoms was rare, and its spiritual tendencies were seen as quaint. The humans of Stormwind would have to fend for themselves.

The reluctance of the other nations to send aid infuriated King Barathen, and he resolved to take matters into his own hands. The gnoll packlord had been bold in attacking Stormwind City. Barathen decided equally bold tactics were needed to defeat him.

The king and a small, elite party of armored knights left the city under cover of darkness and waited for the next gnoll assault to hit the city walls. When the raiding parties attacked, the king and his forces made their move—riding hard *away* from Stormwind City and toward the Redridge Mountains. Barathen's gambit paid off: the packlord had held nothing back for this raid, but he had not accompanied his warriors himself. Like most gnolls, Garfang loved to let others do the hard work for him.

But with all of his armies away, the packlord's camp in Redridge was left exposed and undefended.

Barathen's party battled Garfang and his personal guards for a full day and night. In the end, it was King Barathen himself who sank a blade into the packlord's neck. Half of his knights had died, and the survivors had all been wounded, but Barathen had finally ended Garfang's reign.

When the gnoll forces learned that their leader was dead, they turned on each other. Several would-be packlords battled to take Garfang's place. Yet none had his cunning or guile, and the gnolls thinned their own numbers, leaving them unable to push deep into human lands anymore. King Barathen took advantage of the infighting. He rallied his soldiers and launched his forces into the Redridge Mountains. There they decimated what remained of the gnolls. Although pockets of the hostile creatures would continue dwelling in the region, they would never again threaten Stormwind as they once had.

King Barathen Wrynn, known thereafter as the Adamant, was celebrated as a hero, and the kingdom of Stormwind entered a time of great prosperity. The victory had given Stormwind's people confidence that they could handle any threat that might arise, even if they had to face it without the aid of the other human nations. In the years that followed, Stormwind would become even more distant from the northern kingdoms.

Yet unbeknownst to the greater world, events would soon take place in Stormwind that would change the fate of Azeroth forever.

THE LAST GUARDIAN
45 YEARS BEFORE THE DARK PORTAL

Far from Stormwind, the Council of Tirisfal continued its tireless hunt for the renegade Guardian Aegwynn. Waves of unflagging Tirisgarde scoured the world to find Aegwynn and hold her accountable for her defiance.

Aegwynn, however, remained safe in her sanctum, deep within the sunken ruins of ancient Suramar. Only rarely did she emerge to walk the outside world. At times, she would contact the Council of Tirisfal and observe its activities. Much to her dismay, she found that its practice of interfering with politics had become more overt and troublesome. Now, the Council of Tirisfal was actively practicing statecraft.

It was during one of these sojourns that Aegwynn crossed paths with Nielas Aran, one of the most dogged and unrelenting Tirisgarde ever. He hounded the Guardian for months, using the enchanted artifacts at his command to nullify her magic and hamper her attempts to escape his grasp.

These fierce encounters became like a game of wills and wits between Nielas and Aegwynn. During their protracted duels, the opponents bantered back and forth, seeking insights into each other's strengths and weaknesses. To Aegwynn's surprise, she discovered that Nielas harbored misgivings about the Council of Tirisfal. He was well aware of the order's political machinations—activities that he did not condone.

Nielas realized that Aegwynn was not the traitorous rebel that the Council of Tirisfal had made her out to be. As he discerned more about the Guardian's own motivations, he began to sympathize with her plight. Nielas also sensed that Aegwynn was wrestling with some unseen darkness in her soul. But for all of his brilliance, he would never know that this darkness was actually the lingering presence of Sargeras. Hoping to help Aegwynn overcome her struggle, Nielas laid down his arms and abandoned his hunt.

Before long, an unexpected love blossomed between the two former enemies. They agreed that they would work together to prevent the Council of Tirisfal from ever having control over another Guardian. Knowing she could not maintain her mantle of Guardianship forever, Aegwynn proposed a solution to Nielas. They would bear a child capable of inheriting Aegwynn's *Tirisfalen* powers. Only then could a new Guardian arise free from the Council of Tirisfal's manipulation.

Nielas readily agreed, seeing this plan as a redemptive act for Aegwynn. If she could not purge the darkness within herself, then perhaps she could create an heir who would be free from her own personal burdens.

In time, Aegwynn gave birth to a son. She named him Medivh, or "Keeper of Secrets" in the high elven tongue. The infant possessed an incredible affinity for magic, a natural gift passed down from his parents. Aegwynn also locked her powers away within the boy's spirit, where they would linger until Medivh reached maturity.

There was, however, something much darker in Medivh: the lurking spirit of Sargeras stirred in the child's soul. Though Aegwynn did not know it, the demon lord had possessed the infant while he formed in her womb.

Aegwynn and Nielas searched far and wide for a safe place where Medivh could be raised. They ultimately settled on Stormwind due to its isolated location and tenuous ties with Dalaran and the other northern nations. There, Nielas became the official conjurer of Stormwind's royal court.

Having secured a future for her son, Aegwynn left Medivh in the care of Nielas. He would educate and tutor the boy in the ways of the arcane arts until the time came when Medivh assumed the role of Guardian. Aegwynn herself departed Stormwind, retiring from her duties as Guardian. The long centuries had taken their toll on her, and she could bear no more. She disappeared from sight, but always, she would watch her beloved son from afar.

Nielas's role as official court conjurer meant that the young Medivh was also a part of the royal court. As the boy grew older, he spent much of his time in the company of two other notable children: Anduin Lothar, a descendant of the Arathi bloodline, and Llane Wrynn, the prince of Stormwind. Despite their penchant for mischief and adventure, the three children were adored by the kingdom's populace.

Medivh cherished his friendship with Anduin and Llane, for their activities were often an escape from Nielas's intensive tutoring. Although Medivh excelled in the arcane arts, his father rarely gave him praise. He was a cold and mirthless mentor, constantly pushing his son to achieve more. Nielas eventually revealed why he placed such a burden on Medivh. He told his son of the Council of Tirisfal, the line of the Guardians, and Medivh's own secret heritage. Nielas claimed that one day the boy would assume the role of Guardian. The fate of the entire world would then rest squarely on his shoulders.

The pressures of his destiny and his exhausting studies tormented Medivh's thoughts. The mounting anxiety led to disastrous consequences when the boy finally came of age. On the eve of his fourteenth birthday, the stress building within Medivh ignited his dormant Guardian powers. Fevered dreams assaulted the youth as the *Tirisfalen* energies howled to be unleashed.

Nielas struggled desperately to help his son, but the incredible powers within Medivh lashed out, killing his father. Thereafter the boy fell into a deep coma. For many years, he lay unconscious in Stormwind's Northshire Abbey, tended to by clerics and watched over by his faithful friends Anduin and Llane.

When Medivh finally awoke, he found the world had changed around him. Llane was poised to succeed his father, Barathen, as the king of Stormwind. Anduin Lothar had become a knight in Stormwind's military. As Medivh gradually acclimated to his new life, he recognized the awesome power at his fingertips and resolved to use it to protect the world from evil. Despite his strange coma, he appeared normal, and he assured the clerics that nothing was amiss.

Even Medivh himself was unaware that Sargeras was still hiding within his soul, subtly twisting his every thought and action to a much darker end. At long last, the fallen titan had found the perfect instrument with which to begin the Legion's next invasion of Azeroth.

TO BE CONTINUED . . .

THE TOWER OF KARAZHAN, FUTURE HOME OF THE GUARDIAN MEDIVH

INDEX

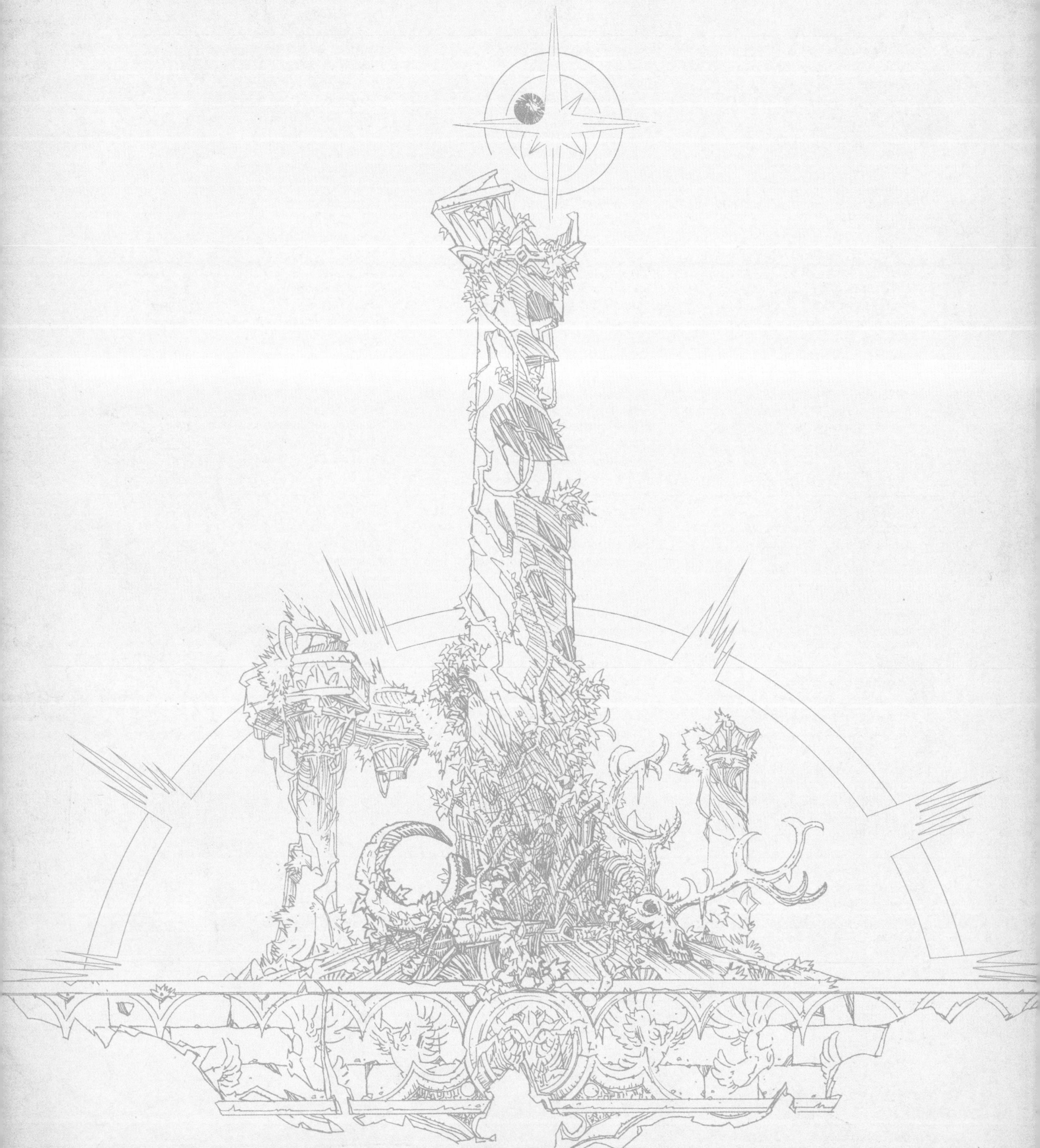

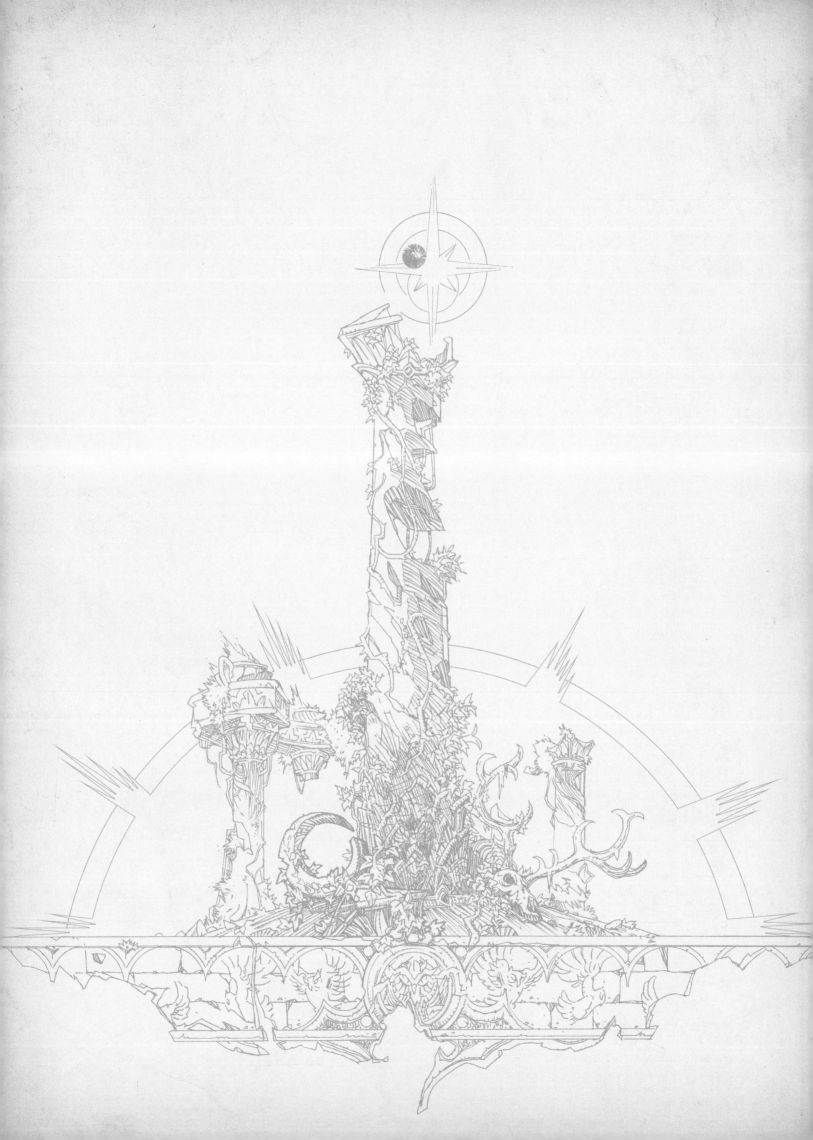